RATIONALE-BASED DEFENCES IN CRIMINAL LAW

Although it is often accepted that rationale-based defences to criminal liability can be justificatory or excusatory, disagreements about how best to conceptualise the categories of justification and excuse have appeared so interminable that some theorists argue that they should be abandoned altogether. This book offers a novel, principled, and intuitively appealing conceptual account of the natures of justifications and excuses, showing how they differ, and why the distinction between them matters.

The monograph breaks new ground by defending a model of rationale-based defences that turns solely on the quality of the defendant's reasoning. This model is shown to generate appealing liability outcomes, advance convincing solutions to questions that have puzzled criminal lawyers for years, and offer suggestions for doctrinal reform that are both normatively sound, and practical. By proposing new ways to think about defences, this book makes an original contribution to criminal law theory that will be of benefit to academics, practitioners, and persons interested in law reform.

Rationale-Based Defences in Criminal Law

– 'I did it. I chose to do it. And here's why…' –

Mark Dsouza

·HART·

OXFORD · LONDON · NEW YORK · NEW DELHI · SYDNEY

HART PUBLISHING
Bloomsbury Publishing Plc
Kemp House, Chawley Park, Cumnor Hill, Oxford, OX2 9PH, UK

HART PUBLISHING, the Hart/Stag logo, BLOOMSBURY and the Diana logo are
trademarks of Bloomsbury Publishing Plc

First published in hardback, 2019
Paperback edition, 2019

A catalogue record for this book is available from the British Library.

Library of Congress Cataloging-in-Publication data

Names: Dsouza, Mark, author.
Title: Rationale-based defences in criminal law : "I did it. I chose to do it. And here's why..." / Mark Dsouza.
Description: Oxford ; Portland, Oregon : Hart Publishing, 2017. | Based on author's thesis
(doctoral - University of Cambridge, 2014) issued under title: A theory of rationale-based defences. |
Includes bibliographical references and index.
Identifiers: LCCN 2016056275 (print) | LCCN 2016057838 (ebook) | ISBN 9781509902958
(hardback : alk. paper) | ISBN 9781509902965 (Epub)
Subjects: LCSH: Justification (Law)
Classification: LCC K5086 .D76 2017 (print) | LCC K5086 (ebook) | DDC 345/.04—dc23
LC record available at https://lccn.loc.gov/2016056275

ISBN: HB: 978-1-50990-295-8
PB: 978-1-50993-214-6
ePDF: 978-1-50990-297-2
ePub: 978-1-50990-296-5

Typeset by Compuscript Ltd, Shannon

To find out more about our authors and books visit www.hartpublishing.co.uk.
Here you will find extracts, author information, details of forthcoming events and
the option to sign up for our newsletters.

For Grandpa and Granny
Still missed

ACKNOWLEDGEMENTS

This book grew out of my doctoral thesis, and along the way I have accumulated several debts of gratitude. Naming my creditors will not begin to discharge these debts, but I will name them anyway, if only to acknowledge how much I owe to them.

My thanks to Antje du Bois-Pedain, Andrew Simester, Andreas von Hirsch, Sandra Marshall, Matthew Kramer, Findlay Stark, Matthew Dyson, the Rajiv Gandhi (UK) Foundation which funded my doctoral studies, the Faculty of Law at the University of Cambridge, the School of Law and Social Justice at the University of Liverpool, and the Faculty of Laws at University College London. I am also grateful to Bill Asquith, the editorial staff at Hart Publishing and the anonymous reviewers who examined my book carefully and saved me from so many missteps and mistakes.

There are many others that deserve my thanks. Fortunately, these are the people closest to me and I can thank them each time I see them.

Mark Dsouza
London
2017

CONTENTS

Part III: Translating Theory into Doctrine

SUMMARY

In this book I describe and defend an account of the theoretical and philosophical differences between paradigm justifications and paradigm rationale-based excuses in the criminal law, which turns solely on the quality of the defendant's reasoning and not at all on the objective outcomes of her actions. I adopt a morally distinctive account of the criminal law and argue that when the defendant's reasons for committing a prima facie offence accord with the morally derived system of norms that underlies the criminal law, she is justified, whereas when her reasons meet societal normative expectations of reasoning without conforming to the criminal law's underlying system of norms, she may be excused.

To make good this thesis, I first argue that offence definitions and rationale-based defences operate at distinct temporal stages in the criminal law, and that their core features ought to be understood by reference to the function that they most centrally perform at their respective stages. In particular, I argue that while offence definitions offer ex ante guidance aimed at preventing identified harms or conduct, rationale-based defences become relevant only after the proscribed harm or conduct has occurred, and therefore the primary focus of all rationale-based defences is the determination of the defendant's blameworthiness. As such, I argue that the occurrence of an all-things-considered wrong should be irrelevant for ascertaining the availability of any rationale-based defence.

I then derive and describe the moral norms relevant to defensive actions that I believe underlie the core tenets of the criminal law and demonstrate how these norms map onto our intuited conceptions of justification. Next, I defend a compatible account of rationale-based excuses. I also outline the contours of the special defence of necessity, which I argue is a deeming justification even though it does not conform to the paradigm of a justification. Finally, I demonstrate the criminal law outcomes that are generated by this model of rationale-based defences.

INTRODUCTION

This is a study of the philosophical foundations of supervening defences in the criminal law. The term 'defence' is used by practitioners to refer to any claim that protects the defendant from punishment. However, different claims preclude punishment by operating at different stages of the criminal adjudication process. One category of defensive claims denies the defendant's status as a responsible moral agent at the time of the offence. This category includes claims of infancy, automatism, insanity and intoxication. Another category works by disputing the existence of the actus reus or mens rea elements of the offence. Examples include claims of alibi or (depending on the mens rea stipulation in an offence) inadvertence. Yet another set of punishment-blocking claims invokes procedural objections against trying the defendant. This set includes claims relating to limitation, diplomatic immunity, autrefois acquit and autrefois convict. All of the foregoing claims, while defensive in a practical sense, are not defences in the sense relevant to this study. This study focuses on those substantive defences that operate once the prosecution has discharged its initial probative burden and has proved beyond reasonable doubt that the defendant is responsible prima facie for committing the offence charged. Defences that operate at this stage 'block the presumptive transition from responsibility to liability', without denying the defendant's responsibility, by claiming that further relevant factors should block liability.[1] I refer to these as supervening defences, and include in this set of defences claims of duress, necessity, self-defence and the like. This set of supervening defences is traditionally subdivided into the categories of justification and supervening excuse. In this book, I will argue that all supervening defences exculpate based on the reasons for which the defendant chose to commit what was prima facie an offence, and therefore that all supervening defences are rationale-based defences.

The philosophy of justifications and excuses in the criminal law has been studied for centuries. In that time, several different and contradictory models of justification and excuse have been proposed and passionately defended. Of course, there is no preordained sense in which the terms 'justification', 'excuse' and their cognates must necessarily be used—these are not pre-existing logical categories that we discover, but rather categories that we invent in the process of using and describing them. So how does one go about proposing a model of justification

---

[1] RA Duff, *Answering for Crime* (Oxford, Hart Publishing, 2007) 263. See also AP Simester, 'Mistakes in Defence' (1992) 12 *OJLS* 295, 296.

and excuse, and how does one evaluate the strengths of a model or compare rival models? Most theories of justification and excuse appear, at heart, to be derived by inductive reasoning, and that is a useful way of approaching the problem. A theorist poses to herself a succession of questions about the outcomes that intuitively she would like her model of justification and excuse to generate. For instance, she may ask herself the following (and more) questions to plot her preferred outcomes:

1. whether the entitlement to supervening defences (or any of them) depends on demonstrating that, 'all things considered', no harm was done;
2. whether the availability of a supervening defence turns on the existence of an actual need for defensive action or on the defendant's perception that defensive action is required;
3. whether a person taking justified or excused action is required first to retreat if possible, even when the threat she faces is wrongful or undeserved;
4. whether a person taking defensive action should compensate the people (or any class of them) affected by such action;
5. whether a person is required to submit to justified or excused action; and
6. whether and, if so, to what extent the classification of a defence as a justification or an excuse affects the set of executive actions that the state is permitted to perform.

Having identified her intuitively preferred responses, she would then construct a theory of justification and excuse that can generate all or most of her preferred outcomes and yet be internally consistent. The outcomes that cannot be consistently accommodated within the preferred theoretical model of justification and excuse may then be rejected in favour of some other less preferred (but still plausible) outcome.

Such a theory of justification and excuse could be critiqued internally, on the basis that it is internally incoherent or contradictory, or externally, on the basis that the intuited answers that the theorist has chosen to accommodate in her theory are themselves implausible. An internal critique offers value by checking the internal logic, but a theory that successfully repels all such critiques still appeals only to those who share the theorist's moral intuitions. An external critique, on the other hand, argues across the model critiqued. If there is a genuine disagreement between the intuitions of the theorist and the critic, then neither can hope to convince the other.

But of course our moral intuitions are more nuanced than this sketch implies. Even if we feel that 'P' is the correct response to one of our outcome-plotting questions, we may still be willing to accept that 'Q' and 'R' are also plausible solutions, even if they are not the solution to which we are most drawn. Hence, it is possible for a person to believe that there are two or more models of justification that are plausible, and it may be possible for a theorist to agree with her external critic, and vice versa, that both the theorist's and the critic's models are plausible, and perhaps that they have different areas of relative strength and weakness. Even so, on balance we may prefer one theory to another, because on the whole we find the intuitions accommodated by one more plausible than those accommodated by the other. And although different people may well form different judgements about which model they prefer, an internally coherent model that can accommodate a greater number of plausible outcomes *and* offer plausible explanations for either rejecting other intuitions or addressing the concerns underlying them in some other way would be especially persuasive. If, in addition, such a model is able to show how its rules link to fundamental and basic intuitions about the nature and purposes of the criminal law, then its claim to being the most useful way to conceptualise justifications would be even more convincing.

All of this is very abstract, but it has a bearing on the methodology and the arrangement of the argument that will appear in this book. Part I sets up the overall shape and scope of the inquiry by outlining the current approaches to theorising justification and supervening excuse, and considering an alternative approach to performing the same task. I start Chapter 1 by describing a hypothesis that almost all criminal law theorists explicitly or implicitly rely upon in order to set up their models of the criminal law in general, and the structural difference between a justification and an excuse in particular. I call this the 'wrongness hypothesis'. Although the wrongness hypothesis is eminently plausible, I argue that it is fundamentally an unprovable assumption based on an intuited view of the structure of the criminal law, and not a conclusion in itself. Moreover, there are good reasons to doubt the usefulness and appropriateness of the wrongness hypothesis approach for the criminal law. Therefore, I rely on some of the other literature on this subject to briefly describe an alternative account of the manner in which the criminal law functions, and I draw out the implications of this model for the divide between justifications and supervening excuses. Specifically, I argue that under this model, the difference between justifications and supervening excuses is the *quality* of the defendant's reasons for committing a prima facie offence. I call this the 'quality of reasoning hypothesis'. This hypothesis too is based on an unprovable assumption—one that incidentally entails the conclusion that the wrongness hypothesis, at least in the form that I describe it, is incorrect. Yet, because the broad outcomes that it generates are at least plausible at first blush, the quality of reasoning hypothesis cannot be dismissed out of hand. Therefore, I set out to explore it in greater detail.

Part II of this book considers what a criminal legal system in which defences were arranged based on the quality of reasoning hypothesis would look like. I start in Chapter 2 by expanding on the proposed alternative model of how the criminal law works. In particular, I describe this model's implications for disputed theoretical issues, such as the way offence definitions ought to be framed and read, and the way we should conceive of culpability and criminal blame. Admittedly, not all of these implications track the conclusions of (some versions of) the more mainstream theories of the criminal law. However, I show that there is sufficient academic support for each of them to suggest that they are at least plausible. Even though neither overall model of the criminal law has a knock-down argument to defeat the other, in the chapters that follow I set out to demonstrate that the alternative model being set up herein offers a preferable account of criminal law. I do so on the basis that it generates outcomes that better track our moral intuitions, especially in respect of putatively justified agents and agents who find it difficult to meet criminal law standards due to learning difficulties and other mental conditions not amounting to insanity.

I begin that endeavour in Chapter 3 by identifying certain propositions that I take to be axiomatic and foundational for a modern system of criminal law. Substantively, I take the state's commitment to liberal principles of non-interference to be axiomatic, and therefore argue that the core of an *ideal* state's criminal law cannot contain rules that regulate matters purely in the private domain. Structurally, I take it to be axiomatic that at least the core of the criminal law in a rule of law state is related to morality. In other words, subject to certain caveats and limitations, the criminal law at core endorses and enforces moral norms.[2] I show that most moral theories build upon an understanding of 'the moral good' that is in some way contingent upon the continued survival of humans. Their axiomatic value statements only make sense if they presuppose the existence of beings that are recognisably human. This makes the ontological identity of humans prior to, and outside the content of, a human morality, and of any normative system, including that of the criminal law, which derives from it. I identify from existing accounts of human nature certain features that are relevant to the operation of criminal law defences and accepted as being constitutive of a generalised instance of the species of human beings. I treat these as setting the main logical limits or boundaries of the guidance that can be offered by a moral criminal law in respect of defensive or self-protective conduct. Next, I describe the set of liberal norms that must exist to support 'constituent rights'—rights created when the state clothes the aforementioned limits of its power with the trappings of a legal entitlement. In doing so, I describe a special immunity from blame that must be recognised in respect of actions arising out of constituently human behaviour, and argue that the criminal law defence made available for actions taken to defend against threats to life, major physical injury and the like is best understood as a translation into law of this special moral immunity from blame. I then extend my analysis to consider 'posited rights'—entitlements entirely contoured by the state in the exercise of its political authority. Using the norm structure described in relation to constituent rights as a template, I describe one set of norms that might plausibly be constructed to support posited rights. I propose that, cumulatively, the normative structures for supporting constituent rights and posited rights constitute a sufficiently (for my purposes) detailed model of the system of norms that underlies the criminal law, even though it addresses only directly victimising acts.

Part III of this book focuses on demonstrating how the aforementioned propositions about the underlying structure of the criminal law translate into

---

[2] Perhaps a better way of describing this move is to say that I choose to restrict my audience to those who share my commitment to core liberal ideals and have a morally distinctive conception of the criminal law, and then set out to describe a model that will appeal to this audience.

recognisable doctrinal rules. In Chapter 4, I explain how the system of conduct norms outlined in Chapter 3 maps onto the doctrinal rules of a modern criminal law. In doing so, I suggest that the paradigmatic forms of justified conduct conform to guidance contained in a certain subset of conduct norms from the criminal law's underlying system of norms and, as such, paradigmatic justifications guide conduct. By contrast, paradigmatic rationale-based excuses, which we do not expect to guide conduct, do not mirror any part of the conduct guidance in the criminal law's underlying system of norms. I also argue that necessity should be understood as a non-paradigmatic form of justification, in that although we expect this justification to guide future conduct, we cannot trace it to any of the criminal law's underlying conduct norms.

Chapter 5 is a more detailed study of the forms of justification that I have identified as being paradigmatic. I set out the scope of these justifications and make arguments about how they should be applied in the criminal law. In particular, I explain why I identify these defences as conforming to the paradigm of a justification, make arguments as to the perspective that ought to be adopted when evaluating a person's claim to a paradigmatic justification, and explore the limits of these justifications.

I focus on rationale-based excuses in Chapter 6 and build upon John Gardner's suggestion that we excuse conduct that conforms to societal normative standards for behaviour even though it falls short of the criminal law's normative standards. I do so by explaining how the notion of hypocrisy in blaming generates the normative pull of rationale-based excuses. I argue that although all rationale-based excuses are united by their underlying appeal to the principled avoidance of hypocrisy in blaming, the model of rationale-based excuses generated on this view is very flexible and therefore rationale-based excuses can look very different in different jurisdictions.

Thereafter, in Chapter 7, I argue that the defence of lesser-evils necessity can and should be conceived of as a special deeming justification, rather than as the paradigmatic justification. I propose a theory as to the source of the necessity defence's exculpatory pull and compare the operation and limits of this defence to those of paradigmatic justifications. I also apply this conception of lesser-evils necessity to many prominent English cases in which this defence has been considered (or might have been considered) in order to demonstrate the sorts of liability outcomes that it generates.

Finally, in Chapter 8, I describe the outcomes generated by this model of justification and excuse in relation to the outcome-plotting questions with which we began (along with a few other such questions). In doing so, I flesh out in greater detail the alternative model of justification and supervening excuse outlined in Chapter 2, and offer suggestions about how the intuitions that cannot be accommodated within this model may nevertheless be addressed by the state using one or more of the other tools of social coordination at its disposal. I argue that each of the outcomes generated by this model of rationale-based defences is plausible, even when it is not the current preferred mainstream response. To my mind of course, these outcomes are more than plausible—I think that they are the most plausible responses to the outcome-plotting questions—but even someone who does not share my intuited preferences might be willing to accept that they are not implausible. If so, then provided that such a reader: (a) accepts the axiomatic assumptions with which I began; (b) broadly accepts the arguments used to reach these conclusions from those initial axioms; and (c) accepts that most conflicting outcome intuitions can be adequately addressed using other tools of governance available to the state, she has a very good reason to adopt my model of the distinction between a justification and a rationale-based excuse.

Even the most convincing philosophical theory relies on the reader being willing to suspend her disbelief long enough to let the roots of the argument take hold. Whether this theory is convincing or not is for the reader to decide, but it is probably true that a reader who is willing to accept that my starting points are at least plausible, even if not wholly appealing to her, has a far better chance of finding something of value in the pages that follow.

Part I

Overview

1

The Proposed Borders of Justification and Excuse

Many a theorist has tried to map the 'perplexing borders of justification and excuse',[1] but no consensus has emerged as to the specific features that differentiate these species of supervening defences. However, notwithstanding the cacophony of dissent, one assumption that is ubiquitous (albeit often unspoken) in the writings of most criminal law theorists is that justifications negate the wrongness of what occurred due to the prima facie criminal conduct, whereas excuses negate the defendant's blameworthiness for engaging in the conduct. In this chapter, I critique this assumption and tentatively set out the contours of an alternative approach to distinguishing between justifications and excuses, which I will defend in the rest of this study.

1.1 The 'Wrongness Hypothesis'

Despite disagreeing on points of detail, a large majority of theorists who have studied the justification/excuse distinction agree on the validity of what I call the 'wrongness hypothesis'. Some background is necessary to understand the content of this hypothesis.

People like Fletcher,[2] John Gardner,[3] Simester,[4] Sendor[5] and Husak[6] agree that in order to be justified, an agent must be motivated by good subjective reasons

---

[1] K Greenawalt, 'The Perplexing Borders of Justification and Excuse' (1984) 84 *Columbia Law Review* 1897.

[2] GP Fletcher, 'The Right Deed for the Wrong Reason: A Reply to Mr. Robinson' (1975) 23 *UCLA Law Review* 293, 320.

[3] J Gardner, 'Justifications and Reasons' in AP Simester and ATH Smith (eds), *Harm and Culpability* (Oxford, Clarendon Press, 1996) 104–05.

[4] AP Simester, 'On Justifications and Excuses' in L Zedner and JV Roberts (eds), *Principles and Values in Criminal Law and Criminal Justice* (Oxford, Oxford University Press, 2012) 99.

[5] BB Sendor, 'Mistakes of Fact: A Study in the Structure of Criminal Conduct' (1990) 25 *Wake Forest Law Review* 707, 766.

[6] DN Husak, 'Justifications and the Criminal Liability of Accessories' (1989) 80 *Journal of Criminal Law and Criminology* 491, 516–17.

when committing what is prima facie an offence. They also insist that no action can be justified if it results in an outcome that is, all things considered, wrongful. At best, such an action may be excused. In his theory, Fletcher uses 'wrongful' as meaning 'contrary to Right', ie, contrary to the objective legal order, or the objective greater good.[7] Similarly, for John Gardner[8] and Simester,[9] an outcome is considered wrongful if there is no non-excluded guiding reason to cause it. In other words, if in the circumstances that truly exist an agent ought not to have brought about a particular outcome, then she cannot be justified in bringing it about, even if she did so in the belief—however reasonable—that circumstances calling for her actions existed. Yet, they also require for justification that the agent act for one of the available guiding reasons. Sendor's theory of criminal conduct employs the concept of 'dual wrongfulness', whereby a violation of the victim's right is one half of wrongfulness, and disrespect for the rights of the victim is the other. A justification negates the first half of wrongfulness, whereas an excuse negates the second half. Thus, for Sendor too, a justification negates the presence of an objectively wrong outcome—the violation of someone's rights. A person who mistakenly thinks she is justified may at best negate the second half of Sendor's conception of wrongfulness.[10] Similarly, Husak conceptualises wrongs in generally 'objective' outcome-related terms and treats justifications as the negation of this wrong.[11]

While Eser subscribes to the proposition that a justification negates a wrong, he is less categorical about his conception of a wrong. Nevertheless, he seems to adopt Fletcher's objective outcome-related conception thereof.[12] Gur-Arye has argued that the use of the justification/excuse distinction in the criminal law is unhelpful,[13] but where she does use it, she too adopts a view that is in line with Fletcher's view.[14] Accordingly, both Eser and Gur-Arye also broadly accept that justifications negate the objective, outcome-dependent wrong, but add that the agent must commit the prima facie offence for subjectively appropriate reasons in order to be justified.

---

[7] GP Fletcher, 'Rights and Excuses' (1984) 3(2) *Criminal Justice Ethics* 17. See also GP Fletcher, 'The Right and the Reasonable' (1985) 98 *Harvard Law Review* 949, 966–67.

[8] Gardner, 'Justifications and Reasons'.

[9] Simester, 'On Justifications and Excuses' 99.

[10] Sendor, 'Mistakes of Fact'.

[11] Husak, 'Justifications and the Criminal Liability of Accessories' 494–96, 504, 509.

[12] A Eser, 'Justification and Excuse' (1976) 24 *American Journal of Comparative Law* 621, 621–23, 635, 637.

[13] M Gur-Arye, 'Should a Criminal Code Distinguish between Justification and Excuse?' (1992) 5 *Canadian Journal of Law and Jurisprudence* 215.

[14] M Gur-Arye, 'Legitimating Official Brutality: Can the War against Terror Justify Torture?' (2003) dx.doi.org/10.2139/ssrn.391580, 21.

Robinson[15] and Westen[16] demur insofar as the agent's subjective reasons for acting is concerned. They argue that irrespective of the agent's reasons for acting, if the outcome the agent brought about was not objectively wrongful, she is justified in causing it (although she might still be convicted of an attempt to commit the crime that she prima facie committed).

Nevertheless, all of the scholars mentioned above are united in that while they are comfortable with excuses being analysed on a subjective basis, they either reject subjectivist bases for justifications altogether or require them to coincide with the negation of the objective, outcome-related 'wrongfulness' of what occurred. At the heart of each of their theories of justification and excuse, then, is the proposition that justifications negate the objective outcome-related 'wrongness'[17] of the prima facie offence committed, whereas excuses relate to factors personal to the actor that negate the actor's blameworthiness for committing the prima facie offence.[18] This is what I call the 'wrongness hypothesis'.

Uniacke and Duff also subscribe to the wrongness hypothesis, but they do so in a slightly different manner. Uniacke's theory is that whether conduct is justified rather than excused depends on the perspective from which it is being evaluated. For Uniacke, moral justification must be judged on the basis of the facts as the agent reasonably perceived them (or, as she terms it, 'agent-perspectivally'). However, a legal justification is an all-relevant-things-considered judgment that it was factually appropriate to have engaged in the particular conduct.[19] Hence, Uniacke would call a putatively justified agent 'perspectivally justified' and would recognise that such an agent has a complete moral justification and a legal basis for a complete excuse. Duff uses slightly different labels—he would say that a putatively justified agent acts in a manner that was 'warranted' and thus morally justified. However, he insists that legal justification requires both warrant and objective

---

[15] PH Robinson, 'A Theory of Justification: Societal Harm as a Prerequisite for Criminal Liability' (1975) 23 *UCLA Law Review* 266, 272–73. See also PH Robinson, 'Rules of Conduct and Principles of Adjudication' (1990) 57 *University of Chicago Law Review* 729, 749–50; and PH Robinson, 'The Bomb Thief and the Theory of Justification Defenses' (1997) *Criminal Law Forum* 387, 394–99.

[16] P Westen, 'An Attitudinal Theory of Excuse' (2006) 3 *Law and Philosophy* 289, 306.

[17] Note that the usage of the term 'wrongness' for the present purposes does not coincide with the sense in which I use the term 'wrong' in advancing my own thesis. For my own preferred usage, see note 22 in Ch 3 below.

[18] Admittedly, this is a gross simplification. However, I believe that the features that each of these scholars associates with justification can be traced to this underlying (and sometimes unspoken) assumption, since these features would not follow if the stated proposition were false. See also RA Duff, 'Rule-Violations and Wrongdoings' in S Shute and AP Simester (eds), *Criminal Law Theory: Doctrines of the General Part* (Oxford, Oxford University Press, 2002) 62; MN Berman and IP Farrell, 'Provocation Manslaughter as Partial Justification and Partial Excuse' (2011) 52 *William and Mary Law Review* 1027, 1032. I might add that I do not think that subscription to the wrongness hypothesis is a necessary feature of any consequentialist, deontological or hybrid account of the ontology of a wrong. That is a further choice. I have identified the theorists named because they do make that further choice and I think that they represent the predominant line of thinking on this issue.

[19] S Uniacke, *Permissible Killing* (Cambridge, Cambridge University Press, 1994) 12.

rightness.[20] As such, for the purposes of legal justification, though not moral justification, both Uniacke and Duff subscribe to the wrongness hypothesis.

The wrongness hypothesis is not universally accepted, of course. Greenawalt[21] and Baron,[22] for instance, theorise the availability of a justificatory defence broadly on the basis of subjective perceptions of facts, and would accordingly allow that an actor whose actions do occasion an objectively wrong outcome can be justified. Nevertheless, it is no exaggeration to state that the dominant explanation of the theoretical distinction between justifications and excuses relies upon the wrongness hypothesis.

1.2 Questioning the Wrongness Hypothesis

Theories premised on the wrongness hypothesis insist that a (legally) justified act does not occasion a legal wrong and that a 'putatively justified' actor who in fact authors a legal wrong cannot be justified in law. In these theories, the label 'justified' communicates (to the public and to the defendant concerned) a composite judgment about the actor and the action—the judgment that the actor did the right thing *and* that objectively the right thing happened. When either one of these statements is not true—ie, either the actor did not subjectively, and in the transitive verb sense, *do* the right thing, or she did, but all things considered the right thing did not happen—the 'justified' label is withheld.

Greenawalt's contrary position is premised on his insistence that a 'person may distinguish his evaluation of the desirability of the act from his evaluation of the actor's conduct'.[23] He argues that:

> So long as one exercises the best possible judgment on the facts he can reasonably acquire, the existence of other facts knowable only in some practically unimportant sense is immaterial for purposes of moral evaluation. His act is justified even if, in retrospect, the estimation turns out to have been wrong. Neither moral relevance nor ordinary usage supports distinguishing between justification and excuse on the basis of a line between unknowable and knowable facts.[24]

This line of argument stems from a counter-definition of justification as being a matter of moral evaluation of the actor and not the act. Thus, in order for the

---

[20] RA Duff, *Answering for Crime* (Oxford, Hart Publishing, 2007) 281–84.

[21] K Greenawalt, 'Distinguishing Justifications from Excuses' (1986) 49(3) *Law and Contemporary Problems* 89, 91–92, 102. See also Greenawalt, 'The Perplexing Borders' 1903.

[22] M Baron, 'Justifications and Excuses' (2005) 2 *Ohio State Journal of Criminal Law* 387, 393, 396–98. See also M Baron, 'The Provocation Defense and the Nature of Justification' (2009) 43 *University of Michigan Journal of Law Reform* 117, 124–30.

[23] Greenawalt, 'Distinguishing Justifications from Excuses' 94. See also his comments at 102 of the same essay, where he explicitly rejects the wrongness hypothesis.

[24] ibid 94–95, footnotes omitted.

actor to have been justified, it is not necessary that the act be justified—ie, that the 'correct' outcome resulted from her actions. This proposition also finds support in the common law, according to which, if a person acts in self-defence on the basis of a genuine belief in facts that, if true, would justify her acting in self-defence, then she is justified, and has a complete defence to a crime of personal violence, even if it transpires that her belief was unreasonable.[25] Baron argues along similar lines.[26] Both, then, reject the wrongness hypothesis.

Which approach is correct? Is justification an evaluation of the merits of both the actor and the act or is it just an evaluation of the actor? Both approaches have some appeal and, to be clear, neither approach has a knock-down argument against the other, since both are premised on intuited understandings of what it is to be justified. However, there are good reasons to doubt the usefulness of the wrongness hypothesis approach. Wrongness hypothesis-based theories use the label 'justified' only when the label can also communicate to the public the finding that the right thing happened—that in some sense the victim has no legitimate grounds to complain about the violation of her rights. However, it does so at the cost of obscuring information about whether the actor *did* the right thing. It uses the same label for actors who *did* the right thing and actors who did not, in cases in which, all things considered, the right thing did not happen. Information about whether the victim deserved the rights violation she suffered or whether the breach of the regulatory provision served a good purpose may well be of interest to the public. However, one doubts that the criminal court's judgments are the appropriate medium to convey this information, especially when they can only do so at the cost of information about the defendant's personal deservingness of blame. Arguably, a criminal conviction or acquittal (whether by way of justification or excuse) should be a ruling about the defendant, because at least in the popular imagination, it assigns a label primarily to the defendant. Any information that it conveys about whether the right thing (all things considered) happened should be purely incidental,[27] and it certainly should not obscure information about the defendant. Intuitively, the sense one gets is that the criminal court's primary purpose is to judge the defendant, and not to judge whether the victim deserved to suffer a violation of her rights. This latter task seems best left to civil courts, which are responsible for determining whether a victim deserves compensation.

However, a lot has been written about justifications and excuses on the basis of the wrongness hypothesis, and so we should also consider the normative

---

[25] *Beckford v R* [1988] AC 130, 144.

[26] Baron, 'The Provocation Defense' 124–30.

[27] In other words, the primary message in a criminal conviction should be 'We have considered the facts of this case and conclude that D is a criminal—she committed φ offence', not 'We have considered the facts of this case and conclude that φ offence has been committed [against V]'.

argument for the appropriateness of the wrongness hypothesis. Since the term 'justification' has no preordained meaning, there is no 'correct' approach to theorising it that is simply waiting to be discovered. Hence, the argument for the most appropriate way to understand justification has to be normative, and the strength of any such argument depends on its rational appeal and the plausibility of the system it generates. The wrongness hypothesis is appealing because it is elegant and simple, and it seems to fit neatly into the structure that we associate with criminal law. The theory taps into our intuition that in the same way as offence definitions can be split up into elements of actus reus and mens rea, the categories of defences can also be split up into those that negate concerns underlying the actus reus stipulation, dubbed 'justifications', and those that negate concerns underlying the mens rea, dubbed 'excuses'.[28] This approach is attractive, but it makes an unsubstantiated logical leap in assuming that by conceiving of offences and defences symmetrically, we can formulate a good description of how criminal laws ought to function. In fact, to the best of my knowledge, there is no (non-intuited) reason that has been offered to substantiate the assumption that the actus reus/justification and mens rea/excuse symmetry has anything to do with normatively establishing the manner in which the law ought to function. True, offence and defence definitions (and, within them, actus reus, mens rea, justification and excuse stipulations) perform different functions within the criminal law, but they are not *how* the criminal law functions. At the very least, they do not found the only account of how the criminal law functions.

Another plausible account, and one that offers more narrative exposition, says that the criminal law functions by ex ante stipulating conduct that should be avoided and ex post evaluating cases in which the conduct happens anyway in order to determine the blameworthiness of the actor.[29] On this account, offence stipulations (which set out the actus reus and mens rea requirements) relate to the ex ante stage of criminal law, and so their features would be adapted to the function that they perform, viz providing prior conduct guidance with a view to avoiding certain harms. On the other hand, supervening defences are raised after the harm has occurred, at the stage of trial, in order to protect the defendant against a blaming judgment. Arguably, then, their features should relate primarily to the function that they perform at this stage, viz undermining the apparent blameworthiness of the defendant. On this view, all supervening defences would function by negating (at least some aspects of) the defendant's blameworthiness, and none of them need necessarily negate the occurrence of a wrong.

One might object that on any plausible moral account of criminal law, there must be *some* moral value ascribed to what happened, such that when a

---

[28] See in this connection Eser's account of the evolution of this approach in German criminal law philosophy: Eser 'Justification and Excuse' 626–29.

[29] See, for instance, AP Simester and A von Hirsch, *Crimes, Harms, and Wrongs* (Oxford, Hart Publishing, 2011) 3.

morally wrong thing happens, some adverse moral judgement of the actor who caused it should follow, even if we decide to excuse the actor on account of her non-culpability. The alternative account I have just outlined seems unable to accommodate this moral value, since it disconnects the question of justification from whether a moral wrong occurred. However, this objection proceeds on the false assumption that the moral value of what happened must be accommodated at the ex post stage of determining the blameworthiness of an actor. There is no reason that this must necessarily be true and if it is not, then this creates the logical space necessary in the alternative account outlined above to ascribe moral value to what actually happened without necessarily connecting justification to the non-occurrence of a wrong. One alternative stage of the criminal process at which the moral value of what happened can be accommodated is the ex ante stage. One might, for instance, frame the ex ante stipulation meant to prevent a moral wrong 'φ' such that it is o nly violated when φ actually happens (as opposed to when the actor tries to cause φ or does not take care not to cause φ). In a system like this, when φ fortuitously did not happen despite the actor's best efforts, the stipulation against causing φ would not be violated and the actor would attract no blame vis-a-vis the stipulation against causing φ (although she may well attract blame vis-a-vis other stipulations). In taking account of the fact that what happened was not φ, this account of the criminal law would ascribe moral value to what actually happened.

Despite its widespread currency, then, the wrongness hypothesis has no argument to conclusively establish its superiority over an account of supervening defences that explains them by reference to the functions they perform at the ex post stage of criminal law. To be fair, the converse is also true. However, since there are good reasons to doubt the usefulness of the wrongness hypothesis, it may be time to consider whether an account of supervening defences that explains them by reference to the functions they perform at the ex post stage of criminal law is more convincing. To this end, I make the assumption, for the purposes of this study, that the wrongness hypothesis is incorrect or, at least, unhelpful. Instead, I describe rationale-based defences in terms of the stages of the criminal law. If the system of justification and excuse that I describe is more persuasive than those predicated on the wrongness hypothesis, then that would go some way towards vindicating my assumption.

1.3 Conduct Rules, Decision Rules and the Stages of Criminal Justice

Let us examine further the proposition that the criminal law functions in discrete temporal stages. In framing their theory about the role of deterrence in criminal justice, Simester and von Hirsch observe that the criminal justice system operates in stages and that it has different functions at each stage.[30] The first stage of criminal justice is forward-looking or prospective. It has to do with the criminal law's purely norm-setting function. At this stage, the criminal law is concerned with ex ante proscribing harmful conduct. The second stage of criminal justice is adjudicatory and evaluative, or backward-looking. After a general criminal law norm is violated, the criminal justice system must evaluate the prima facie offender's conduct to see whether, in view of her conduct, she deserves a blaming judgment. If that is the case, it must also evaluate whether she deserves punishment and, if so, how much.

A closely related and overlapping—arguably even congruent—concept to which Dan-Cohen draws attention is the 'old but neglected idea that a distinction can be drawn in the law between rules addressed to the general public and rules addressed to officials'.[31] The former set of rules are 'conduct rules' and the latter set are 'decision rules'. Dan-Cohen argues that any given rule may be a conduct rule, a decision rule or both.[32] In general, he explains that conduct rules give notice to the public about conduct that is proscribed and subject to criminal sanction, whereas decision rules guide decision-makers like the police, prosecutors and judges in assessing the blameworthiness of, and imposing sanctions upon, conduct rule violators.[33] Conduct rules, then, are concerned with ex ante guiding behaviour, so as to prevent the occurrence of a particular harm, whereas decision rules are concerned with allocating blame appropriately after the harm has occurred.

Because the primary rationale of conduct rules is to give notice, it is argued that they should be intelligible to the public and must clearly stipulate legal requirements so that people can avoid committing criminal offences. Accordingly, they should be simple, brief and grounded in objective criteria in order to avoid unpredictability, vagueness and ambiguity.[34]

Decision rules are addressed to officials empowered and trained to make judgments. They are routinely broad and open-ended, allowing the decision-maker to take into account the complex and varied situational factors of a particular case,

---

[30] Simester and von Hirsch, *Crimes, Harms, and Wrongs* 3. The authors divide the operation of substantive criminal law into three stages: criminalisation; adjudication and conviction; and punishment. This study is concerned with the first two stages. See also PH Robinson, *Structure and Function in Criminal Law* (Oxford, Clarendon Press, 1997) 125.

[31] M Dan-Cohen, 'Decision Rules and Conduct Rules: On Acoustic Separation in Criminal Law' (1984) 97 *Harvard Law Review* 625. See also M Dan-Cohen, 'Reply' in PH Robinson, SP Garvey and KK Ferzan (eds), *Criminal Law Conversations* (Oxford, Oxford University Press, 2009).

[32] Dan-Cohen, 'Decision Rules and Conduct Rules' 631.

[33] For a summary of Dan-Cohen's argument and a general overview of the conduct rule/decision rule idea, see MR Gardner, '"Decision Rules" and Kids: Clarifying the Vagueness Problems with Status Offense Statutes and School Disciplinary Rules' (2010) 89 *Nebraska Law Review* 1, 4–7. See also Robinson, 'Rules of Conduct' 731; MN Berman, 'Justification and Excuse, Law and Morality' (2003) 53 *Duke Law Journal* 1, 32–36. It is not only rules that proscribe conduct that can be conduct rules—rules that permit conduct that is otherwise proscribed may also be addressed to, and attempt to guide the conduct of, the general public. So the rule that one may use reasonable force in self-defence is also, at least partly, a conduct rule. I will discuss permissive conduct rules in greater detail in section 2.1 in Ch 2.

[34] Gardner, '"Decision Rules"' 5–6. See also Robinson, 'Rules of Conduct' 732.

as well as to apply subjective criteria inviting individualised discretion and normative assessments.[35] This is why decision rules are, and ought to be, framed in relatively indeterminate terms. Decision rules do not aim to provide notice; their primary rationale is to define the rules by which cases can be decided.

It is immediately apparent that conduct rules find a natural home in the ex ante stage of the criminal law, which deals with giving notice of rules meant to prevent harmful conduct.[36] Offence definitions may be viewed as being primarily[37] conduct rules, giving notice of conduct (in the form of actus reus and mens rea[38] stipulations) that should be avoided. They are therefore grounded in objective criteria and state rules of prospective guidance for all persons governed by the criminal justice system. Our experience of crime definition rules tells us that they are usually stated as rules for immediate application, as opposed to rules the application of which is contingent upon the existence of specified circumstances, and that they are usually impersonal, in that they are addressed to all people generally, without reference to the particular characteristics or circumstances of the individual addressees of the norm.[39] Furthermore, since they are principally concerned with giving prior notice to the general public in order to prevent harm, they are not primarily concerned with making personal blaming judgments in respect of a person violating the rule.

It is also apparent that the adjudicatory stage of criminal justice is populated by decision rules.[40] A violation of a general criminal law conduct norm which results in the proscribed outcome (that is, the commission of a prima facie offence) activates the jurisdiction of the criminal justice system to punish.[41] The system's

---

[35] Gardner, '"Decision Rules"' 6.

[36] H Stewart, 'The Role of Reasonableness in Self-Defence' (2003) 16 *Canadian Journal of Law and Jurisprudence* 317, 333–34. See also M Thorburn, 'Justifications, Powers, and Authority' (2008) 117 *Yale Law Journal* 1070, 1095.

[37] Primarily, but not solely. Offence definitions also function as one of the decision rules in play when determining the blameworthiness of the actor after she has committed a prima facie offence.

[38] The appropriateness of including a mens rea stipulation in a conduct rule has been debated, with GP Fletcher, *Rethinking Criminal Law* (Boston, Little Brown & Company, 1978) 475–79, 553–54, 694–97 arguing that it is essential; Robinson, *Structure and Function* 129–37 arguing that it is mostly unnecessary; and Duff, 'Rule-Violations and Wrongdoings' 68–74 arguing that both views have their flaws. Although I cannot enter into this debate here, I prefer and adopt Fletcher's views, which appear to have gained the most currency.

[39] These characteristics, while generally true of offence definitions, need not be true of all conduct rules, or even all conduct rules within the criminal law.

[40] For instance, Dan-Cohen, 'Decision Rules and Conduct Rules' 637–38 argues that duress and some instances of necessity are decision rules that would, in a world of acoustic separation, be conveyed only to officials. I will argue in this book that other defences too are best viewed as decision rules. See also Stewart, 'The Role of Reasonableness' 10.

[41] By 'activates', I mean that it is only once it is established that a prima facie offence was committed that the judge has the jurisdiction to hold the defendant guilty of committing a crime and, thereupon, to punish her. This jurisdiction may be exercised fully, partially or not at all. See M Gur-Arye, 'Justifying the Distinction between Justifications and Power (Justifications vs. Power)' (2010) 5 *Criminal Law and Philosophy* 293, 296, who explains that this is in line with the German criminal law's structure of criminal offences, as per which: 'Conduct that does not satisfy all elements of the definition of the offense remains outside the scope of the criminal law. Conduct that satisfies the elements of the definition

officials must now evaluate, by reference to decision rules addressed to them, the prima facie offender's conduct to determine whether she deserves a blaming judgment and, if so, whether she also deserves punishment. These decision rules include rules relating to the appreciation of evidence, the procedure to apply at trial, the appropriate sentence to pass and—critically for the purposes of this study—the availability of defences.

This is not to suggest either that offence definitions are solely conduct rules or that defences are necessarily solely decision rules. As Dan-Cohen recognises, the same rule can be both a conduct rule and a decision rule. However, I do make a more limited assertion here—in an account of the criminal law that is sensitive to the temporal stages in which it functions, the characteristic feature of an offence definition is its nature as a conduct rule, and the characteristic feature of a defence, qua defence, is its nature as a decision rule. I will rely upon this stipulation about the characteristic features of offence definitions and defences as I attempt to derive and describe the nature of supervening defences.

1.4 From Supervening to Rationale-Based Defences

The rejection of the wrongness hypothesis has important implications for how we conceive of supervening defences. Consider the following alternative statements made by a defendant who admits to having committed the actus reus of an offence with the stipulated mens rea:

1. 'I am entitled to a defence because, even though this formed no part of my reasons for acting, my actions did more good than harm.'
2. 'I am entitled to a defence because, even though this formed no part of my reasons for acting, my victim happened to be in the process of attacking me with lethal force and my actions had the effect of repelling the attack.'
3. 'I am entitled to a defence because of my reasons for having acted.'

In principle, all three statements are claims that the defendant is entitled to a supervening defence. However, not all of these claims are compatible with the rejection of the wrongness hypothesis. Statements 1 and 2 above assert (for different reasons) that although the prima facie offence was committed, in fact, no wrong (depending on how one defines a wrong) meriting criminal law intervention occurred. But the rejection of the wrongness hypothesis as the basis of supervening defences means that such assertions, even if they are true, cannot

---

constitutes a criminal wrongdoing which may be negated by justifications.' Hence, the acceptance of a justification is a (negative) exercise of the jurisdiction to blame and punish rather than an acknowledgement that no such jurisdiction ever arose.

themselves ground a supervening defence. In other words, no supervening defence can operate solely by demonstrating that in fact there was no wrong meriting criminal law intervention. Statement 3 is wide enough to include both cases in which on the whole no wrong occurred and cases in which a wrong did occur. Its exculpatory force derives from the defendant's reasons for acting. Only statement 3 can ground a supervening defence that is compatible with the rejection of the wrongness hypothesis.

Another way of looking at this is that at the time that the defendant makes a claim to it, a supervening defence functions purely as a decision rule. At this time, the harm proscribed by the conduct rules has already come to pass and we are now at the ex post stage of blame evaluation. To make the argument at this stage that in the instant case, the harm done is not one that merits criminalisation (as opposed to criminal sanction) is as out of place as an argument that raises as a defence to a charge of theft the proposition that theft should not be a criminal offence. Such an argument is an appeal for individual and retroactive legal reform rather a claim to a defence.

The rejection of the wrongness hypothesis then reduces all supervening defences to rationale-based defences, and I think that this is a morally defensible reduction in the scope of the defences available.[42] Indeed, for many theorists, including those who subscribe to the wrongness hypothesis, a supervening defence is only available if the defendant acts for the right reasons.[43] Accordingly, I will henceforth use the term 'rationale-based defence' instead of 'supervening defence', except where the latter is more appropriate for the context.

1.5 A Rationale-Based Alternative to the Wrongness Hypothesis

The rejection of the wrongness hypothesis for justifications means that the standard account of excuses being based on factors that negate the culpability of the agent no longer convinces, since it can no longer explain the distinction between justifications and excuse. Excuses do negate the culpability of the agent, but then so do justifications. What then sets justifications apart from rationale-based excuses?

My hypothesis builds on Karl Binding's suggestion that the normative system that characterises and underlies core rules of the criminal law operates independently

---

[42] I will qualify this assertion somewhat in section 3.2.1 in Ch 3.
[43] See, for instance, Greenawalt, 'Distinguishing Justifications from Excuses' 95; Fletcher, 'The Right Deed' 320; J Gardner, 'The Gist of Excuses' (1998) 1 *Buffalo Criminal Law Review* 575, 588; AP Simester, 'Wrongs and Reasons' (2009) 72 *MLR* 648, 659, 664.

of the doctrinal law designed by different jurisdictions to capture its content.[44] I will describe my understanding of the morally derived system of norms that I argue underlies the criminal law[45] and will then propose that an agent who violates an offence stipulation despite acting for reasons that comport with the criminal law's morally derived normative foundations acts with justification.[46] In fact, I will argue that this is the paradigmatic form of a justification. However, situations may still arise in which although the normative guidance underlying the criminal law requires that a person act in a particular manner, it would be hypocritical for society to demand this of the person, given that it would not demand the same of itself. In such cases, I propose that the defence made available to the defendant should be classified as an excuse.[47] In paradigm cases, the grant of an excuse records our judgment that the defendant's reasoning as revealed by her conduct, though morally lacking, conformed to standards that we as a society normatively expect from ourselves when performing the same role as her and that therefore it would be hypocritical for us to single her out for the label of 'evil' or 'criminal'.

My hypothesis, then, is that we can distinguish between justifications and rationale-based excuses on the basis of the quality of the reasoning displayed by the defendant. I therefore refer to it as the 'quality of reasoning hypothesis'. In order to make good my hypothesis, I must demonstrate the following:

1. the manner in which conduct rules and decision rules operate in the criminal law;
2. that the normative system that characterises the core of the criminal law derives from moral norms;
3. the actual structure of the normative system that characterises the core of the criminal law; and
4. the implications of this structure of underlying norms for the contours of justifications and rationale-based excuses, as set up in terms of my hypothesis.

I will attempt to do so in the subsequent chapters of this study.

Only thereafter will I be able to explore in greater detail the manner in which supervening defences ought to work in practice, and the corollaries and limitations generated by the hypothesised view of justifications and defences. The success of the argument will depend in part upon the intuitive plausibility of the entire framework of supervening defences that it generates and in part upon the appeal of the intuitions on which it is founded.

---

[44] Because Binding's argument was made in German (in his treatise *Die Normen und ihre Ubertretung*), I rely on Eser's summary of it in Eser, 'Justification and Excuse' 625. Binding separates the notion of 'unlawfulness' from the statutory text intended to capture it, thereby giving unlawfulness an autonomous function. He argues that what is truly violated by a criminal act is not the penal provision which provides a sanction, but instead the commands and prohibitions of the legal system, ie, its norms, which in theory are logically prior to the written law. Accordingly, the concept of wrongfulness must be oriented to and conceived out of the substance of the norms.

[45] See Ch 3.

[46] See Chs 4 and 5.

[47] See Ch 6.

Part II

Defences in the Structure of the Criminal Law

2

Reasons and Perspective in the Criminal Law

In this chapter, I further explore the distinction made between the criminal law's conduct rules and its decision rules, and examine arguments relating to the choice of perspective to be adopted in framing and applying these rules. I argue that the special relationship between criminal law and morality requires that criminal law conduct rules be framed by reference to objective facts. In analysing the perspective that should be adopted when applying decision rules, I distinguish between two threads of the rational process, viz, the process of observing facts and reaching reasoned factual conclusions and assessments on their basis ('functional reasoning'),[1] and the process of inculcating and displaying commitment to normative rules of conduct ('norm-reasoning'). I argue that different blaming judgments flow from flaws in a person's functional reasoning and flaws in her norm-reasoning, and, further, that the quality of the defendant's norm-reasoning ought to be assessed by reference to the defendant's subjective perspective. This view of the structure of blaming judgments will have a direct bearing on the arguments I make about how we should conceive of the difference between a justification and a rationale-based defence.

2.1 Reasons and Objectivity in Conduct Rules

Raz's analysis in the seminal *Practical Reason and Norms* is based on the fundamental claim that: 'Reasons are referred to in explaining, in evaluating, and in guiding people's behaviour.'[2] The relationship of reasons to guiding and evaluating

---

[1] The cognitive and intellectual processes that I pick out with the term 'functional reasoning' are a subset of the processes generally referred to as 'epistemic reasoning'. However, this subset excludes moral epistemology. In addition, although norms themselves can be facts, they are not the kind of facts I have in mind when talking about the process of observing facts. Therefore, I adopt non-standard terminology here. Nevertheless, when discussing existing literature on the subject and in the interests of clarity, I will occasionally need to refer to 'epistemic mistakes' and 'epistemic reasoning'. These references should be understood in context.

[2] J Raz, *Practical Reason and Norms* (Oxford, Oxford University Press, 1999 [1975]) 15–16.

behaviour can reveal a lot about how the criminal law functions, because these are amongst the essential functions of the criminal law.

One area of particular interest is whether there is any difference between the logical bases for conduct rules and decision rules. Raz argues that 'reasons are used to guide behaviour, and people are to be guided by what is the case, not what they believe to be the case'.[3] He further argues that:

> Only reasons understood as facts are normatively significant; only they determine what ought to be done. To decide what we should do, we must find what the world is like, and not what our thoughts are like. The other notion of reasons is relevant exclusively for explanatory purposes and not at all for guiding purposes.[4]

If one broadly accepts these assertions, then certainly norms to guide behaviour (ie, conduct rules) should be based on reasons that are facts rather than beliefs. In making the implicit assertion that (at least) conduct rules ought to refer to facts and not beliefs, Raz acknowledges and addresses the obvious counter by arguing that:

> To be sure, in order to be guided by what is the case a person must come to believe that it is the case. Nevertheless it is the fact and not his belief in it which should guide him and which is a reason. If p is the case, then the fact that I do not believe that p does not establish that p is not a reason for me to perform some action. The fact that I am not aware of any reason does not show that there is none. If reasons are to serve for guiding and evaluating behaviour then not all reasons are beliefs. It may seem that reasons which are neither the beliefs nor the desires of the agent cannot be used in explaining his behaviour, but this is a mistake. The explanation depends on his belief that the reasons obtain, but again this does not establish that his belief is the reason. All it shows is that this type of explanation of a person's behaviour turns on his belief that certain reasons apply rather than on the fact that they do apply. We can understand his behaviour even if we think he was wrong in believing that there were good reasons for him to do what he did.[5]

Raz's argument on this point makes a subtle appeal to our evaluation of the outcome of the behaviour, and invites us to make a similar evaluation of the behaviour that caused it. The resulting evaluation is one that refers to a standard of 'ought', based on a 'god's eye' awareness of all the contextual circumstances. The adoption of such a reference point assumes that conduct norms in the criminal law are meant to guide agents to achieve ideal and absolute goals (even if, on occasion, they cannot possibly be aware of the circumstances that make the guidance applicable) rather than to set attainable goals. This presupposition is not self-evidently correct.

Stewart, on the other hand, argues that since conduct rules must be capable of guiding conduct, they cannot demand knowledge of facts that one could not

---

[3] ibid 17. See also PH Robinson, 'Competing Theories of Justification: Deeds versus Reasons' in AP Simester and ATH Smith (eds), *Harm and Culpability* (Oxford, Clarendon Press, 1996) 64–65.

[4] Raz, *Practical Reason and Norms* 18. See also Robinson, 'Competing Theories' 64–65.

[5] Raz, *Practical Reason and Norms* 17.

reasonably have been expected to know.[6] Hence, he views the role of criminal law conduct norms as providing attainable rather than abstract guidance, and consequently insists that the conduct norm refer to accessible rather than absolute truths. Again, he makes a linking assumption that is not self-evidently correct. His implicit assertion is that framing conduct rules by reference to objectively true facts rather than subjective perceptions of the facts necessarily prejudices their ability to offer useful guidance. However, if one does not bind oneself to the view that in every case, being in violation of a conduct rule automatically attracts blame (or even prima facie blame) for disobedience of its guidance, conduct rules can offer useful normative guidance even when framed by reference to objective facts. While the legal provisions that typify criminal law conduct rules also have symmetrical decision rule aspects directing the decision-maker to evaluate reported behaviour by reference to the conduct rule, these are rarely the only decision rules operating in the evaluation of the behaviour. In fact, only in the exceptional set of strict liability state-of-affairs crimes does the mere circumstance of being in violation of a conduct rule ipso facto translate into a blaming evaluation of the violator. Blameworthiness usually requires more. If one admits the possibility that these other decision rules that operate in the criminal law may require reference to perceived rather than objective facts, then it is possible to imagine conduct norms that refer to the 'objective facts', and nevertheless offer useful normative guidance to the addressees of the rule, without necessarily generating unfair blaming judgments. I will make the argument that, in fact, key decision rules dealing with making personal blaming judgments do require reference to perceived rather than objective facts in section 2.2.4.

However, the question remains: should we prefer to frame conduct rules by reference to objective facts or to facts as perceived? We can start by considering when it is legitimate for the state to offer guidance in the form of criminal law conduct rules. Humans naturally and constituently possess purposive agency[7]—the ability to choose one's willed actions, even in defiance of one's biological needs and instincts. In the absence of legitimate guidance about *how to exercise* this purposive

---

[6] H Stewart, 'The Role of Reasonableness in Self-Defence' (2003) 16 *Canadian Journal of Law and Jurisprudence* 317, 333–36.

[7] ME Bratman, 'Planning Agency, Autonomous Agency' in *Structures of Agency: Essays* (New York, Oxford University Press, 2007) 197–98 treats purposive agency as one of the core features of human agency. In addition, he also treats reflectiveness, planfulness and a conception of our agency as temporally extended as core features of human agency. However, for the purposes of the present study, it is sufficient to focus on purposive agency. This is because, as Bratman notes elsewhere, we can sometimes do things that are merely purposive and that do not involve the other three capacities identified. See ME Bratman, 'Reflection, Planning, and Temporally Extended Agency' in *Structures of Agency: Essays* (New York, Oxford University Press, 2007) 21–22. Since our experience of criminal justice systems is that criminal liability can attach even to such 'merely' purposive actions, and this study concentrates on the criminal law, it is appropriate to focus on 'mere' purposive agency. See also A Gewirth, *Reason and Morality* (Chicago, University of Chicago Press, 1978) 26–42, who bases his principle of generic consistency on the fundamental assumption that all morally salient actions are voluntary and purposive. It is a human's innate capacity for voluntary and purposive action that I refer to as purposive agency.

agency, each person enjoys the archetypical Hohfeldian liberty[8] to do as she pleases, and how she chooses to act is entirely her own business.[9] But although her capacity to exercise her purposive agency as she pleases is normatively unrestrained, there is no legitimacy implied by the absence of such normative restraint. A person who exercises this Hohfeldian liberty acts neither legitimately nor illegitimately—the absence of constraint is merely a starting point that may be altered by legitimate normative guidance.

In liberal states, we avoid giving people guidance in respect of conduct that is purely their own business.[10] Accordingly, I will treat only conduct that is not purely a private individual's business as being potentially subject to legitimate guidance. If a person's behaviour can be shown not to be the business of anyone else, it will be outside the domain of any legitimate guidance. Of course, it remains to be seen how broadly we define the scope of one's own business and the business of others, but in principle, the assertion is that legitimate liberal guidance is only possible in respect of conduct which is also the business of some natural or legal 'bearer' of business other than the actor. Where this is not the case, any guidance offered is illiberal, busybody guidance.

So, when are a person's actions not purely her own business? Since we are looking for an explanation that logically precedes legal norms, for the present we may ignore purely 'legal' persons—they do not exist in a pre-norm world. Now even in a world logically prior to legal norms, each person is possessed of certain elements that constitute her as a human. I will argue in sections 3.1 and 3.2.1 that each person is constituently entitled to possess and defend these elements, and is not subject to guidance to the contrary.[11] Even if the enumeration of the constituent elements that I propose seems unappealing, so long as one agrees that each human has *some* constituent elements and that even pre-legally, she may possess and defend these elements without being subject to legitimate guidance to the contrary, the argument may proceed. At the core of what is pre-legally a person's business are these constituent elements. Now although prior to any legitimate guidance to the contrary a person's chosen actions are entirely her own business,

---

[8] WN Hohfeld, *Fundamental Legal Conceptions as Applied in Judicial Reasoning and Other Legal Essays* (New Haven, Yale University Press, 1919) 35–49, particularly at 42–43.

[9] J Locke, *Two Treatises of Government and A Letter Concerning Toleration* (New Haven, Yale University Press, 2003 [1690]) 109–10 makes a similar, but not identical, proposition when he argues that prior to the state's laws, man is free to do as he pleases, subject only to the law of nature. The proposition made here is even more foundational—I argue that in the absence even of what Locke calls the law of nature, a human would be free to act as she pleases, simply because she is capable of doing so, and there is nothing to tell her not to do so.

[10] This was the broad view argued for by JS Mill, *On Liberty* (New Haven, Yale University Press, 2003 [1859]) 80–81, 121, 139–44. Although Mill's views have been shown to need some qualification over the years, it remains a broadly acceptable synopsis of the limits of the guidance that may be offered by a genuinely liberal state.

[11] T Hobbes, *Leviathan* (New Haven, Yale University Press, 2010 [1651]) 79–80 identifies a fundamental 'right' of nature that inheres in each person to preserve her own nature, and argues (at 81–82) that this right is inalienable.

when this person's actions affect the constituent elements of another, even without a system of legitimate guidance, it is clear that these actions are legitimately the business of the affected party as well.[12] The latter can legitimately complain about the former's actions and therefore can legitimately offer non-busybody guidance to the former in respect of these actions. The affected person's standing arises pre-legally and is a deviation from the default absence of such standing. Her pre-legal standing to legitimately offer guidance to restrict the conduct of others stems from and is limited to the effect that such conduct would actually have on her constituent elements. The only normative restrictions that can be supported by such a narrow pre-legal standing is guidance against *actually affecting* (as opposed to guidance requiring a person to try not to affect, or even guidance against trying to affect) the constituent elements of others.[13] Anything more than that would be illiberal, busybody guidance.[14]

The set of circumstances in which *the criminal law* can legitimately offer guidance will necessarily be some subset of all the cases in which at least *someone* can offer legitimate guidance.[15] It follows that a liberal criminal law's standing to offer normative conduct guidance is at least as narrowly drawn as the standing enjoyed by the person affected. In our pre-legal world, therefore, it is also, at least, limited to the actual effects that a person's behaviour has on the constituent elements of others. Accordingly, reference to the intended, (incorrectly) believed or possible effects of some behaviour in framing a norm relating to it is inappropriate.

---

[12] Contrast this with a situation in which two persons exercising their unrestrained capacity to act find themselves interfering with each other without affecting their respective constituent elements, because their actions are mutually contradictory or incompatible—say, both are trying to pick up and take away the same stone. On these facts, neither would be interfering with the actions of the other legitimately (or illegitimately), since their respective actions are themselves neither legitimate nor illegitimate; they are merely an exercise of their Hohfeldian liberties—their unrestrained capacity to act. Although conflict also arises in such cases, since the actions of both parties are entirely their own respective businesses, no non-busybody guidance can be offered to either.

[13] In this connection, see also HM Hurd, 'What in the World is Wrong?' (1994) 5 *Journal of Contemporary Legal Issues* 157, who also argues at length that for deontological moral theory, the most convincing and internally coherent way to identify a wrong is by reference to actually doing morally prohibited actions rather than trying to do them, or intending to do them, or deliberating about doing them, or being motivated to do them.

[14] The same proposition can, and I will argue in section 3.3 should, be extended by analogy to apply to a world in which the law has vested upon its subjects additional rights. These rights expand the set of matters that are the 'business' of each subject. Therefore, more cases will arise in which it is legitimate for a person to comment upon the conduct of others.

[15] For the present purposes, it is not necessary to adopt a concluded view on the characteristic features of that subset, but Duff and Marshall's explanation that only those wrongs that are 'public wrongs' ought to fall within the (potential) domain of the criminal law points us in the direction of a plausible answer. By 'public wrongs', Duff and Marshall mean wrongs that are properly the concern of 'the public', ie, all members of the polity, by virtue simply of their shared membership of the political community. See RA Duff and SE Marshall, 'Public and Private Wrongs' in J Chalmers, F Leverick and L Farmer (eds), *Essays in Criminal Law in Honour of Sir Gerald Gordon* (Edinburgh, Edinburgh University Press, 2010) 71–72; SE Marshall and RA Duff, 'Reply' in PH Robinson, SP Garvey and KK Ferzan (eds), *Criminal Law Conversations* (Oxford, Oxford University Press, 2009) 250; SE Marshall and RA Duff, 'Criminalization and Sharing Wrongs' (1998) 11(1) *Canadian Journal of Law and Jurisprudence* 7, 13–14.

In other words, an ideal liberal criminal law's guiding norms must necessarily be framed by reference to objective outcomes rather than subjective perceptions or anticipations of outcomes. Since we have already noted that the mere circumstance of being in default of a conduct rule need not necessarily lead to a blaming judgment, this idea is palatable.

We have so far considered only conduct rules that imperatively restrict a person's original unfettered capacity to act as she chooses, and since we start from a position of absolute unfettered capacity, the majority of conduct rules that we encounter will be of that nature. However, it is also possible to have conduct rules that permit, or at least recognise an immunity from contrary guidance in respect of, certain conduct.[16] Such conduct rules would effectively expand the scope of their addressees' liberty, since they would operate as overriding carve-outs from imperative conduct restricting rules. The philosophical constraints on the scope of imperative conduct restricting rules stem from the fact that they modify the default position of absolute unrestricted capacity to act as one chooses. But as 'permissive conduct rules' are not exceptions to this absolute unrestricted capacity to act as one chooses, they are not subject to the same philosophical constraints that rein in imperative conduct-restricting rules. They therefore need not necessarily be framed by reference to objective facts. For reasons that will become clear in sections 2.2.4 and 5.1, it is my view that in practice, it makes no difference whether such rules are framed by reference to objective facts or by reference to perceptions of facts.

On the primary argument made above, there can be no liberal moral criminal law conduct norm proscribing conduct that will not actually affect (in the sense of harm or perhaps offend) any person other than the actor. Moreover, even after such a norm is set in place, if the actor's disrespect for the conduct rule does not actually affect any other person (ie, when the disrespect of the conduct norm does not translate into a violation of it), the norm does not give the liberal criminal legal system any claim to a moral voice in censuring such behaviour. This hints at an explanation for why many modern criminal legal systems tend to differentially punish two people who attempt the same offence when only one of them succeeds, despite their equal personal culpability. The attempter simply does not affect other people in the same way and to the same extent as the person who completes the offence. Hence, the moral voice available to the criminal law in censuring an attempter is the relatively weak voice generated by the harm actually caused by the attempt (arguably, the expressive effect of the attempt and the example set by it) instead of the strong moral voice that harm constitutive of the completed offence would have generated.[17] An alternative way of looking at

---

[16] A similar distinction is also made in J Hruschka, 'Justifications and Excuses: A Systematic Approach' (2005) 2 *Ohio State Journal of Criminal Law* 407, 408. Rules of this sort will be discussed in greater detail in sections 4.1 and 5.1.

[17] J Dressler, 'Reassessing the Theoretical Underpinnings of Accomplice Liability: New Solutions to an Old Problem' (1985) 37 *Hastings Law Journal* 91, 99–100.

the same proposition is that in a retributive criminal legal system, the outer limit of the law's moral jurisdiction to censure for an offence 'φ' is directly correlated to a generalisation as to how much other people are affected by the offence.[18] While a mere attempt to commit φ may also be an objectively bad thing, it is bad only in a comparatively limited sense and therefore a failed attempt is less serious than the completed offence, and ought to be censured less strongly than a completed offence. Hence, the punishment prescribed for an attempt to commit φ tends, in many jurisdictions, to be lower than the punishment prescribed for actually committing φ.

In summary, in the context of the criminal law system, I generally agree with Raz's conclusion that conduct rules, at least to the extent that they restrict liberty, should be framed on the basis of facts as reasons for action. Once φ is identified as conduct to be avoided on pain of criminal sanction, the criminal law should say 'You should not φ' rather than 'You should not do what you believe to be φ', 'You should not try to φ' or 'You should try not to φ' when framing the conduct norm.

2.2 Reasons and Subjectivity in Decision Rules

Raz notes that reasons are used to evaluate a person's behaviour.[19] On that basis, we may explore the possibility that a rational agent can be adjudged blameworthy if her actions, in her circumstances, reflect poorly on the quality of her reasoning.[20] This suggestion is consistent with the accepted dogma that one prerequisite of any blaming evaluation of an agent's actions is that she must have been capable of exercising rational facilities while performing them.[21] Duff too recognises the link between the quality of reasoning and blame when he argues that a putatively justified agent acts in a 'warranted' and therefore not blameworthy, manner:

> An agent whose beliefs and actions are both epistemically and normatively reasonable is at least warranted in what she does … Whether warranted or justified, she can answer for

---

[18] For instance, AP Simester and A von Hirsch, *Crimes, Harms, and Wrongs* (Oxford, Hart Publishing, 2011) 3 argue that by criminalising an activity, the state declares that it is morally wrongful, instructs citizens not to do it and warns that upon default they are liable to be convicted and punished within specified limits. According to the authors, these limits signal the seriousness with which the act is regarded. See also A von Hirsch and A Ashworth, *Proportionate Sentencing* (Oxford, Oxford University Press, 2005) 131–32, 135–37; and Dressler, 'Reassessing the Theoretical Underpinnings' 104. GP Fletcher, 'The Right and the Reasonable' (1985) 98 *Harvard Law Review* 949, 961 also argues that 'in each type of retributive theory, the primary issue is wrongdoing. The gravity of the wrong determines the maximum severity of the punishment'. While I cannot argue for it here, I proceed on the basis that in victimising offences, the seriousness with which an act is regarded—ie, the gravity of the wrong—is directly related to how much it affects others.

[19] Raz, *Practical Reason and Norms* 15–16.

[20] V Tadros, *Criminal Responsibility* (Oxford, Oxford University Press, 2005) 65–66 supports a similar proposition, but argues from partly intuited notions of responsibility instead.

[21] This fact actually suggests an even stronger connection between reasoning and blame: although we may well be able to attribute causal responsibility to a person who is incapable of reasoning, such a

her actions with a clear conscience, even when they involved the commission of a crime: *her practical reasoning was impeccable*, and she acted reasonably in accordance with its conclusions; she acted either as she had sufficient reason to act, or at least as she had good reason to believe that she had sufficient reason to act.[22] (Emphasis added)

2.2.1 The Threads of Reasoning

It is useful to consider two threads of a person's reasoning separately. The first has to do with the person's exercised capacity to observe facts and reach reasoned factual conclusions and judgments on the basis of them. Let us call this functional reasoning. The second relates to the person's understanding and responsiveness to normative guidance. Let us call this norm-reasoning.[23]

To understand the distinction that I am proposing here, consider the following examples. First, consider the case of the pub landlord:

> T, a burly drunk, begins to act aggressively at a pub. D, the pub landlord asks T to leave, but this just makes T more aggressive. T starts to swing his arms around threateningly. At this, D pins T's arms to his side and bundles T onto the landing outside the pub door. Because D uses a bit too much force in doing so, T loses his balance, falls down a short flight of five steps into the street and strikes his head. T sustains a head injury, from which he dies.[24]

When questioned, D might explain why he used that amount of force by saying that he did not intend to use as much force as he had ended up using. Or perhaps he made a mistake about how strong he was, or how heavy T was, or how drunk and off-balance T was, or how slippery the floor was, and so underestimated the effect that the force would have. D employs functional reasoning in order to make all of these assessments, and so if D uses any of these explanations, he admits to exhibiting *functional reasoning* that was arguably, in some sense, deficient. Alternatively, D might explain that he intended to use exactly as much force as he used, but that he either believed that he was entitled to use that much force or didn't care whether or not he was entitled to use that much force. In reaching these

---

person is not blamed for causing harm. This indicates (albeit not conclusively) that it might be possible to argue that an agent can be considered blameworthy vis-a-vis a system of norms *only* if her actions, in her circumstances, reflect poorly on the quality of her reasoning. At this stage, I will not attempt to defend this stronger claim, but I believe that the overall tenor of my argument does support it.

[22] RA Duff, *Answering for Crime* (Oxford, Hart Publishing, 2007) 296; see also the more general views expressed at 267–71. Similarly, see AP Simester, 'A Disintegrated Theory of Culpability' in DJ Baker and J Horder (eds), *The Sanctity of Life and Criminal Law* (Cambridge, Cambridge University Press, 2013) 190.

[23] This distinction runs along similar lines to the one briefly described by Hruschka, 'Justifications and Excuses' 409. I do not make any claim that these threads are always mutually exclusive—as will become clear, although they are conceptually distinct, there may well be significant areas of overlap.

[24] These were the facts in the case of *R v Scarlett* [1993] 4 All ER 629.

conclusions, D employs norm-reasoning, and so if D offers these explanations, he admits to exhibiting *norm-reasoning* that was arguably, in some sense, deficient.

Consider also the case of the policeman in hot pursuit:

> D, a policeman, is called to a house to investigate a report of a dangerous gunman terrorising someone there, and on arrival, he sees T running away with what appears to be a gun. He chases T and, coming upon him as he rounds a corner, shoots T dead. At the time, T is unarmed, on his knees with his hands in the air, begging not to be shot.[25]

When questioned, D might explain that at the time, he genuinely (albeit wrongly) believed that T was about to shoot at him. Or perhaps he might say that he had aimed to fire a warning shot above T's head, but had missed his target and ended up killing T. In making judgments like whether T was about to shoot at him or whether he was aiming correctly and safely above T's head, D exercises his functional reasoning. Any mistakes he makes in doing so potentially reveal his functional reasoning in a poor light. Alternatively, D might explain that he intended to shoot T dead despite knowing that T was not trying to shoot at him because he either believed that he was entitled to shoot with deadly intent at suspects who had fled or because he didn't care whether or not he was so entitled. In reaching these decisions, D employs norm-reasoning, and so any mistakes he makes potentially reveal his norm-reasoning in a poor light.

A person who is poor at functional reasoning potentially invites blaming judgments that reflect that shortfall in exercising her exercised capacity to reason—she is careless or perhaps objectively reckless.[26] Such a person exhibits deficient functional reasoning in failing to observe situational facts that she should have observed, or in reaching unwarranted conclusions on the basis of those facts, or in erroneously underestimating or overestimating the potential risks of a course of action, or the extent of the consequences it might generate. The common thread in all these errors of reasoning is that (in the absence of any normative guidance as to how good the person's functional reasoning should be) they do not reveal the person in a bad light in respect of her commitment to, and appreciation of, normative rules of conduct; they merely show that the person made an error of judgment in her assessment of aspects of the physical world.

---

[25] These were the facts in the case of *Beckford v R* [1988] AC 130.

[26] The exact meaning of recklessness is subject to some dispute. Some authorities suggest that a person is reckless when she is actually aware of the potential adverse consequences of her planned actions and, in the circumstances actually known to her, it is unreasonable to take the risk of causing these consequences, but she goes ahead anyway. This test is one of advertence. In this context, see *R v G* [2004] 1 AC 1034, which built upon the subjective approach to recklessness set out in *R v Cunningham* [1957] 2 QB 396. Other authorities suggest that a person who goes ahead with her planned actions without actually being aware of the unreasonable risk of adverse consequences, even though such risk would have been obvious to a reasonable person, is also reckless. See, for instance, *R v Caldwell* [1982] AC 341, which laid down this standard of 'objective recklessness'. English law has since distanced itself from *Caldwell*-style recklessness, but to the extent that this formulation is plausible, the blaming judgment stems from not being careful enough. Objective recklessness is therefore a blaming judgment stemming from poor functional reasoning.

A person who is poor at norm-reasoning does not obey the normative guidance given to her either because she inculcates contrary normative values or because she chooses to ignore the norms.[27] She accordingly invites blame as someone who displays an inappropriate attitude towards the normative guidance given to her. Recall that the normative guidance contained in conduct rules is meant to guide behaviour—a conduct rule is not a mere stipulation of the consequences that are likely to ensue from being causally connected to specified undesirable outcomes or occurrences. So described, a person is norm-blameworthy if her *behaviour* demonstrates a failure to be guided by the norm, whether or not the harm that the norm was aimed at preventing actually occurs. Conversely, if a person's behaviour demonstrates acceptance of the guidance offered, she is not norm-blameworthy, whether or not the ideal consequences ensue. Within the context of substantive criminal law relating to core offences, it is generally accepted that the core norms at play are morally derived, and hence a person who acts because she does not believe, for instance, that killing is bad, or who reacts to a threat by choosing to respond to it in a manner that is excessive, invites the judgment of being morally bad or evil.

If blameworthiness (as opposed to attribution of legal causation) depends on the quality of a person's reasoning, then we must ask: to what standard should the defendant's reasoning be compared? By dividing the defendant's reasoning into functional and normative reasoning, we can treat this as two separate questions vis-a-vis the two different types of reasoning. It is immediately clear that for the purposes of attributing blame, there is no point in comparing the defendant's functional reasoning to the perfect functional reasoning of someone with a 'god's eye' awareness of all the circumstantial facts. Since no human can possibly attain a 'god's eye' awareness of everything, this is an unreal standard by reference to which to judge a human. Any person who makes an epistemic mistake falls short of the 'god's eye' standard of functional reasoning, but even outside legal contexts, when we call someone careless or objectively reckless, we are not just saying of her that she happened to make an epistemic mistake—we are asserting that she fell short even of the less demanding standards of functional reasoning that are expected of her by us in the context of her actions. The context within which the agent acts often determines how demanding the applicable standard of functional reasoning is—a trained professional is societally expected to meet higher standards of functional reasoning when acting within the scope of her training

---

[27] There is of course the third possibility, viz that she is unaware of the content of the norm. In most cases, ignorance of the norm is usually dealt with by a post-moral (and posited) meta-rule, which usually, but not inevitably, deems a person to be informed of all conduct guidance in the criminal law. Theorists like A Ashworth ('Ignorance of the Criminal Law, and Duties to Avoid it' (2011) 74 *MLR* 1) and DN Husak ('Mistake of Law and Culpability' (2010) 4 *Criminal Law and Philosophy* 135) criticise the intransigence of such a meta-rule, but I cannot enter into that debate here. Where such a meta-rule exists, the explanation that one was ignorant about the applicable norm is unavailable to the agent, and where there is no such meta-rule, ignorance of the applicable norm may exempt the agent from norm-blame.

than a layperson.[28] Even outside the realms of special training, we may declare that the agent was careless when she failed to meet the standards that we would expect of an ordinary member of society acting in the agent's place. The law often refers to such standards, particularly in adjudicating civil liability, but it is important to remember that these benchmarks exist as societal facts that are logically independent of any institutionalised stipulation of standards[29] (including those institutionalised in a legal system). In other words, independently of the law, there exists normative but non-institutionalised guidance in societal norms as to how good one's functional reasoning should be. The violation of purely societal norms about the quality of functional reasoning expected exposes a person to a form of societal disapprobation, and I will call this subset of societal disapprobation 'functional blame'.

We turn now to identifying the appropriate benchmark for assessing norm-reasoning. Should the quality of norm-reasoning be assessed by reference to the norms applicable to the facts as they objectively exist or by reference to the norms applicable to the facts as perceived by the defendant? The first thing to note here is that since norm-reasoning and functional reasoning are conceptually distinct, in principle, the evaluation of the quality of a person's norm reasoning is distinct from and should not be influenced by the quality of her functional reasoning. To unpack this proposition, consider the following permutations:

1. Because of her poor functional reasoning, D misidentifies the applicable normative guidance. However, she exercises her capacity to follow the (misidentified) norm guidance. She does not display poor norm-reasoning, even though on the whole, she does the wrong thing in the circumstances. Her error here is purely one of functional reasoning.
2. D correctly identifies the applicable normative guidance, but does not exercise her capacity to follow it. Again, on the whole, she does the wrong thing in the circumstances, but this time she displays poor norm-reasoning and not poor functional reasoning.
3. D exhibits poor functional reasoning in misidentifying the applicable norm guidance and is not guided even by those norms. Here too she does the wrong thing in the circumstances, but this time she displays both poor functional reasoning and poor norm-reasoning.

    There is one other relevant permutation that I will only mention at this stage, but will expand on a little later in section 2.2.3.
4. There is normative guidance directing D to meet a certain standard in terms of her functional reasoning—say the standard of a reasonable person, which also

---

[28] See in this context, the discussion of role-specific expectations as to the quality of functional reasoning in J Gardner, 'The Gist of Excuses' (1998) 1 *Buffalo Criminal Law Review* 575, 579–81, 584–85.

[29] By 'institutionalised stipulation of standards', I mean standards that might exist within the broad set of what Raz calls 'institutionalized systems'. See Raz, *Practical Reason and Norms* 123–31. Standards also exist in society per se, but society is not an institutionalised system.

happens to be the expected societal standard. D's functional reasoning does not meet the societal standard. In this case, the same exercise of D's rational capacities attracts both functional blame and blame arising from poor norm-reasoning (which I will call 'norm-blame'). But even here, although D's desert of norm-blame and functional blame coincides, her functional reasoning and norm-reasoning remain distinct, and are benchmarked against different standards set by different systems. The benchmark for D's functional reasoning is the non-institutionalised system of societal expectations, whereas the benchmark for her norm-reasoning is the institutionalised normative guidance directing her to meet the standard of the reasonable person in her functional reasoning.

As a practical matter, a person can only apply her norm-reasoning capacities to the norms that apply to the facts as she perceives them.[30] Hence, the quality of a person's norm-reasoning (ie, her responsiveness to conduct norms) can only be assessed by reference to her beliefs (where the term includes her perception of the facts and her reasoned factual conclusions and assessments on that basis, but not her normative beliefs).[31] Therefore, even if the applicable conduct norm is framed by reference to objective facts, norm-blame should only be apportioned by evaluating the defendant's reasoning by reference to the normative guidance applicable to the facts as she perceived them.

2.2.2 Norm Blame and Criminal Culpability

Keeping the two threads of reasoning distinct gives us the conceptual tools to make an important proposition about culpability in the criminal law. Traditional theories of culpability or blameworthiness attempt to link a moral agent, D, and a proper blaming judgment for causing some prohibited consequence 'φ'.[32] For instance, in Hart's modified choice theory of culpability:

> What is crucial is that those whom we punish should have had, when they acted, the normal capacities, physical and mental, for abstaining *from what it forbids*, and a fair opportunity to exercise these capacities.[33] (Emphasis added)

Michael Moore, who rejects Hart's shift from pure choice to the capacity to exercise choice as the basis for culpability, also refers to the choice made in causing

---

[30] Raz, *Practical Reason and Norms* 17 also concedes that: 'To be sure, in order to be guided by what is the case a person must come to believe that it is the case.' See also the observations made in section 2.1 in respect of Raz's assertion that reasons (as facts and not beliefs) can and should be used to evaluate behaviour.

[31] I exclude the defendant's normative beliefs from an evaluation of her norm-blame because we are not testing the mere internal consistency of her normative reasoning. See n 27 above as to why erroneous beliefs about the content of the normative system are usually irrelevant to the outcome of an assessment of norm-blame.

[32] Simester, 'A Disintegrated Theory' 180.

[33] HLA Hart, *Punishment and Responsibility* (Oxford, Oxford University Press, 1968) 152.

the evil which the norm seeks to prevent[34] rather than in disobeying the norm. Similarly, Gur-Arye says, 'respecting offenders' dignity requires that they will not be held liable for offenses whose commission does not express their negative attitude (mental state) *towards other persons' protected interests*' (emphasis added).[35] Simester too argues that: 'The burden for ascribing culpability [both for choice-based and character-based culpability theories] lies in justifying that evaluative link between *act* and defendant—that link which allows us to transmit judgments of *the deed* across to the person' (emphasis added).[36]

This approach wrongly identifies the basic challenge of culpability *at the evaluative stage of the criminal law* because it fails to note the centrality of the criminal law's system of conduct rules to ex post culpability rulings.[37] Because of this, choice theorists find it difficult to link the prohibited consequence, φ, to the moral agent, D, in the absence of anything as unequivocal as advertent choice,[38] and character theorists, in suggesting that something like 'insufficient concern for the interests of others' is a blameworthy *character trait*,[39] attract criticism for defining the 'in principle' domain of *criminal* culpability too broadly.[40] But in the criminal law's institutionalised normative system, *criminalisation theory* is directly concerned with φ, and *it* draws the link between φ and the criminal law's normative guidance to behave so as not to cause φ. This link often depends on φ being an undeserved violation of some victim's interest. Yet it remains true that a person may choose[41] to accept the criminal law's normative guidance, and still commit φ, and, conversely, that she may reject the normative guidance, but still fail to commit φ. Once the prohibiting norm is in place, culpability theory need only provide an account of the link *between D and the applicable norm*. The challenge

---

[34] MS Moore, 'Choice, Character, and Excuse' (1990) 7(2) *Social Philosophy and Policy* 29, 57. See also P Westen, 'An Attitudinal Theory of Excuse' (2006) 3 *Law and Philosophy* 289 who expressly pegs his theory of excuses to the actor's expressed attitude toward what the criminal statute declares to be the legitimate interests of persons.

[35] M Gur-Arye, 'Human Dignity of "Offenders": A Limitation on Substantive Criminal Law' (2012) 6 *Criminal Law and Philosophy* 189, 201.

[36] Simester, 'A Disintegrated Theory' 180.

[37] I expand in detail on this idea in M Dsouza, 'Criminal Culpability after the Act' (2015) 26 *King's Law Journal* 440. For the present purposes, the condensed summary of the argument presented in that article will suffice.

[38] See, for instance, the choice-based theories proposed in Moore, 'Choice, Character, and Excuse'; CO Finkelstein, 'Responsibility for Unintended Consequences' (2005) 2 *Ohio State Journal of Criminal Law* 579; MS Moore and HM Hurd, 'Punishing the Awkward, the Stupid, the Weak, and the Selfish: The Culpability of Negligence' (2011) 5 *Criminal Law and Philosophy* 147. See also in this connection Simester, 'A Disintegrated Theory' 185, 191; AP Simester, 'Responsibility for Inadvertent Acts' (2005) 2 *Ohio State Journal of Criminal Law* 601, 603.

[39] See, for instance, Simester, 'A Disintegrated Theory' 192–94; RA Duff, 'Choice, Character, and Criminal Liability' (1993) 12 *Law and Philosophy* 345, 362; Tadros, *Criminal Responsibility* 82–85, 90.

[40] See Duff, 'Choice, Character, and Criminal Liability' 368; Simester, 'A Disintegrated Theory' 195. I emphasise the reference to *criminal* culpability in the main text because the aforementioned 'in principle' domain of culpability may well apply unobjectionably in respect of *non-criminal* culpability.

[41] I refer to choice here since even character theorists agree that choice does supply a link between our judgment about a wrong φ and our evaluation of D, albeit via a disclosure about D's character.

of culpability, in the sense of ex post blame*worthiness*, then, is to explain why D's violation of the prohibiting norm results in a negative evaluation of D. I think that culpability theories that try to trace our negative evaluation of the outcome φ back to D at the ex post stage of blame evaluation start at the wrong place.

At the ex post stage, if we start with the criminal law conduct norm, it is easy to trace our negative evaluation of the fact that D acted contrary to the norm back to our evaluation of D. Conduct norms are meant to guide conduct or behaviour, and so D shows due regard to them when she is guided by those norms in choosing her actions. She is not culpable (ie, blameworthy) in these circumstances. Conversely, D acts culpably when she does not let the conduct rules guide her behavioural choices. Accordingly, D's in-principle[42] criminal culpability depends on her attitude[43] towards the criminal law's conduct rules. It does not depend on her having caused (or not caused) a consequence that an applicable conduct rule sought to avoid.[44] This approach differs significantly from traditional approaches to understanding culpability, because expressing an inappropriate attitude towards a norm is not synonymous with causing the harm that the norm was designed to prevent. Although a choice to ignore or behave contrary to a norm usually coincides with bringing about the outcome that the norm is calculated to avoid (at least where the conduct rule is well formulated), it need not. Similarly, although the bringing about of an outcome that a norm is calculated to avoid usually involves a failure to be guided by the conduct rule in question, it need not be. D may display a deplorable attitude towards the norm guidance without bringing about the proscribed

---

[42] By in-principle culpability, I mean only *whether* D deserves criminal blame. How much criminal blame she deserves is a separate question that is not directly relevant to the present argument, and so I leave that to one side for now.

[43] My reference to an 'attitude' towards a conduct rule should be understood in contradistinction to Sendor's usage of the same term in his explanation of the desert of criminal liability. Sendor is concerned with the defendant's attitude (in particular, the attitudes of respect or disrespect) towards the right protected by a norm rather than the norm itself. His reference to the defendant's attitude allows him to consider, in addition to mens rea factors, aspects of the defendant's mental state generally relevant at the supervening defence stage. My own usage of the term is both broader and narrower: it is broader in that it refers to an attitude towards the norm rather than the interests protected by the norm; and it is narrower in that since I am unconcerned with any actual outcomes, respect or disrespect to the norm may be established without referring to considerations relevant to establishing supervening defences to liability for causing the outcome. See BB Sendor, 'Mistakes of Fact: A Study in the Structure of Criminal Conduct' (1990) 25 *Wake Forest Law Review* 707.

[44] A similar argument was also made by Karl Binding in German in *Die Normen und ihre Ubertretung*. For the present purposes, I rely on Eser's summary of Binding's thesis in A Eser, 'Justification and Excuse' (1976) 24 *American Journal of Comparative Law* 621, 625. For Binding, the norm breached by criminal acts was drawn from a set of norms separate from, and underlying, doctrinal law, and a person was guilty of acting wrongfully when she directed her will towards violating these underlying norms. Duff, 'Choice, Character, and Criminal Liability' 363–64 also considers in passing the possibility that an improper attitude towards the criminal law's norms may be the basis for culpability, although he identifies the having and acting upon that attitude as a character trait. Thus, he would explain that an agent's criminal culpability arises from her possession of that character trait. Although this move is open to him, it seems somewhat unnatural to identify the 'having and acting upon of an improper attitude towards the criminal law's norms' as a character trait. It bears little resemblance to other (more recognisable) character traits that Duff also identifies—traits such as honesty, dishonesty, courage, cowardice, generosity, meanness, compassion and callousness.

outcome, as in the case of a failed attempt to φ, or she may cause the feared outcome without displaying a blameworthy attitude towards the concerned norm, as in the case of negligent or accidental commission of φ. The argument made here recognises the distinctness of the enterprise of criminalisation and the enterprise of determining blameworthiness, and is sensitive to it. We criminalise the bringing about of φ by creating an appropriate criminal law conduct norm 'π' because, for instance, φ is a harm. Having done that, it is redundant to once again refer to the occurrence (or otherwise) of φ when determining an agent's blame*worthiness* in respect of norm π. The agent's blame*worthiness* should depend instead on her attitude towards π.

By the yardstick suggested, a person may deserve criminal blame depending on her attitude towards the criminal law's norms even if the apprehended outcome does not materialise.[45] Intuitively we do think that two persons who do their utmost to commit murder are equally bad persons, even when due to blind luck, only one succeeds,[46] and the understanding of culpability proposed here explains why. Yet, as explained in section 2.1, the entitlement or standing to offer liberal guidance and award criminal blame arises only when harm occurs. In other words, the outcome of the agent's actions creates the (blamer's) entitlement to blame, whereas the agent's attitude to the norm creates her own desert of blame.[47] Perhaps this is how all blame, criminal or otherwise, works. Perhaps the assertion that we blame D for committing φ is just convenient shorthand for the fuller explanation that we blame D because her actions resulted in φ happening, and she was blameworthy for not following some normative guidance designed to prevent φ from happening. However, I need not defend those propositions here. For the present purposes, it is sufficient to say that the criminal law, as an enterprise of the state, assigns blame in the public domain of citizenry, and that in that special institutionalised context, when it assigns criminal blame, both blameworthiness and something for which to blame are necessary (but not independently sufficient) preconditions.

The importance of the shift in focus from blaming based on the outcome contemplated by a norm to blaming based on the agent's responsiveness to the norm is best showcased by what it suggests about whether criminal blameworthiness can

---

[45] In this context, see the general discussion of failed attempts and unmaterialized risks in MH Kramer, *The Ethics of Capital Punishment: A Philosophical Investigation of Evil and Its Consequences* (Oxford, Oxford University Press, 2011) 204–06. I do not adopt Kramer's view without reservations—in particular, I have reservations about his assertion that the degree of harm that actually occurs in some way positively correlates with the degree of evilness associated with the conduct. Nevertheless, I agree with the underlying assertion that moral blame may be deserved even when no harm actually materialises.

[46] In fact, L Alexander and KK Ferzan, 'Results Don't Matter' in PH Robinson, SP Garvey and KK Ferzan (eds), *Criminal Law Conversations* (Oxford, Oxford University Press, 2009) argue that equal criminal liability should ensue in such cases.

[47] This is a conclusion with which I think that Michael Moore would agree, given his views on the independent moral significance of wrongdoing. See MS Moore, *Placing Blame: A Theory of the Criminal Law* (Oxford, Oxford University Press, 2010) 191–247.

stem from inadvertence. I will briefly outline my views on this issue, although I cannot enter into a complete defence of my views on this issue here.

If norm-blameworthiness depends on the agent's attitude towards the norm, then criminal blame is that subset of norm-blame that arises in respect of the norms contained in the criminal law. A person's criminal blameworthiness then ought to be predicated on her displaying an inappropriate attitude towards the criminal law's normative guidance. It seems unlikely that one can display an attitude towards a norm without adverting[48] to it. The obvious rebuttal to this proposition is that 'If D can display an "attitude" of "I cannot be bothered to be careful not to be in violation of a right (ie, by causing the prohibited outcome)", surely she can also display the attitude of "I cannot be bothered to be careful not to be in violation of a norm"'. This argument fails because an attitude towards 'being in violation of a norm' is not the same as an attitude towards the norm itself. To be in violation of a norm is to have caused the harm that the norm was designed to prevent. As previously explained, causing or avoiding harm is not coterminous with accepting or rejecting the corresponding norm's guidance.[49] Of course, one can be careless about finding out the normative guidance available. However as pointed out earlier,[50] as a general (and fairly uncontroversial) rule, that does not exculpate a defendant from norm-blame.

In order to truly deserve norm-blame, then, a person should at least be subjectively reckless about, or wilfully blind to, the possibility of disobeying the normative guidance applicable. In other words, the minimal requirement for norm-blame is that the agent advertently chose not to exercise her capacity to avoid violating the norm. Inadvertent norm violations are not norm-blameworthy, and where the normative system concerned is that of the criminal law, inadvertent norm violations ought not to be criminally blameworthy.[51] Ordinarily, a person who inadvertently brings about that *outcome* is most functionally blameworthy and, in principle, the criminal law should not punish for this kind of blameworthiness. This conclusion fits well with the fact that the mens rea stipulations in most core criminal law offence definitions require advertence, in the form of either intention,

---

[48] For a sophisticated account of what it means to advert to something (in that case, a risk of harm, as opposed to my proposed alternative focus on the norm guidance), see Moore and Hurd, 'Punishing the Awkward' 152–56, who also, citing different arguments, conclude that liability in the criminal law ought to be predicated only on advertence, and that criminal liability based on inadvertence is normatively illegitimate.

[49] The same logic also tells us that the attitude of 'I cannot be bothered to be careful not to be in violation of a right' is not an attitude towards the right. This difference is the difference between negligently causing harm and advertently causing harm. Sendor errs in treating carelessness as an attitude towards the underlying right. See Sendor, 'Mistakes of Fact' 727. Carelessness is actually an attitude towards being in violation of a right, and that is why, vis-a-vis the underlying right, it is inadvertent. Blame for inadvertently causing φ derives from poor functional reasoning and not (or at least not without stipulating additional norms) from poor norm-reasoning.

[50] See n 27 above.

[51] Moore, 'Choice, Character, and Excuse' 58 also tentatively suggests the same conclusion.

knowledge or subjective recklessness.[52] Mens rea stipulations may be seen as one filter in a process geared towards isolating norm-blameworthy persons (rationale-based defences being another).

But if criminal blameworthiness is explained in this way, then it must stem only from poor norm-reasoning. It cannot arise from poor functional reasoning and so, in principle, criminal liability should not flow from functional blameworthiness. This conforms to the general intuitive association of the label 'criminal' with wickedness or evil rather than having poor observational skills or being poor at interpreting the facts that one does observe.[53] Nevertheless, the criminal law regularly convicts people for bringing about φ negligently or in a manner that is 'objectively reckless'.[54] In doing so, it appears to designate the convict criminally blameworthy because of her poor functional reasoning. Since negligence-based liability is fairly commonplace in the criminal law and a finding of negligence is an indictment of the actor's functional reasoning, it would appear that poor functional reasoning (ie, functional reasoning found to be deficient by reference to societal norms) can, and regularly does, found criminal liability. This would therefore suggest that the normative position that I adopt is implausibly revisionist. In fact, it is not.

2.2.3 Criminal Liability Apparently Linked to Functional Reasoning

Most cases in which the criminal law appears to impose liability for poor functional reasoning may be explained in a manner that is compatible with the normative proposition I make. The key is to see these cases as instances in which, in addition

---

[52] In relation to 'subjective recklessness', see n 26 above. Intention, knowledge and subjective recklessness are appropriate bases for making criminal convictions because they reveal flaws in the defendant's norm-reasoning vis-a-vis the criminal law's norms.

[53] As Kramer (*The Ethics of Capital Punishment* 188) notes: 'Numerous wrongs are committed through negligence. Although some negligent wrongs are extremely harmful ... none of them is properly classifiable as wicked. Carelessness is a vice, and it can lead to horrifically injurious consequences in some settings; but the gravity of the culpability of a careless action, even when calamitous results ensue therefrom, is not sufficient to render the action evil.'

[54] As Sendor ('Mistakes of Fact' 714) and Tadros (*Criminal Responsibility* 81) note in other contexts, negligence is an adequate threshold for blame. Since the criminal law is, amongst other things, a tool for social regulation, the extension, for regulatory reasons, of the criminal law to making blaming judgments in respect of functional reasoning is tempting, and indeed some would say pervasive in modern legal systems. On this point, see also Lord Rodger's separate concurring judgment in *R v G* [2004] 1 AC 1034. For the reasons I have stated, I consider such a use of the criminal law to be philosophically inappropriate. Lord Bingham's comments in *R v G* [2004] 1 AC 1034, 1055 reflect the same idea: 'it is not clearly blameworthy to do something involving a risk of injury to another if (for reasons other than self-induced intoxication ...) one genuinely does not perceive the risk. Such a person may fairly be accused of stupidity or lack of imagination, but neither of those failings should expose him to conviction of serious crime or the risk of punishment'. Nevertheless, I do accept that there is some scope for legitimate criminal liability when the criminal law chooses to offer normative guidance as to how one should exercise one's functional reasoning.

to a primary conduct rule (which directs its addressees not to bring about a pro-scribed outcome φ), the criminal law also adopts an institutionalised benchmark for the quality of functional reasoning that it expects the said addressees to employ in being guided by the primary conduct rule. This benchmark is often (though not invariably) set by reference to the objective reasonable person, who is sometimes attributed a selection of the defendant's capacity-limiting characteristics. There is copious literature addressing the topic of exactly which characteristics of the defendant should be so selected, but I do not propose to comment on that issue at this stage. Instead, I propose that in adopting an institutionalised benchmark, the criminal law supplements its primary conduct norm with a secondary con-duct norm. Since an agent can choose to be more, or less, careful while gathering facts about a given situation and when extrapolating conclusions on the basis of these facts, it is conceptually possible to have normative guidance as to this aspect of the agent's behaviour. Moreover, it is easy to see that an agent who chooses not to follow such normative guidance displays a flaw in her norm-reasoning and that this flaw can support norm-blame. Consider, for instance, special regulations that require persons who offer adventure-sports activities to take special care to ensure the safety of their equipment. When the subject of this normative guidance chooses not to take such care as is required by the norm, she invites norm-blame.

So when the criminal law proscribes causing φ and institutionally requires that each person's functional reasoning in seeking not to cause φ must meet the bench-mark set by the reasonable person, it is offering the following cumulative norma-tive guidance to the addressee:

> Primary Norm: do not cause φ; and
> Secondary Norm: take as much care as a reasonable person would, not to inadvertently cause φ.

These norms are violated only when D (advertently) does not choose her behav-iour by reference to them.[55] D violates the Primary Norm when she advertently chooses not to exercise her capacity to avoid committing φ (whether or not she actually commits φ). She only violates the Secondary Norm when she advertently chooses not to exercise her capacity to comply with the Secondary Norm, ie, to take as much care as a reasonable person would not to inadvertently φ. Of course, the same failing might also attract functional blame, but when criminal liability is imposed for the failing, it is best understood as liability based on norm-blame relatable to the Secondary Norm rather than liability based on functional blame. Hence, in such cases, the finding of blameworthiness in relation to the defendant can also be traced to an advertent failure to be guided by a conduct norm.

This explanation of blaming decisions within the institutionalised system of the criminal law helps us to make sense of cases involving advertent wrongdoing as well as of most cases that have hitherto been seen as involving criminal liability for inadvertent wronging. It does this without abandoning the certainty of the link

---

[55] Or is treated as having done so in terms of a meta-rule of the type described in n 27 above.

offered by choice-based approaches to culpability between our judgments about what the agent did and our judgments about the agent herself. So, for example, where φ is 'causing the death of a person', the criminal law gets the standing to blame an agent when she causes another person to die. However, criminal blame *for murder* ensues if the causal agent was norm-blameworthy in advertently violating the criminal law norm against killing another,[56] whereas criminal blame *for gross negligence manslaughter* ensues if she was norm-blameworthy in advertently violating a secondary criminal law norm requiring each person to take care not to be grossly negligent in the performance of their duties, when such negligence might result in the death of a person. Similarly, consider the law of rape (and many other sexual offences) in England and Wales. Prior to the Sexual Offences Act 2003, in terms of the notorious case of *Morgan*, the mens rea requirement in relation to the complainant's lack of consent was the absence of an *honest belief* that the complainant was consenting.[57] Accordingly, a defendant who honestly believed that the complainant had consented did not commit rape. This formulation treated poor functional reasoning in identifying the complainant's consent as irrelevant to the sort of blame apportioned by the criminal law of rape. The normative guidance offered in relation to consent in the *Morgan* era was as follows:

Primary Norm: do not have sexual intercourse with V without her consent.

If D genuinely believed that V was consenting, then however unreasonable that belief, D was not norm-blameworthy in relation to the Primary Norm and so could not be convicted of raping V. This outcome was compatible with the proposition that at its core, a criminal conviction signifies at least that the convict did not have due regard for the criminal law's conduct rules.

The law on this point has been changed by the Sexual Offences Act 2003, and under section 1(c) thereof, the mens rea now required in relation to consent for the rape offence is an absence of *reasonable* belief in the complainant's consent. In addition, section 1(2) explains that: 'Whether a belief is reasonable is to be determined having regard to all the circumstances, including any steps [D] has taken to ascertain whether [V] consents.' With some slight simplification for explanation, the normative guidance now offered in relation to consent to sexual intercourse ought to be parsed as follows:

Primary Norm: do not have sexual intercourse with V without her consent.
Secondary Norm: if you believe that V is consenting, take as much care as a reasonable person would to ensure that your belief is correct.

In terms of this guidance as well, where D genuinely believes that V was consenting, then no matter how unreasonable that belief is, D does not incur norm-blame

---

[56] I ignore for the moment doctrinal oddities that mean that in jurisdictions like England and Wales, a person can be convicted of murder even without intending to kill the deceased if she intended to inflict serious injury upon the victim and death resulted.
[57] *DPP v Morgan* [1976] AC 182.

in relation to the Primary Norm. However, if D refuses the guidance of the Secondary Norm and does not take as much care as a reasonable person would have taken to ensure that his evaluation about V's consent is correct, then D *is* norm-blameworthy in respect of the Secondary Norm. If in these circumstances the proscribed consequence (ie, non-consensual sexual intercourse) occurred, then D could suffer norm-blame (and a criminal conviction) relatable to a criminal law conduct rule.

Unpacking the conduct norms for a criminal offence that appears to blame for poor functional reasoning in this way helps us avoid reaching some unfortunate conclusions. Consider, for instance, the case of *R v B (MA)*.[58] In that case, the court held that under the Sexual Offences Act 2003, the reasonableness of D's honest but mistaken belief that V had consented to sexual intercourse must be judged by reference to the strictly objective standard of what a reasonable person would have believed, even if D's actual belief was caused by mental conditions not amounting to insanity in law (such as delusional psychotic illnesses or personality disorders) which affected his ability to understand whether V was consenting to sexual intercourse. In other words, if D suffers from a delusional psychotic illness that does not answer to the law's idiosyncratic conception of insanity, and because of this illness he has intercourse with V mistakenly believing that she is consenting to—even welcoming—sexual intercourse, he should be labelled a rapist. This is the case even if he subjectively made every effort to ensure that V was actually consenting, because an objectively reasonable (ie, not mentally ill) person would not have believed that V was consenting.[59] Keeping aside for a moment our sympathy for V's plight, there is surely something deeply disturbing about this labelling outcome. The court concluded that D should be labelled a rapist, even though D might never have dreamed of forcing himself upon another, and might in fact have tried his best to ascertain that his prospective sexual partner was consenting. It held that the label of 'rapist' was appropriate even where D's main problem was that mental illness has affected his ability to correctly analyse his situational perceptions. This label is highly stigmatic and yet the court held that D should share it with other persons who are unambiguously contemptuous of the sexual autonomy of others.

This disturbing outcome can be avoided by recognising that even where the criminal law seems to blame for poor functional reasoning, it is actually issuing normative guidance requiring addressees to take special care in forming epistemic judgments, and blaming for a person's failure to choose her actions by reference to the guidance in this norm. On that account, D incurs blame relatable to the Secondary Norm only if he chooses not to exercise his capacity to achieve the standards of functional reasoning that a reasonable person would have attained.[60]

---

[58] *R v B (MA)* [2013] 1 Cr App R 36.

[59] Strictly, this part of the ruling was obiter. However, it does flow from the belief that the criminal law may punish for poor functional reasoning.

[60] This is a slight modification of the standard account of choice-based culpability proposed by theorists like Moore ('Choice, Character, and Excuse' 57) and Finkelstein ('Responsibility for

Even assuming, as was the case in *R v B (MA)*, that incapacity-based defences are unavailable, if D tried but was unable to achieve the prescribed standards of functional reasoning, D would not deserve norm-blame relatable to the Secondary Norm, because he accepted the guidance in the Secondary Norm. Such an outcome has intuitive appeal, and doctrine has tried to accommodate it to some extent by picking and choosing certain features of the defendant by reference to which the benchmark set by the law is moderated. Hence, the reasonable person is often attributed the defendant's age, gender and physical disabilities. But this solution is inelegant and inadequate. Attempts to exhaustively enumerate the features of the defendant that ought to be attributed to the reasonable person have consistently proved inadequate, and no convincing principled defence of any such list of features has been forthcoming. So when cases like *R v B (MA)* arise, courts that proceed on the basis that the criminal law blames for poor functional reasoning continue to have to reach conclusions that they themselves find disturbing[61] in order to preserve doctrinal integrity. The alternative approach described herein sidesteps these problems. It offers a clear and principled basis for exonerating any person who has tried to meet the standards of functional reasoning prescribed by the law, even when she fails.

This idea may be scaled up further to take into account additional complexities in the law. For example, the criminal law may additionally adopt a Tertiary Norm relating to behaviour that might cause D to become unable, or less able, to achieve the standards prescribed in other norms. In fact, it often does just that. Consider, for instance, the defendant who fails to comply with a norm of the criminal law because she is intoxicated or is in an uncontrolled automatic state. When this intoxication or state of automatism is self-induced (ie, voluntary), the criminal law often treats the defendant as being criminally blameworthy, provided that the outcome (or conduct) proscribed by the Primary Norm occurs. The subtext of rules that inculpate voluntarily intoxicated persons[62] (or, if you prefer, prevent them from raising evidence of their voluntarily intoxicated state to negate mens rea),[63] rules that prevent defendants from relying on mistakes attributable to their voluntarily intoxicated state[64] and rules that inculpate persons who offend in a

---

Unintended Consequences'), and recounted by others like Simester ('A Disintegrated Theory' 185). The standard account proposes that a moral agent, D, is (prima facie) culpable or blameworthy for causing the proscribed outcome, φ, only if she chooses not to exercise her capacity to avoid causing φ. In the argument made in this section, I have replaced the reference to the causing of the proscribed outcome φ with a reference to the violation of the norm that proscribes committing φ.

[61] See, for instance, the manner in which the Court of Appeal in *R v B (MA)* (n 58) tried to moderate the effect of its statement of the law in paras 40–41.

[62] See, for instance, *DPP v Majewski* [1977] AC 443, 474; *R v Kingston* [1995] 2 AC 355, 369; and AP Simester, 'Intoxication is Never a Defence' [2009] 1 Crim LR 3. *cf R v Heard* [2007] 3 WLR 475, 484–85.

[63] AP Simester, JR Spencer et al, *Simester and Sullivan's Criminal Law: Theory and Doctrine* (Oxford, Hart Publishing, 2016) 717–19.

[64] See, for instance, in England and Wales, s 76(5) of the Criminal Justice and Immigration Act 2008.

self-induced state of automatism[65] is that there is tertiary normative guidance in the criminal law against choosing to do something that jeopardises the effective exercise of one's capacity to be guided by other applicable criminal law norms. Someone who does not exercise her capacity to avoid breaching this Tertiary Norm deserves norm-blame by reference to the Tertiary Norm. Of course, even such a norm would not inculpate a defendant of the sort contemplated in the dicta in *R v B (MA)*, and that, I think, is a good thing.

Embracing an acquittal in *R v B (MA)* does not commit us to denying that V suffered a wrong. Whether V suffered a wrong and whether the person who was the author of that wrong deserves to be criminally blamed for authoring it are separate questions. Conceptually, the fact that the criminal law exonerates D from criminal blame does not prevent us from recognising that V nevertheless suffered a wrong. On that basis, civil law remedies may continue to be available to V for the wrong she suffered.[66] Neither is an acquittal necessarily worrying from the perspective of crime prevention. Even where criminal blame is ruled out for a person suffering from delusional psychotic illnesses or personality disorders of the sort considered in *R v B (MA)*, the state can empower the court to require the person to undergo treatment. This is the sort of power that is regularly exercised by courts in respect of defendants who are found not guilty of a charged offence by reason of insanity.

It appears to me that a large majority of seemingly negligence-based offences can be explained on this basis. As for the minority of offences that cannot, the arguments made herein offer a normative case for rejecting them. I therefore propose that philosophically, criminal blameworthiness ought to be understood as norm-blame arising from the failure to show due regard to the guiding norms of the institutionalised system of the criminal law. This, coupled with the actual causation of a proscribed outcome, should be understood as amounting to criminal blame. Further, one should only be taken to have not shown due regard to a norm if one has adverted to it and then chosen not to exercise one's capacity to accept its guidance.

2.2.4 The Choice of Perspective in Decision Rules

A court's jurisdiction to evaluate behaviour that violates conduct norms is regulated by decision rules. These govern the general trial procedure, the substantive determination of liability in a particular case and the consequential determination of the punishment for a liable person. At least the last two categories of these decision rules deal with the agent in a personal manner—they make personal norm-blaming judgments in respect of the particular case and that particular

---

[65] See, for instance, *R v Quick* [1973] QB 910; *R v Bailey* (1983) 77 Cr App R 76; and *R v Coley* [2013] EWCA Crim 223.
[66] I touch upon this possibility in section 8.5.3.

agent. As I have argued, the general nature of a norm-blaming judgment requires reference to perceived facts rather than objective facts. For this reason, I maintain that decision rules dealing with the substantive evaluation of personal norm-blame ought generally to be denominated in terms of reasons that are beliefs (ie, perceptions of facts) rather than objective facts. Furthermore, there is no special normative reason to even formally peg such decision rules to objective factual bases. The decision rules relating to these blaming judgments are addressed to judges (or, where applicable, the jury) who are required to assess the behaviour of an agent after it has happened. As we have already noted, they are concerned with the evaluation and censure of conduct after it has occurred, and not with providing prior guidance for behaviour. Therefore, while Raz is right in arguing that conduct rules should be framed by reference to objective facts, his reasons for insisting that norms should be based on facts and not beliefs do not apply when rules are referred to in the context of evaluating past conduct.[67] Raz himself proceeds on the contrary basis that reasons as facts should be used to evaluate behaviour.[68] However, there are several types of evaluating judgments one can pass with respect to behaviour, and while the application of Raz's methods may well tell us whether behaviour was objectively beneficial, they would be inappropriate for telling us (as is the enterprise of decision rules in the criminal law) whether the person engaging in the behaviour acted in a criminally blameworthy manner. Alternatively, if one accepts that the special liberal moral context of the criminal law generates reasons to ground conduct norms in objective facts, it still does not follow that criminal law decision rules should also be grounded in objective fact. The criminal law already has a moral voice since it adopts moral conduct norms. When it evaluates conduct, it does so by reference to morally predicated standards and therefore it can speak with a moral voice simply by virtue of that fact.

As explained in section 2.2.3, even when the criminal law appears to blame for poor functional reasoning, it should in fact be understood as making a norm-blaming judgment relatable to a norm requiring the agent to meet an institutionalised qualitative benchmark for functional reasoning when being guided by

---

[67] As M Dan-Cohen, 'Decision Rules and Conduct Rules: On Acoustic Separation in Criminal Law' (1984) 97 *Harvard Law Review* 625, 672–73 observes: 'according to Dr. Raz, the various arguments for the rule of law all spring [from] the basic intuition that "the law must be capable of being obeyed" and that hence "it must be capable of guiding the behaviour of its subjects. It must be such that they can find out what it is and act on it". But this idea, with its seemingly unassailable logic, applies only to conduct rules: by definition, conduct rules are all one needs to know in order to obey the law. Decision rules, as such, cannot be obeyed (or disobeyed) by citizens'. Similarly, Stewart, 'The Role of Reasonableness' 333–34 argues that: 'It is uncontroversial that some legal rules, such as the rules of the road, are meant to guide the conduct of citizens, while other legal rules, such as the rules governing the application of the insanity defence, do not. The instrumental demands of the rule of law that Raz identifies apply more urgently … to the first kind of rule, but not to the second: a rule that people are supposed to follow must be reasonably clear, promulgated in advance, publicly available, and so forth, while a rule that determines when an offender will be declared insane rather than responsible would never be relied upon and so need not always be promulgated in advance or clear to the public.'

[68] Raz, *Practical Reason and Norms* 15–16.

another conduct rule. Hence, even in these cases, the quality of the agent's norm-reasoning should be evaluated from a subjective perspective. If the agent did not realise that she was in a situation in which the 'meet the institutionalised benchmark for functional reasoning' norm applied to her, she would not have displayed poor reasoning vis-a-vis that norm.

As such, all decision rules that deal with the apportionment of norm-blame require the decision-maker not to take notice of circumstantial factors that the agent did not perceive. Concomitantly, all decision rules that deal with the apportionment of functional blame require the decision-maker to ascertain whether the agent perceived at least all circumstantial factors that that society normatively expected her to have perceived, and to decide whether the assessments she made based on those factors were at least as good as those that that society normatively expected her to have made.[69] Thus, if the decision rule is stated as 'The agent was not blameworthy in doing X if Y happened' (where Y is a specified circumstantial contingency), then while applying it, the decision-maker must mediate the harshness of the rule at least to the extent that the agent should not be found to be norm-blameworthy in doing what she believed to be X if she did it because she believed that Y had happened, and she should not be found to be functionally blameworthy if her beliefs that she was doing X, or that Y had happened, were appropriate on the basis of facts that she knew or was normatively expected within that society to have known. Indeed, a failure to use these perspective-adjusted standpoints when applying any rule that deals with the attribution of personal blame would invariably result in an unfair assessment of the reasoning of a person. The law's expressive capacity should not be used to convey such an unfair personal blaming judgment, since that would amount to lying about the defendant.[70]

2.2.5 The Reasonableness of Beliefs and 'Imperfect Self-Defence'

I have argued that although norm-blame should only be assessed on the basis of the agent's norm-reasoning within the context of the facts as the agent perceived them, where there is normative guidance, whether explicit or implicit, requiring the agent to be especially meticulous in her functional reasoning, the agent may deserve norm-blame for failing to be adequately guided by *that* norm.

---

[69] The standard may be higher or lower depending on the role performed by the agent (a doctor would have to exercise better medical judgment than a layperson) or the development of her mental capabilities (an infant is not required to be as reasonable as a mature person).

[70] See also BS Byrd, 'Till Death Do Us Part: A Comparative Law Approach to Justifying Lethal Self-Defense by Battered Women' (1991) 1 *Duke Journal of Comparative & International Law* 169, 176; and BS Byrd, 'Wrongdoing and Attribution: Implications beyond the Justification-Excuse Distinction' (1987) 33 *Wayne Law Review* 1289, 1301–02, who agrees that '[a] completely objective standard is appropriate only for defining norms of conduct and making factual determinations but is never appropriate for judging the actor's responsibility for objectively determined wrongs'. Along similar lines, see Robinson, 'Competing Theories' 64–65; and MN Berman, 'Justification and Excuse, Law and Morality' (2003) 53 *Duke Law Journal* 1, 55–56.

When deciding on whether such norm-blame is appropriate, a comparison of the perceived facts with the facts that the agent would have perceived if she had exercised her functional reasoning with the requisite care would provide evidence of the failure to be appropriately guided. Can it be argued that there is always implicit normative guidance requiring persons who claim a rationale-based defence to have taken special care to meet objective standards of reasonableness in their functional reasoning?

Simester seems to imply that this is the case. He says that a person who sets out to act on the basis that she is entitled to a rationale-based defence knowingly commits a prima facie offence and so can be expected to conform to a higher standard of reasonableness in claiming the defence.[71] The presence of such implicit normative guidance would also fit well with Uniacke's theory as to the perspective that must be adopted while making any moral assessment of a person. Uniacke argues that the moral assessment of a person must be agent-perspectival, by which she means that the person's deservingness of moral blame must be assessed by examining her conduct in the context of facts that she actually knew and the information reasonably available to her.[72] Something like the implicit normative guidance hypothesised by Simester seems to also be implicitly assumed in Uniacke's qualification requiring reference to information reasonably available to the agent. Greenawalt too argues for a perspectival approach mediated by a reasonableness standard. In his view: 'So long as one exercises the best possible judgment on the facts he can reasonably acquire, the existence of other facts knowable only in some practically unimportant sense is immaterial for purposes of moral evaluation.'[73] Stewart also adopts a similar position when he argues that:

> We would have to say to [the 'putatively justified' actor], that he should have done something else; but we would not be able to tell him what that something else was; we would be blaming him for not knowing and not acting upon a fact he could not reasonably have been expected to know. Assigning blame in circumstances such as these is akin to imposing absolute liability, which is repugnant to any account of criminal law that takes issues of fault and responsibility seriously (as [John] Gardner's and Fletcher's certainly do). In short, a person who acts reasonably in response to the reasonable appearance of a deadly threat to himself or one under his protection has done nothing which attracts the kind of blame the criminal law requires. [The 'putatively justified' actor] is entitled to say, and we should say, that he did the right thing in the circumstances. A fact he could not reasonably have known—the suspect's gun was an imitation—does indeed mean that his

---

[71] AP Simester, 'Mistakes in Defence' (1992) 12 *OJLS* 295, 308–09. Admittedly, 'can be expected to' is not the same as 'is cautioned to'. In that sense, perhaps Simester is arguing that the requirement that an agent meet a higher standard of reasonability is purely a decision rule and not a conduct norm at all. I will consider this possibility a little later in this section.

[72] S Uniacke, *Permissible Killing* (Cambridge, Cambridge University Press, 1994) 42. See also S Uniacke, 'Rights and Relativistic Justifications: Replies to Kasachkoff and Husak' (2000) 19 *Law and Philosophy* 645, 646.

[73] K Greenawalt, 'Distinguishing Justifications from Excuses' (1986) 49(3) *Law and Contemporary Problems* 89, 94.

conduct was, from some perspective, wrong; but this is not the kind of wrong that should affect our legal assessment of his conduct. From the point of view of the criminal law, he did nothing wrong, and we should therefore not say that his conduct was merely excused rather than justified.[74]

However, none of these arguments are premised on the existence of words to suggest normative guidance to conform to objective standards of reasonableness in the offence definition, or the rationale-based defence stipulation. It therefore seems difficult to support the assertion that it is nevertheless implied. Moreover, if the pre-legal standing to legitimately comment upon the conduct of others stems from the actual effect of such conduct on another human's constituent elements, then in order for a pre-legal basis to proscribe the negligent or objectively reckless conduct of others, there must be a constituent element that creates a pre-legal entitlement not to be exposed to risk (or, more specifically, risk above a certain threshold deemed 'reasonable'). This seems exceedingly unlikely, since risk is a human-authored, rational and relational concept rather than something that exists in nature as part of what makes a human. Thus, I doubt that there can be any implicit pre-legal guidance requiring people to conduct themselves with care. The argument that such normative guidance can be read into institutionalised systems of criminal law seems to stem purely from dismay at completely exonerating a defendant who acted carelessly or even grossly negligently, rather than from any actual flaw of reasoning that it reveals in the defendant's attitude towards the system of normative guidance. If this is the basis of the argument, then it is a prudential and not a moral argument and, if accommodated, it would be another dilution of the moral foundations of the criminal law. Conversely, rejecting the argument for implicit guidance universally applicable to all persons who claim a rationale-based defence need not necessarily result in the complete exoneration of the defendant. It would only mean that the blame that should be affixed is functional rather than moral blame. In such cases, it is conceivable (though not necessarily desirable) that criminal consequences may be imposed by stretching the criminal justice system. Furthermore, it is certainly possible (and more morally appropriate) to impose civil liability upon the agent for her blameworthiness vis-a-vis a separate set of institutionalised civil law norms that more closely track societal norms relating to the functional standard of functional reasoning.

Even if we abandon the idea that there is always implicit moral normative guidance requiring persons who claim a rationale-based defence to have taken special care to meet objective standards of reasonableness in their functional reasoning, we may still insist that as a pure decision rule, a person's access to a rationale-based defence should be made contingent on her meeting objective standards of reasonableness in their functional reasoning.[75] However, such a model would undermine the conduct rule's guidance by blaming persons who subjectively complied with

---

[74] Stewart, 'The Role of Reasonableness' 333.
[75] As may have been Simester's intent in the text accompanying n 71 above.

the conduct rule. Although it is quite possible for a decision rule not to mirror a conduct rule, generally, such decision rules operate to the benefit rather than the detriment of the defendant in not mirroring the conduct rule. A 'higher standard of reasonableness' stipulation that is purely a decision rule would be illegitimate because it would unfairly assign norm-blame to persons who complied with the norms that they believed were applicable. It would generate blaming decisions that took people by surprise. Furthermore, the moral judgments it would generate in respect of persons who are careless in claiming a rationale-based defence would be false. It would label such persons as having displayed deficient moral reasoning, whereas in fact they had demonstrated only poor observational or logical reasoning skills. It is not enough to respond that making such a judgment encourages people to be more careful when they know that they are committing a prima facie offence. The system's moral assessment of the particular defendant would still be wrong, and making the questionable claim that making such a wrong assessment has positive deterrent consequences does not change that fact.

For this reason, I think that it would be illegitimate to read into the criminal law either any general normative guidance requiring that a person claiming a rationale-based defence must have met objective standards of reasonableness or a decision rule to that effect. A person who explains her actions as conforming to the norms applicable to the situation in which she mistakenly, but honestly believed herself to be should be completely absolved of norm-blame, even if her mistake was unreasonable. Instead, she should suffer a judgment that holds her functionally blameworthy. Such a person should not be labelled an evil person, but rather a negligent, careless or objectively reckless person.[76] To the extent that we wish to affix liability for such blameworthiness, non-criminal liability is most appropriate.[77] Nevertheless, if, for prudential reasons, we prefer to attach criminal responsibility to persons who cause harm due to extreme carelessness, this should ideally be done by ex ante positing express norm guidance imposing upon such persons a duty to take care to avoid the harm concerned.[78] A failure to take due care would then attract norm-blame.

Something similar (though not quite identical) to this possibility is considered in passing by Duff, who suggests that:

> [W]e should ... recognise that one who acts on a carelessly formed, epistemically unreasonable and mistaken belief is neither warranted in nor excusable for acting as she does: the question is whether she should be convicted of the same offence as one who acts

[76] See also Gardner, 'The Gist of Excuses' 575–76, who gives the example of the English law prerequisite that a person's actions be dishonest for the system to label her a thief, instead of meddlesome, puerile, presumptuous or thoughtless.

[77] In this context, see the views expressed by L Alexander and KK Ferzan, 'Against Negligence Liability' in PH Robinson, SP Garvey and KK Ferzan (eds), *Criminal Law Conversations* (Oxford, Oxford University Press, 2009) 274; and Alexander and Ferzan, 'Results Don't Matter'. Although these views are far from undisputed, I share the authors' opinion that there is no convincing non-consequentialist, *moral* argument to criminally punish negligence.

[78] Something like this can be seen in the Model Penal Code, as per §§3.04–3.08 of which, a good-faith belief in justificatory facts gives rise to a justification, subject to the rider in §3.09(2) that a

without a belief in facts that would justify his action; or of a lesser offence to mark the distinctive, and less serious, character of the wrong she commits.[79]

The same intuition also finds expression in the approach of some jurisdictions in the US to unreasonable mistakes in claiming a rationale-based defence, at least in the context of causing death.

One such jurisdiction is California, where the doctrine of imperfect self-defence is applied to such cases. This doctrine is explained in the following terms:

> [W]hen the trier of fact finds that a defendant killed another person because the defendant actually, but unreasonably, believed he was in imminent danger of death or great bodily injury, the defendant is deemed to have acted without malice and thus can be convicted of no crime greater than voluntary manslaughter.[80]

A more recent formulation of the effect of this doctrine may be found in the case of *People v Humphrey*, wherein it was explained that:

> [F]or killing to be in self-defense, the defendant must actually and reasonably believe in the need to defend. If the belief subjectively exists but is objectively unreasonable, there is 'imperfect self-defense,' i.e., 'the defendant is deemed to have acted without malice and cannot be convicted of murder,' but can be convicted of manslaughter.[81]

In simple terms, this doctrine has to do with the manner in which the law is posited in California. Murder is defined as the unlawful killing of a human being with malice aforethought, whereas manslaughter is the unlawful killing of a human being without malice. 'Malice' is understood in a manner that covers more conceptual ground than the concepts of 'intention' and 'knowledge' in a typical mens rea stipulation. It seems to require an intent to act unlawfully.[82] Thus, a person who kills another under the honest but unreasonable mistake that she was legitimately acting in self-defence undoubtedly intends to (or at least knows that she is very likely to) cause the death of her victim. Nevertheless, she is not doing so out of malice, since she has no intent to act unlawfully. In the absence of malice, the level of guilt declines[83] and the defendant must be convicted of manslaughter instead of murder.

---

recklessly or negligently formed belief cannot support a justificatory defence to an offence for which recklessness or negligence suffices to establish culpability.

[79] Duff, *Answering for Crime* 293–94.
[80] *In re Christian S* (1994) 7 Cal 4th 768, 771.
[81] *People v Humphrey* (1996) 13 Cal 4th 1073, 1082.
[82] *In re Christian S* (n 80) 775–80. The court concluded that despite an amendment to the statutory definition of 'malice', which stated that an awareness of the obligation to act within the law was not a sine qua non for establishing malice, the concept of malice nevertheless requires an intent to act unlawfully.
[83] ibid 773.

The doctrine of imperfect self-defence treats an unreasonable mistake in claiming the right to kill in self-defence as the negation of a posited element of the offence, rather than as a matter relating to the appropriate background considerations in light of which to assess norm-reasoning. Thus, the doctrine of imperfect self-defence works in a completely different way from the approach that I advocate for dealing with unreasonable mistakes while assessing norm-blame. Moreover, it is considerably more limited in scope and only applies to reduce a murder conviction to a manslaughter conviction, because it is constrained by the words of the posited law. Even so, its very existence is significant, since it suggests a wider intuitive reluctance to brand a person who has merely been careless 'evil' or 'malicious'.

My arguments as to why conduct rules must refer to objective facts and as to why there is no implicit general normative guidance requiring that a person claiming a rationale-based defence must have met objective standards of reasonableness make reference to and depend upon the existence of certain pre-legal, moral normative standards of what conduct is wrong. To make good these arguments, I need to demonstrate that the presumed connection between the criminal law and pre-legal standards of right and wrong is plausible, and that is my endeavour in the next chapter.

3

The Normative Guidance
Underlying the Criminal Law

When examining the system of conduct-guiding norms underlying the criminal law, the first question to ask is: 'To what end may the criminal law issue guidance?' Locke argued that: 'The great and chief end ... of men's uniting into commonwealths, and putting themselves under government, is the preservation of their property [ie, their lives, liberties and estates].'[1] The different branches of a good system of law serve this end in different ways. The criminal law contributes to the state's central enterprise of preserving the entitlements of people primarily by guiding people so as to prevent them from intentionally or recklessly harming one another.[2] This chapter is therefore concerned with whether, and how, a good criminal law's system of norms is geared towards preserving the entitlements of the people.

The most obvious way in which legal norms preserve the entitlements of persons is by granting them rights and by providing them with remedies in cases of violations of these rights. In the criminal law context, however, legal norms can preserve the entitlements of persons in another way too: by recognising that certain actions taken in defence of an entitlement are unrestricted by the criminal law. In this regard, entitlements provide the foundation of criminal law defences. This chapter sets out the basic structure of a person's entitlements by distinguishing between two types of rights: rights by which the state confers upon the constituent elements of persons the normative character of a right ('constituent rights'); and rights created by the state in exercise of its political authority in respect of things that humans do not already constituently possess, but which are considered valuable for a good life ('posited rights'). It then maps out the defensive entitlements generated by each type of right.

In this enterprise, I take as being axiomatic the proposition that legal norms ought not to direct people to act in ways that run counter to what morality asks of them. Since I adopt a morally distinctive account of the criminal law and I am

---

[1] J Locke, *Two Treatises of Government and A Letter Concerning Toleration* (New Haven, Yale University Press, 1690/2003) 136–37, 141, 154–55.
[2] J Feinberg, *The Moral Limits of Criminal Law Volume 1: Harm to Others* (Oxford, Oxford University Press, 1987) 31. See also JS Mill, *On Liberty* (New Haven, Yale University Press, 2003 [1859]) 80–81, 121, 139–44.

interested in the criminal law that is related to morality, I am also interested in the *conduct-guiding* part of such a criminal law, and so, in this chapter, I also focus on moral rules meant to guide conduct, setting to one side moral rules that guide the evaluation of it.[3] Furthermore, although some theorists believe that morality demands that one obey the law, this is not the sense of morality that is relevant to the position I develop. If morality feeds into sources or limits the criminal law's guidance, it must, at least in part, be logically prior to the guidance of the criminal law, and I aim to identify and work with this pre-legal portion of morality. Note that although the pre-legal morality I refer to is logically prior to human authorship, it is not logically independent of human existence. As will emerge in section 3.1 below, this morality is contingent upon the continued existence of humans—it dwells within the domain of humanity and is good only for humans, and not for other animals.[4]

Furthermore, as an enterprise of a liberal rule-of-law state, the criminal law must, at least at its core, restrict itself to guidance that is not repugnant to liberal principles. Its core guidance must therefore not extend to conduct that is purely an individual's own business. As Duff and Marshall explain, in liberal states the criminal law is centrally concerned with activities in the public as opposed to the private realm.[5] It follows that guidance against purely self-facing behaviour (including, arguably, some behaviour made private to two or more people by way of consent) has no place, at least at the core of a liberal criminal law, even when the behaviour concerned results in harm. The criminal law should only concern itself with behaviour that is already legitimately the business of others.

I have previously suggested that a person's actions are the business of someone other than herself if they affect the constituent elements of some other person.[6] This chapter develops this point further in two different directions: first, it builds upon the notion of constituent elements to develop the concept of a constituent right; and, second, it argues that by positing further (non-constituent) rights, the state may legitimately expand the scope of actions that are another person's business. Both types of rights affect what actions should count as justified in the criminal law.

---

[3] The idea that rules for guiding conduct and rules for evaluating it can operate independently and be subject to different considerations has already been explored in Ch 2. Of course, the evaluation of conduct will not be independent of the guidance of it, but the two should not be conflated.

[4] In the terminology developed by Kramer to describe the various types of objectivity, such a moral code would be called weakly objective qua mind-independence. See MH Kramer, *Objectivity and the Rule of Law* (Cambridge, Cambridge University Press, 2007) 3–4; and MH Kramer, 'Is Law's Conventionality Consistent with Law's Objectivity?' (2008) 14 *Res Publica* 242–43.

[5] RA Duff and SE Marshall, 'Public and Private Wrongs' in J Chalmers, F Leverick and L Farmer (eds), *Essays in Criminal Law in Honour of Sir Gerald Gordon* (Edinburgh, Edinburgh University Press, 2010) 71–72; SE Marshall and RA Duff, 'Reply' in PH Robinson, SP Garvey and KK Ferzan (eds), *Criminal Law Conversations* (Oxford, Oxford University Press, 2009) 250; SE Marshall and RA Duff, 'Criminalization and Sharing Wrongs' (1998) 11 *Canadian Journal of Law and Jurisprudence* 7, 13–14. See also RA Duff, 'Towards a Modest Legal Moralism' (2014) 8 *Criminal Law and Philosophy* 217.

[6] See section 2.1. See also more generally Mill, *On Liberty* 80–81, 121, 139–44.

3.1 Constituent Elements and the Limits of Moral Guidance

Most moral theories accept that 'the moral good' is in some way contingent upon the continued survival of humans.[7] These axiomatic value statements presuppose the existence of beings that are recognisably human. It follows that the features that identify a being as human are logically prior to any guidance that such moral theories can offer. These features have no moral value, positive or negative; they are simply part of the background to the rules for moral guidance. This necessarily implies that the moral guidance in these moral codes cannot self-consistently impinge upon the essential humanity of any human. It cannot therefore command a person to shed, or to suffer the shedding of, any of her constituently human attributes.[8] Since the same also applies to the guidance in morally derived normative systems like the criminal law, a moral criminal law's guidance is also similarly restricted.

To fully delineate this boundary of the criminal law's normative guidance, we would have to identify all the features that constitute a typical human. This, of course, is too big a task for this study. I will instead restrict myself to sketching an appropriate moral underpinning for the structure of criminal law defences by referring to human features that are generally accepted in the literature as being constituently human. In particular, since this study is situated within a broadly rights-based liberal tradition, I will refer in this enterprise to the picture of the typical human painted by combining Hobbes' traditional rights-based liberalism with Hegel's compelling critique thereof.

Hobbes suggests that a typical human is constituted with certain innate faculties of the body and the mind.[9] For him, the innate faculties of the body include

---

[7] For instance, Aristotle explicitly treats 'the good' as being logically subsequent to human existence. Book 1 of his *Nicomachean Ethics* is even titled 'The Human Good'. See Aristotle, *Nicomachean Ethics* (D Ross and L Brown trans, Oxford, Oxford University Press, 2009 [350 BC]) 3–22. Hobbes too says that there is nothing that is absolutely good or evil—whatever is the object *of a person's desire* is good, whereas whatever is the object *of a person's aversion* is evil. T Hobbes, *Leviathan* (New Haven, Yale University Press, 2010 [1651]) 34. Similarly, HLA Hart, *The Concept of Law* (Oxford, Clarendon Press, 1994 [1961]) 199–200 reserves a place within his conception of the institution of law for a certain minimum content of natural law characterised by statements 'the truth of which is contingent on human beings and the world they live in retaining the salient characteristics which they have'. See also AJ Lisska, 'Finnis and Veatch on Natural Law in Aristotle and Aquinas' (1991) 36 *American Journal of Jurisprudence* 55, 58; and O Curry, 'Who's Afraid of the Naturalistic Fallacy?' (2006) 4 *Evolutionary Psychology* 234, 241.

[8] This assertion is compatible with Hobbes' argument based on his understanding of human nature that each human enjoys an inalienable 'right of nature' 'to use his own power, as he will himselfe, for the preservation of his own Nature; that is to say, of his own Life; and consequently, of doing any thing, which in his own judgment, and Reason, he shall conceive to be the aptest means thereunto'. Hobbes, *Leviathan* 79–82. In Lockean political theory too, this right is of foundational importance. See Locke, *Two Treatises* 104, 107, 111, 155–56.

[9] 'Nature hath made men so equall, in the faculties of body, and mind.' Hobbes, *Leviathan* 76.

features like life and the human form, whereas the innate faculties of the mind include features like purposive agency.[10] In addition, he also treats some actual behaviour (as opposed to mere tendencies of appetite or aversion) as being quintessentially, even constituently, human. The most crucial such behaviour for him is acting to preserve one's natural features, which he identifies as a human being's inalienable 'right of nature' to preserve her own nature (ie, her constituent features), using any means she judges to be apt.[11] For him, this 'right of nature' is innate to humans and no human can be directed to forgo or to act contrary to it. Of course, there is no reason to imagine that this is the only form of actual behaviour that is in the very nature of being human.[12] For instance, one way in which Hegel critiques the Hobbesian account of the human natural state is by giving us a compelling account of why it is also intrinsically human to recognise the humanity of other humans and to be aware of their recognition of our humanity.[13] Hegel's proposition is in fact also corroborated by the Aristotelian recognition that humans are *by nature* political (or, more fundamentally, social) animals,[14] who must, in order to form cooperating social and political groups, recognise other humans as being eligible for membership. In other words, it is in

---

[10] Hobbes would call this 'Will', which he described as 'the last Appetite, or Aversion, immediately adhaering to [an] action, or to the omission thereof'. Hobbes, *Leviathan* 39. Because humans have purposive agency, they are capable of choosing their actions, and if there were no legitimate guidance as to how they should exercise their choice, they would enjoy unrestricted and absolute freedom to do as they autonomously pleased. See in this connection n 9 in Ch 2 above. This proposition does not confirm or deny either Hobbes' intuition that a human would tend to make selfish and anti-social choices, or Locke's intuition that a human would tend to make choices that are generally conducive to social aggregation.

[11] Hobbes, *Leviathan* 79–82. The existence of this right is also of foundational importance to Lockean political theory. See Locke, *Two Treatises* 104, 107, 111, 155–56. I believe that Hobbes was speaking loosely when he characterised this 'right of nature' as a right. I will return to this point at a later stage in the argument. See also in this context KK Ferzan, 'Self-Defense and the State' (2008) 5 *Ohio State Journal of Criminal Law* 449, 457–58.

[12] In fact, while setting out Hegel's criticism of Hobbes' thought experiments about the state of nature, Eubanks notes that Hobbes himself treats human beings as being possessed of a highly sophisticated notion of reciprocal exchange, even in the primal state. This is how they can come to form a social contract. Eubanks rightly asks why Hobbes did not treat this as empirical evidence of the intrinsic sociality of human beings. See CL Eubanks, 'Subject and Substance: Hegel on Modernity' (2005) 6 *Loyola Journal of Public Interest Law* 129, 149. See also SB Smith, 'Hegel's Critique of Liberalism' (1986) 80 *American Political Science Review* 121, 125.

[13] GWF Hegel, *Phenomenology of Spirit* (HP Kainz trans, Pennsylvania, Pennsylvania State University Press, 1994 [1807]) paras 178–96; A Honneth, 'From Desire to Recognition: Hegel's Account of Human Sociality' in D Moyar and M Quante (eds), *Hegel's Phenomenology of Spirit* (Cambridge, Cambridge University Press, 2008) 76–90; P Redding, 'Georg Wilhelm Friedrich Hegel' (2012) *The Stanford Encyclopedia of Philosophy*, http://plato.stanford.edu/archives/sum2012/ entries/hegel. In addition, Hegel would also require us to be aware of our mutual recognition of the humanity of others. See also in this connection A Garza Jr, 'Hegel's Critique of Liberalism and Natural Law: Reconstructing Ethical Life' (1990) 9 *Law and Philosophy* 371, 383

[14] As Aristotle, *Nicomachean Ethics* 10–11 also notes: 'the final good is thought to be self-sufficient. Now by self-sufficient we do not mean that which is sufficient for a man by himself, for one who lives a solitary life, but also for parents, children, wife, and in general for his friends and fellow citizens, since man is born for citizenship'.

the nature of a human to identify other humans as being human like oneself, and not mere articles that may be turned to one's use.

Each of the features identified in this very brief list must logically stand outside the realm of moral guidance and assessment. It makes no sense to ask whether it is moral for us to have opposable thumbs, or to be capable of walking on two feet, or to be able to choose our willed actions. Similarly, and critically for the present purposes, it makes no sense to ask whether it is moral for a human to have behaved in a manner that was constituently human, even when doing so harms others. The human features, including constituently human behaviour, are in Hohfeldian terms immune—or, as I call them, 'existentially immune'—to moral or morally derived guidance and any consequent blaming judgment.[15]

The range of actions placed outside the realm of contrary moral and criminal guidance by virtue of being attributable to constituently human behaviour is narrowed by the fact that the same actions may be impelled by one constituently human behaviour, but suppressed by another. For instance, the exercise of a human's Hobbesian 'right of nature' may conflict with her constituent behaviour of recognising the humanity and non-instrumental nature of other humans. Humans exercise their 'right of nature' by responding to a threat to their 'nature' by all means possible. We can unpack this proposition in the following manner: humans are impelled to respond to any threat to their constituent elements. These threats may be inanimate objects, animals or other humans. They may respond by using any means available to them. These means include all the articles (including animals and plants) in the physical world. In some cases, they may also include other humans. Yet, it is also constituent human behaviour to recognise that other people are equally human and therefore are not available as mere articles to be turned to one's own ends. Hence, treating other people as means to one's end of continued survival goes against constituently human behaviour.

That said, in preserving oneself *against a threatening person*, the defender addresses the threatening person as an end (qua threat) in herself and not as a means to neutralise some other threat. For this reason, any existential immunity for self-preservation[16] extends only to actions that affect the constituent elements

---

[15] In his recent attempt to situate self-defence (which is related to the constituently human 'right of nature' to defend oneself against a threat) within the Hohfeldian jural relations, Steinhoff concludes that in the absence of a better explanation, self-defence is a claim right, supplemented by an act-specific agent-relative prerogative to prefer one's own interests when they conflict with a duty not to harm others. Steinhoff's argument avowedly works backwards from the intuited conclusion that prohibiting self-defence wrongs the victims of attack. To that extent, he takes on the burden of excluding all alternative explanations (or, at least, applying Occam's razor, all alterative simpler explanations) in order to support his chosen conclusion, and Steinhoff freely admits that. However, he does not eliminate the possibility that self-defence (or the 'right of nature') is an immunity, and hence his argument fails to convince. See U Steinhoff, 'Self-Defense as Claim Right, Liberty, and Act-Specific Agent-Relative Prerogative' (2016) 35 *Law and Philosophy* 193.

[16] Conceptualising the normative space to act in self-preservation as an immunity rather than a right brings with it the added benefit that we avoid puzzles like the one with which C Finkelstein, 'A Puzzle About Hobbes on Self-Defense' (2001) 82 *Pacific Philosophical Quarterly* 332, 333–34 grapples in relation to why this 'right' of nature cannot be voluntarily abandoned. The answer simply is

of a human qua threat, but does not extend to any action by which the threatened person uses any other human as an article in responding to the threat. Any such action will in principle remain subject to normative guidance or assessment.

Although the list of actions that can legitimately be attributed to constituently human behaviour is likely to be very short, this is a good thing, because this account of existentially immune actions is purely qualitative. It refers only to the quality of the behaviour as being constituently human and is not reined in by post-moral considerations of the non-disproportionality or parsimoniousness[17] of the action taken. Therefore, even actions that may seem grossly disproportionate or excessive will, if they are attributable to constituently human behaviour, be existentially immune to moral and criminal law guidance and assessment.

To illustrate the points made, imagine that Adam and Yves are adrift in the middle of the ocean with only one plank nearby. The plank can support only one of them, and Yves is clinging to the plank. Adam can only avoid drowning by shoving Yves off the plank, thereby causing Yves to drown instead. Here one aspect of Adam's constituently human behaviour would impel him to act in self-preservation by shoving Yves off the plank. However, another constituently human behaviour would impel him to recognise the equal humanity of Yves and not to treat him as a mere article to be turned to his (Adam's) business (of surviving) by being removed from the plank.[18] In this sort of case, it would seem that either course of action would require Adam to defy some constituently human behaviour, and whatever choice Adam makes, he cannot be described as 'merely being true to what constitutes him as human'. If so, then neither course of action would be existentially immune to moral and criminal guidance, and either would, in principle, be subject to moral and criminal blame.

Now consider the situation from Yves' perspective. When Adam tries to remove Yves from the plank, Yves' constituently human self-preservation behaviour would impel him to prevent Adam from snatching the plank. There is no conflict of constituent behaviours if Yves does so. By preventing Adam from snatching the plank, perhaps even by killing him to do so, Yves does not act contrary to the constituently human behaviour that impels him to recognise the equal humanity of Adam, because when Adam authors a threat to Yves' constituent elements, Adam *himself becomes* Yves' business. In responding to Adam qua threat, Yves does not treat Adam as a means towards avoiding or averting some other threat. He does not objectify Adam by turning Adam to his (Yves') business, because Adam is already his business.

---

that acting in self-preservation is immune to blame. So although a person can voluntarily choose not to preserve herself, if she does not so choose, she cannot (subject to a few qualifications that will emerge presently) be blamed for preserving herself.

[17] See sections 3.3.2 and 8.2 for detailed explanations of what I mean by these terms.

[18] JJ Thomson, 'Self-Defense' (1991) 20 *Philosophy & Public Affairs* 283, 289–90 would identify this example as a 'riding-roughshod-over-a-bystander' case and would also agree with my eventual conclusion that if Adam tried to remove Yves from the plank, he would be morally and criminally blameworthy. The same conclusion would also follow if (on different facts) Adam substituted Yves for himself in pursuit of his (Adam's) business of preserving his life or used Yves in pursuit of his business of survival.

The example of Adam and Yves encapsulates the conflict of constituent behaviour that is most important for the criminal law. The net effect of the foregoing analysis may be captured by the following rule: the normatively externalising effect of constituent self-preservation behaviour extends to actions involving doing whatever it takes *to the threat* by whatever means (other than the instrumental use of humans) necessary in order to prevent harm to one's constituent elements. Potentially, similar conflicts that might arise between other (unenumerated) aspects of constituent behaviour could also be analysed in the same way. Note that the word 'authors' is used in the foregoing paragraph to connote playing an active causative role and that although it is capable of accommodating fault judgments, by default the word is fault-neutral. However, nothing in the analysis so far generates a requirement for fault, whether advertent or inadvertent, in authoring a threat. In fact, even if there were no other humans in the world, a person could still protect her constituent elements against animals or falling rocks without needing to identify any external fault. The only limitation is that the person must act to respond to a threat and must not, in the course of so responding, use any human instrumentally.

3.2 From Constituent Elements to Constituent Rights

Features that are constitutive of a typical member of the human species are not susceptible to moral (and morally derived criminal) evaluation. They are neither good nor bad—they simply cannot be judged by reference to any normative system that (directly or indirectly) derives from them. In addition to being outside the domain of normative evaluation, constituent elements mark the boundaries of the positive guidance that can be given by any moral criminal law. This means that no moral criminal law can direct a person to act otherwise than she is impelled to act by her constituently human behaviour.

When we move from a pre-legal world to a world of legal guidance and subsequent evaluation of actions that detrimentally affect others, pre-legal notions of constituent elements and existentially immune behaviours need to be translated into the legal order. Inevitably, modern liberal states that claim to be moral recognise rights relatable to the human constituent elements identified in section 3.1. Furthermore, they inevitably treat wrongs relatable to constituent rights as being public wrongs. So when D's actions affect the constituent rights of V, D commits a public wrong of the nature that is in the criminal law's domain. The criminal law is therefore legitimately concerned with D's actions. In offering guidance related to these actions, the state must not transgress the limits described in section 3.1 and must work towards its ultimate aim of preserving the entitlements of its subjects.[19]

---

[19] Locke, *Two Treatises* 136–37, 141, 154–55.

One of the main ways in which the state uses its criminal law to protect entitlements is by issuing advance guidance to people as to how they should behave in order to minimise instances of harm to entitlements. It uses imperative, conduct-restricting norms of the nature described in section 2.1 to do so, and I will argue in section 4.1 that such norms underlie the criminal law's doctrinal creation of criminal offences in respect of conduct that harms protected interests.[20]

But what do these norms actually say? Consider T, who authors a threat to D's life. We know that this sort of situation is a liberal criminal law's business and that, as such, it may be able to offer guidance aimed at preserving the entitlements in play. We also know that the criminal law cannot guide D not to perform actions impelled purely by her constituent human behaviour. So let's start by identifying the entitlements in play. D's constituent right to her life is material here. On the other hand, T has no entitlements in play. Although T's act may be an exercise of her constituent purposive agency and no state can purport to dispossess T of that, T is not entitled to *exercise* her purposive agency however she pleases. Her constituent right is the *possession* of purposive agency; prior to any relevant legitimate guidance, the actions she chooses in the *exercise* of her purposive agency exist in a norm-vacuum. Hence, prior to legitimate normative guidance on the subject, she is neither entitled nor unentitled to choose to attack D's life. However, since the criminal law must aim to preserve entitlements, it must intervene in this situation so as to protect the only entitlement genuinely at threat. It must therefore guide T against performing (non-consensual) actions that are incompatible with the preservation of D's life. This is the guidance that underlies the criminal law's doctrinal declaration that it is a crime to kill D.

Since this sort of guidance applies universally to all subjects in relation to all constituent rights, we may generalise it in order to arrive at one general guiding norm of the criminal law in relation to constituent rights. This norm reads 'Do not affect the constituent rights of any other human'. It cannot read 'Do not try to affect the constituent rights of any other human' or 'Try not to affect the constituent rights of any other human' because such directions would also extend to actions that do not actually affect the constituent rights of other humans and would, to that extent, be busybody guidance.[21] Since this duty is an exception to the default state of unrestricted capacity to choose one's actions, outside its domain, the default state continues to apply.

---

[20] See in this connection Feinberg, *Harm to Others* 31; Mill, *On Liberty* 80–81, 121, 139–44.

[21] The first alternate formulation of the rule would extend to actions by which no other person's constituent elements are affected, provided that the actor was *attempting* to affect the constituent elements of another human. Since T's (unsuccessful) attempt to affect D's constituent elements does not actually affect D's entitlements, neither D nor the state on D's behalf may legitimately complain about T's actions. If either issues guidance relating to mere attempts, they would be acting as busybodies. The second alternate formulation would extend to actions by which no other person's constituent elements are actually violated, provided that the actor had deliberately refused to try not to affect the constituent elements of any other human. Once again, the same objection lies—T's mere failure to try not to harm the constituent entitlements of others (without resulting actual harm) does not affect D, and so neither

Since the criminal law's conduct norms are meant to guide human behaviour, the duty not to affect the constituent rights of any other human is only obeyed by someone who refers to and chooses to behave in compliance with it, and it is only violated by someone who refers to it and chooses to behave contrary to its guidance. In either case, it does not matter whether the agent's actions actually affect the constituent rights of another human. Thus, a person who violates this duty commits a wrong related to it, even if in fact her actions affect no other person's constituent elements.[22] (The existence of an institutional basis for making a blaming judgment in relation to such a wrong is a separate matter altogether and, as explained in sections 2.1 and 2.2.2, in the absence of actual harm, no authority to impose blame arises.) This dissonance between the result-based stipulation of the duty and the behavioural choice-based stipulation of when the duty is violated mirrors (and possibly sources the intuitions grounding) the distinction between the bases of conduct rules and blaming decision rules discussed in Chapter 2. Conduct rules like the duty not to affect the constituent rights of any other human are meant to preserve entitlements. Blaming decision rules like the stipulation of the conditions under which this duty is violated are meant to evaluate a person's commitment to the system of conduct rules.

An aspect of this duty that might escape notice initially is that it includes a duty not to interfere with another person exercising her existential immunities, including the existential immunity relating to the preservation of her constituent elements. In other words, one cannot prevent another person from acting according to her constituently human self-preservation behaviour when faced with a threat (whether the threat be natural or human-authored) and claim not to have violated one's duty not to affect the constituent rights of any other human since the threat came from some other source. This is because the very defensive behaviour is itself a component of the affected person's humanity and thus acting in accordance with it is itself a constituent right. Preventing such actions would therefore amount to an independent attack on the constituent rights of the affected person and, accordingly, would fall foul of the duty not to affect the constituent rights of any other human.

When a person (advertently) violates her duty not to affect the constituent rights of any other human, this is a wrong not only against the person directly

---

D nor the state can object to T's actions or issue non-busybody guidance relating to mere failures to try. Admittedly, one does not obey guidance against affecting the constituent rights of any other human when one tries, even unsuccessfully, to harm such rights. However, this section is solely concerned with the statement of conduct rules. The judgment of when a conduct rule would be violated has to do with the applicable decision rules and, as I explained in Ch 2, these two, though connected, do not necessarily coincide. See also HM Hurd, 'What in the World is Wrong?' (1994) 5 *Journal of Contemporary Legal Issues* 157 and the text accompanying n 13 in Ch 2 above.

[22] As used in this context, the phrase 'commits a wrong' refers to transitive sense of D violating a duty. Critically, this is not coextensive with authoring harm to another's constituent rights with fault. In this sense, one may 'commit a wrong' without actually harming another's constituent elements.

affected; as noted above, the state inevitably treats this as a public wrong and so it is the business of the citizenry. How then may the affected party, and others, respond?

3.2.1 Existential Justifications: The Defence of Constituent Rights

The scope of intervention for a person directly threatened (D) can be identified relatively easily. To the extent that D's constituent elements are threatened, she can exercise her existential immunity to defend them. As previously discussed, under this existential immunity, D may respond to a threat by doing whatever it takes to deflect the threat, using all means necessary,[23] and she would face no adverse moral evaluation in respect of her actions. In fact, this immunity arises even if the author of the threat was not a wrongdoer and was acting entirely without blame. As explained in section 3.1, a person acting under an existential immunity may well harm the rights of others. To that extent, such actions are other-regarding and are the legitimate business of a liberal criminal law. Nevertheless, a criminal law that accepts the ontological priority of its addressees cannot issue guidance that detracts from their ontology and so cannot blame humans for merely being human. I propose therefore that the existential immunity forms the basis of a special justification in the criminal law. This justification often takes the form of the plea of justified self-defence in liberal criminal laws. To be clear, the criminal law category of 'self-defence' is generally understood to also apply to cases other than existential immunity cases. It also applies to the use of force to protect rights to one's person, even when the threat is not to an entitlement that is constituently human. These include, for instance, the right that moral liberal states inevitably grant their subjects against assaults that do not threaten their constituent elements.[24] It is also loosely used in relation to the defence of property. The existential immunity that I have proposed does not explain why these other cases of self-defence are treated as being justified and not meriting a blaming judgment. I will address these other cases at a later stage. At this stage, however, I argue simply

---

[23] As previously explained, the existential immunity does not apply where the defender ('D') uses another human ('V') instrumentally. However, if D decides to use V instrumentally but without affecting V's constituent elements, D's does not violate her duty not to affect the constituent rights of any other human although her actions fall outside the existential immunity. In such cases, her actions are not (unless we add in other applicable norms) per se wrong. Consider the following example: D can save her life by causing a lever that is out of her reach to be depressed. She pushes V onto the lever. In doing so, she does not affect any of V's constituent elements. She has nevertheless used V instrumentally. Her action will not fall under the existential immunity. However, D will not incur any blame for a violation of her duty not to affect the constituent rights of any other human, since her actions have not affected any of V's constituent elements. The instrumental use of a person may well be prohibited by a posited rule, even where it does not affect the used person's constituent elements. However, before positing such a rule, the concerned conduct falls under the residual category of things done in the exercise of unconstrained purposive agency.
[24] See, for instance, *R v Scarlett* [1993] 4 All ER 629, in which D used force to defend himself against V's threat to, inter alia, strike him and successfully claimed self-defence.

that exculpation in the identified subgroup of justified self-defence cases, ie, existential immunity cases, is theoretically best explained by the proposition that such cases involve actions that are existentially immune to blame. I will call the defence available in existential immunity cases an 'existential justification'. Note that since we are concerned with whether the actor concerned was behaving in a constituently human manner when seemingly violating the criminal law norm, we are concerned not with the objective situational facts, but with whether subjectively, in prima facie violating the criminal law norm, the actor was impelled by constituently human behaviour. If so, then she is immune from moral blame, or morally predicated criminal blame, in respect of those actions, even if in reality no such behaviour was required.

Treating the use of force in defence of constituent rights as a separate category of self-defence allows us to explain why we might have different expectations and intuitions about how self-defence should work in cases involving the defence of different types of rights. Consider, for instance, our intuitive response to cases in which D is defending a right that is not a constituent right—say, T is attacking D's right against minor assaults which do not affect her bodily integrity by threatening to pinch her. We would tend to agree that D may not shoot her potential attacker T dead to preserve her right not to be assaulted, because this response would be disproportionate, even if T was unambiguously at fault. Contrast this with a case in which the right being defended is a constituent right; say, D's right to life. If D is being attacked by 100 people bent on killing her, then we may be willing to accept that D is entitled to save her life even if she can only do so by killing all 100 attackers, despite the fact that in doing so, D causes much more harm overall than if she had just let herself be killed. Some theorists are even willing to grant that D may defend herself if all her attackers were 'innocent', in that they were infants or had been hypnotised,[25] and I concur. We respond differently to these cases because in existential justification cases, the proportionality of the response is a non-issue—a moral criminal law simply does not have the option of criminally blaming a person for existentially immune actions. By contrast, where the right being defended is not a constituent right, there is no reason why a moral criminal law cannot blame the defender for defensive measures that cause disproportionate harm.

Existential justifications are a special kind of rationale-based justification[26]—they recognise, based on the agent's reasons for having acted, that certain actions are external to the criminal law's blaming enterprise altogether. In claiming an existential justification, an agent provides a rational account of her actions. However,

---

[25] Thomson, 'Self-Defense' 284–89.

[26] To the extent that I concede that existential justifications are somewhat different from other rationale-based defences, I must qualify somewhat my assertion in section 1.4 that the rejection of the wrongness hypothesis reduces all supervening defences to rationale-based defences. Note, however, that in terms of the structure of the criminal process, existential justifications remain supervening defences since they supervene between the establishment of a prima facie offence and a conviction.

unlike other rationale-based defences, exculpation depends not on an evaluation of how good the agent's reasoning was, but rather on the simple determination of the nature of the reasons for having acted that she offers. If she acted for reasons deriving from existentially immune behaviour, her actions were existentially immune to criminal blame. Existential justifications are available in cases like *Beckford v R*,[27] where D claimed that he killed V in response to a perceived threat from V to his own life. However, as explained in section 3.1, they are not available in cases like *R v Dudley and Stephens*,[28] where D1 and D2 killed V (thereby violating V's constituent rights) to avert a threat to their own lives, because in that case V had not authored the threat. In nevertheless using V to further their own business of self-preservation, D1 and D2 treated V as an object liable to be turned to their use, thereby dehumanising him. Since it is against human nature to dehumanise others, D1 and D2 were not merely being human in killing and cannibalising V. Accordingly, they were eligible for (and deserving of) blame. Analogously, a person who, while being threatened at gunpoint, harms a non-threatening third party is not entitled to an existential justification, even though we may wish to exculpate that person on other grounds.

Although at first glance this sounds like an extreme position to adopt, in fact, it is not. First, existential justifications are available only in respect of a particular type of defensive response, viz those that are genuinely impelled by constituently human behaviour. Calculatedly disproportionate or vengeful acts are not impelled by constituently human behaviour even when the actor is facing a threat to her constituent rights, and so these remain subject to criminal blame. Genuine constituently human behaviour tends not to be of the nature that we would intuitively describe as excessive or disproportionate, and even when it is, there is evidence of intuitive support for an exoneration from criminal blame. Consider, for instance, the German Penal Code, whose way of dealing with persons who exceed the limits of self-defence out of confusion, fear or terror is to completely excuse them from criminal liability.[29] Like the grant of an excuse for such conduct under German law, the finding that a person was existentially justified does not convey any normative approbation of her actions—despite the use of the label 'justification', existentially justified conduct is actually immune or external to normative guidance and assessment. Second, existential justifications are only available for threat-directed actions in defence of the very small set of constituent rights. Given the fundamental nature of the constituent rights, most modern liberal states do not condemn persons who protect these rights by using force against the threat, no

[27] *Beckford v R* [1988] AC 130. For now, we may leave aside the fact that the defendant in this case was mistaken, and unreasonably so, about the existence of a threat to his life. I will consider whether such a mistake should have an effect on the availability of the existential justification later in this section and in section 5.2.

[28] *R v Dudley and Stephens* (1884–85) LR 14 QBD 273.

[29] See §33 of the German Strafgesetzbuch, as translated by Professor Dr Michael Bohlander, available at www.gesetze-im-internet.de/englisch_stgb.

matter what the competing political and practical interests.[30] A person is thus not morally blameworthy when her constituently human behaviour impels her to use lethal force against a threat to her life, whether that threat be one evil person or 100 sleepwalking children.[31] Third, the principled stance that *any* genuinely constituently human behaviour, no matter how objectively uncalled for, is immune to criminal blame does not preclude the court from simply disbelieving that a particular act might genuinely have been impelled by a constituently human behaviour. In principle, the trial court could, consistently with the model of existential justification proposed here, have simply found the defendant's claim that he had shot V to avert a perceived threat to his life so outlandish that it could not possibly have been true, and hence it raised no reasonable doubt as to the defendant's guilt.[32]

3.2.2 Defending the Constituent Rights of Others

Let us consider now the normative guidance generated by the commission of a wrong related to the duty not to affect the constituent rights of any other human in respect of persons not directly threatened. Since the wrongdoer's conduct is the business of the entire citizenry, each citizen may legitimately criticise and intervene into the conduct of the wrongdoer. In technical terms, each person has a

---

[30] Unless, of course, she had also inculpated herself by some prior fault. However, such a case is best characterised as one in which the blame arises due to the prior fault, and the consequences generated by the subsequent defensive actions are considered direct consequences of the initial blameworthy act. This explanation of the rules in criminal legal systems that deny a defence to someone who provokes the attack necessitating the defensive action is entirely compatible with the overall argument being made.

[31] *cf* L Alexander, 'Lesser Evils: A Closer Look at the Paradigmatic Justification' (2005) 24 *Law and Philosophy* 611, 630, who argues that in the latter case, the agent must submit to the loss of her life and is not justified in defending herself. Alexander's is very much the minority opinion and is not supported by the doctrine in modern criminal laws. Admittedly, if we stack up enough numbers on the side of the attackers and vest them with features that attract sympathy, we will at some point hope that the agent would simply submit to her attackers. But should she do so, we would not think that she did only what she was required to do—we would praise her for an act of heroism. Heroism is more than almost all modern criminal laws demand of a person.

[32] As a separate matter, this defence would probably not be too difficult to explain to a jury. Juries would be required to consider only whether the defendant genuinely perceived a threat to a constituent human element and whether her response was purely constituently human behaviour. Admittedly, they would need some explanation in respect of these concepts, but in the vast majority, simplified explanations would suffice. So, for instance, juries could usually be given merely a simple list of human constituent elements including life, bodily integrity and the capacity for autonomous choice. Further, in order to determine whether the defendant's response was purely constituently human behaviour, juries would usually need to consider only whether the defendant's actions were in the nature of innate self-preservation behaviour and, if so, whether they involved using a person other than the author of the threat instrumentally. Juries are already required to consider something like this in England and Wales, where s 76(7) of the Criminal Justice and Immigration Act 2008 states that 'evidence [that the defendant did only what she] honestly and instinctively thought was necessary' is probative while assessing the proportionality of defensive action taken. Significantly, juries would no longer have to concern themselves with assessing the magnitude of the threat faced, its imminence and the magnitude of the defensive force used, since the reasonableness of the response would be irrelevant.

Hohfeldian authority[33] to criticise and intervene in relation to such conduct. But how, to what extent and what end, may this authority be exercised? We can exclude for now suggestions that a person exercising this authority may judge or punish the wrongdoer or intervene to enforce and compel conformity with the duty. These responsibilities are generally reserved for the state.[34] But may such a person intervene to repel threats arising from the violation of the duty?[35]

Where such an 'intervention' does not affect the constituent rights of another, any person—not just one exercising this particular authority to intervene—may undertake it by virtue of her initial unrestrained capacity to act, simply because she is (as yet) under no duty not to. Obviously, for this special authority to intervene to have any meaning, it must create a wider normative space for interference with the actions of a wrongdoer. The most logical way for it to do so is by authorising more persons to intervene even when such interventions affect the constituent entitlements of the threatening human. A person acting under this authority may choose to gain access to the threatened person's existential immunity for defensive actions and may then exercise it on behalf of the threatened person. Accordingly, she may intervene only to repel any threat to the constituent rights of another (non-consenting) human. Note that the authority to intervene permits an agent only to exercise the threatened person's existential immunity in a derivative capacity and *on her behalf.* It does not confer on the agent any independent standing to intervene and does not allow any person to override the constituent purposive agency of someone who has chosen to submit to a threat to her constituent rights. Hence, if the authorised agent believes that the person threatened ('V') has chosen to submit to the materialisation of a particular threat, she cannot nevertheless 'protect' V against the threat.

Because a person exercising this authority to intervene actually exercises the threatened person's existential immunity on her behalf, someone who interferes with the intervenor's intervention is actually interfering with the constituent existential immunity of the person who is directly threatened. In doing so, the interferer violates the duty not to affect the constituent rights of another human (the original threatened party). She would thus also be a wrongdoer, and all participants in the system would be able to exercise the original victim's existential immunity (through their own authority to intervene) against the interferer as well.

---

[33] On the characteristic features of a Hohfeldian authority, see WN Hohfeld, *Fundamental Legal Conceptions as Applied in Judicial Reasoning and Other Legal Essays* (New Haven, Yale University Press, 1919) 50–60.

[34] Note that in exceptional circumstances, the state may delegate some of its authority to its subjects. See in this connection Thomson, 'Self-Defense' 285. I will examine the limited instances of such delegations in section 8.2.

[35] Note that violating the duty not to affect the constituent rights of other does not necessarily imply the creation of an actual threat to the constituent elements of any human. For instance, a person who attempts to harm another without knowing (as the victim and the onlookers know) that the attempt cannot possibly succeed nevertheless violates her duty. Yet, this violation does not actually threaten any human's constituent elements. Hence, the set of interventions necessary to repel threats is smaller than the set of interventions necessary to enforce compliance with the aforementioned duty.

In the context of constituent rights, I will argue in section 4.1 that the authority to intervene is the basis for doctrinal criminal law rules permitting a person to commit prima facie offences in defence of the constituent rights (usually the life and bodily integrity) of others.

3.2.3 Guidance to the Threatening Person

Nothing in the analysis suggests that a person suffering defensive action is required not to protect herself against it. Consider the following situation: a villain pushes an innocent fat man (T) off a cliff such that he will fall on D, who is sunbathing below. If D does nothing, she will break T's fall, thus saving him, but getting crushed to death herself. D can save herself by shooting at T, thereby changing his trajectory, but also killing him instantly. However, T also has a gun and is capable of shooting the gun out of D's hand first.[36] Since T is the threat to D's life, D may shoot T in the exercise of her existential immunity and remain exempt from adverse moral evaluation. But what about T's own existential immunity? Since that is a human constituent element, it is logically prior to any normative system addressed to humans generally, and no such normative system can direct its curtailment or forfeiture for any reason, including that it belongs to a person who authored a threat to another. If T defends himself against D's defensive action, T's action will also be exempt from moral evaluation. In fact, nothing in the analysis hitherto shows why even an active violation by a person of her duty not to affect the constituent rights of any other human has—or, indeed, can have—any effect on her constituent elements and existentially immune behaviour. Since all constituent elements (including constituent behaviours) are predicated only on the humanity of the bearer thereof, they continue to be immune to guidance and evaluation in a moral state, even in respect of a wrongful aggressor. Hence, no moral criminal law can demand that a person who violates her duty not to affect the constituent rights of any other human must submit to justified defensive action. Such a person may continue to defend her rights and exercise her immunities as before against all threats to them, whether wrongful or not. While her prior fault in violating her duty would continue to cast her actions in a poor moral light (which is of relevance to a body tasked with dispensing blaming judgments), it cannot generate guidance requiring her to submit to defensive actions that would curtail her constituent elements. The only direct adverse effect of the aggressor's violation of her duty is that other people can now exercise a threatened person's existential immunity on her behalf and be exempt from moral evaluation for actions affecting the aggressor's constituent elements.

---

[36] This example is a modified version of the 'Innocent Threat' example used by Thomson, 'Self-Defense' 287.

3.2.4 In Summary

So far, it has been argued that when the state recognises a constituent element as a right that deserves protection under the criminal law, it creates a system of underlying norms that includes a duty not to affect the constituent rights of any other human (which underlies the doctrinal criminalisation of harming the constituent rights of others) and a contingent authority to intervene (which underlies the permission to act in defence of another's constituent rights). The existential immunity for actions defending constituent rights remains unfettered and forms the basis of a special form of justified self-defence called an existential justification. While an existential justification exempts people who protect themselves against a threat to their constituent elements from adverse moral judgment, the authority to intervene grants people in the public domain of citizenry access to the direct victims' existential immunity in order to protect the victims against threats to their constituent elements.

3.3 Positive Normative Guidance for Posited Rights

Apart from the very small set of constituent rights, all rights with which we are familiar are posited rights. These are the products of human rationality applied to improve the quality of human private and social life. The state identifies particularly valuable interests of the people, defines the contours thereof and by authoritative declaration confers upon them the normative character of a right. In doing so, the state does not merely recognise the moral limits of its own powers—it actually creates rights that are not derived from the ontology of humans. Many posited rights are protected by, amongst other things, the criminal law. A liberal moral criminal law therefore issues norms providing the citizenry with guidance relating to these posited rights, and these norms must not exceed the limits of the state's powers described in section 3.1. In the discussion that follows, I take it that a moral state will posit familiar non-constituent rights, such as a right to liberty,[37] a right against assaults that do not harm our constituent elements (there already being a constituent right against assaults that do harm our constituent elements) and the right to property.[38] Although there is no reason to believe that the framework

---

[37] Recall that in section 2.1, it was explained that the 'normatively unrestrained capacity to act as one chooses' is a Hohfeldian liberty and not a right. However, when the state declares that it will provide a right to liberty, it creates a posited right which is both granted and guaranteed by the state.

[38] This position does not require the rejection of the Lockean theory of property as a natural right. On Locke's terms, the creation of value gives rise to a normative claim to a right, which lies in the realm of political philosophy. This study works with a different understanding of rights, one which categorises them on the basis of their authoritative source. In this study, a right that the polity is required to grant (as opposed to merely recognise) is a posited right, whereas on Lockean terms, since the polity is *required* to grant it, this is a natural right.

of norms that the state must create to support posited rights will be identical to the one that supports constituent rights, the latter does supply a template of norms by reference to which we may examine the structure of norms supporting posited rights. In this section I describe one set of norms relating to the defence of posited rights that would be compatible with both the limits of the state's powers described in section 3.1 and the norms supporting the constituent rights.

When positing rights, the state also defines the contours of the entitlement granted. Unsurprisingly, different jurisdictions do this differently. One state may stipulate that all its citizens may own as much property as they can acquire; another may limit the right to personal property, but instead guarantee all citizens free healthcare. Rights may be made defeasible (for instance, property may be subject to compulsory state acquisition) or conditional (for instance, access to healthcare may be made conditional upon registration with the local clinic), or may be definitionally limited (for instance, by allowing private persons the right to private ownership over anything except nuclear materials). Each of these stipulations will shape the normative framework that supports the right concerned, and therefore there is no standard structure of norms that must inevitably exist to support such rights. Nevertheless, there must be *some* plausible norm structure for core criminal law posited rights[39] that is consistent with the norm structure described for constituent elements, or else the entire hypothesis about the normative structure underlying the criminal law becomes suspect. I therefore attempt here to describe such a compatible norm structure for posited rights.

3.3.1 The Defence of Posited Rights

I start with the defence of a posited right by the right-holder. Although many theorists refer to a 'right' to protect one's rights,[40] I doubt that the best way to characterise the normative space for actions in defence of one's claim rights is also as a claim right. It seems pointless to tell someone who demonstrates scant regard for her victim's rights by being an aggressor in the first place that she should at

---

[39] I do not restrict my understanding of the core of the criminal law to just the protection of constituent rights—that would be a very narrow and artificial proposition. Offences such as theft, assault (even if it does not affect any constituent right) and wrongfully confining a person are all typically seen as *mala in se* offences and none of them relates to constituent rights. For the purposes of this study, I treat all offences generally recognised as *mala in se* as being at the core of criminal law, even if some of them do not involve wrongs related to constituent rights.

[40] See, for instance, SH Kadish, 'Respect for Life and Regard for Rights in the Criminal Law' (1976) 64 *California Law Review* 871, 884–88; GP Fletcher, 'The Right and the Reasonable' (1985) 98 *Harvard Law Review* 949, 954, 966–68, 973; MN Berman, 'Lesser Evils and Justification: A Less Close Look' (2005) 24 *Law and Philosophy* 681, 693–94; KK Ferzan, 'Justifying Self-Defense' (2005) 24 *Law and Philosophy* 711, 728–48; Ferzan, 'Self-Defense and the State' 456, 468. See also E Colvin, 'Exculpatory Defences in Criminal Law' (1990) 10 *OJLS* 381, 390–91; RL Christopher, 'Mistake of Fact in the Objective Theory of Justification: Do Two Rights Make Two Wrongs Make Two Rights...?' (1994) 85 *Journal of Criminal Law and Criminology* 295, 330.

least respect the victim's 'right' that she (the aggressor) submit to defensive action. Moreover, theorists who consider the appropriate defence of rights a right in itself generally argue that it operates against the whole world and that no person ought to interfere with appropriate defensive action. However, this may not correspond to our intuitions where the defensive action is taken against a person innocently authoring a threat or where a third party can defuse the threat more efficiently than the direct victim of the threat. Consider the following example:

> Anne and Brian are model train enthusiasts who are attending the annual working-order model locomotive convention and displaying their prized engines at the event. Anne's locomotive is a sturdy replica of the Flying Scotsman, and Brian's locomotive is a delicate and beautifully detailed replica of the Mallard. Both are equally rare and valuable. Each model locomotive at the convention is displayed on a network of tracks laid down by the organisers, who use a computerised system to ensure that each engine is running at a safe distance from other locomotives and that there will be no collisions. Unfortunately, someone has hacked into and tampered with the organisers' control system, and now Anne's and Brian's locomotives are hurtling headlong into each other. If they collide, Anne's locomotive is likely to be relatively unharmed, but Brian's locomotive will be destroyed. Brian has a gun and can shoot Anne's locomotive off the track, thus saving his own locomotive. However, this will destroy Anne's locomotive. Anne is close at hand and in a position to stop Brian from using the gun.

Here Anne's locomotive innocently poses a threat to Brian's locomotive. If Brian's has a 'right' to defend his property against this threat, then everyone, including Anne, has a duty not to interfere with Brian's defensive action. Yet, it is at least intuitively plausible to think that Anne should be permitted to do so, given first that she was not at fault for having created the threat to Brian's locomotive and, second, that her locomotive is as valuable as Brian's. Whatever one's ultimate view of the merits of such a suggestion, it seems unsatisfactory to foreclose the argument by definitionally stipulating that Brian's proposed defensive action is a right.

Conceptualising the normative space for defensive actions as a Hohfeldian authority is equally implausible. An authority allows the holder to change (or create) some other jural relation.[41] However, someone who defends her posited right does more than change or create jural relations—she vindicates her right against a threat. Moreover, we tend not to see the normative space to defend rights as an optional extra benevolently added on to the right itself by the state. For most, the freedom to defend the right is implicit in the very concept of a posited right.[42] The

---

[41] Hohfeld, *Fundamental Legal Conceptions* 51.

[42] A Brudner, 'A Theory of Necessity' (1987) 7 *OJLS* 339, 360–66 would disagree and would point to the decision in *Vincent v Lake Erie Transport Co* 109 Minn 456 (1910) to say that we can be required to submit to an infringement of right, provided that we can claim compensation for it. He argues that the fact that we can claim compensation for an infringement of right to which we are required to submit affirms the existence of that right. I discuss the decision in *Vincent* in greater detail in section 3.3.3 below, but briefly, if a person is required to submit to an infringement in respect of her claim to something and receive compensation in lieu thereof, then I would characterise that person's right as a right to compensation rather than a right to the thing itself.

law does not grant us a right to property and then separately grant us the authority to defend our property against threats by objects, phenomena, animals and persons. Arguably, a right one cannot defend is not recognisably a right at all.[43] Conceiving of the freedom to defend a right as a Hohfeldian authority would therefore imply the emptying of the right of its content qua right. Nor is the norm allowing the defence of a right a Hohfeldian liberty. A liberty is simply an absence of constraint and, intuitively, it is obvious that the normative claim a person makes when she defends her posited right—say, her jewellery—against a threat is stronger than 'There's nothing telling me not to stop the thief from taking it away'.[44] Moreover, a liberty implies the absence in all others of a right that the person with the liberty refrain from acting. When Anne (faultlessly or otherwise) authors a threat to Brian's rights such that Brian is required to take defensive action affecting Anne's rights, characterising Brian's defensive action as an exercise of liberty would prima facie suggest that all other people, *including Anne*, have no right that Brian not so act. But surely, at least prior to any fault analysis, Anne has a normative claim against Brian's action arising out of her own rights, and so calling Brian's defensive action an exercise of liberty would also require us to explain how (and for how long and to what extent) Anne forfeits her rights. The myriad problems with the forfeiture theory are examined in a bit more detail later in this section, but for now, it suffices to say that these might be sidestepped if we can avoid characterising Brian's defensive actions as falling under a Hohfeldian liberty.

Analogy with the norms supporting constituent rights suggests that the normative space for actions in defence of posited rights is best characterised as a posited immunity from blame.[45] An immunity from blame for appropriate defensive actions implies a divestiture of the state's very power to condemn for such actions,[46] and although this divestiture is posited, it is inseparable from the right. A state cannot posit a right without positing a corresponding immunity for appropriate actions taken to defend the right. Furthermore, in the example of the locomotive enthusiasts Anne and Brian discussed above, characterising Brian's

---

[43] This sort of 'irreducible core' argument has also been made in other contexts. For instance, in response to the increasing creativity of various tax haven jurisdictions in defining their conceptions of a trust, a school of trust law theory has developed which emphasises that the recognition of an institution as a trust is a social fact. On that basis, it identifies certain features that must exist in any institution for holding property for it to be recognisable as a trust. These features form the irreducible core of a trust. See, for instance, D Hayton, 'The Irreducible Core Content of Trusteeship' in AJ Oakley (ed), *Trends in Contemporary Trust Law* (Oxford, Oxford University Press, 1996); D Fox, 'Non-excludible Trustee Duties' (2011) 17 *Trusts & Trustees* 17; *Armitage v Nurse* [1998] Ch 241. At the level of abstraction relevant to this study, the recognition of a juridical relation to something as a right is also a social fact. I argue that a right that cannot be defended is not recognisably a right.

[44] See also in this connection CO Finkelstein, 'On the Obligation of the State to Extend a Right of Self-Defense to its Citizens' (1999) 147 *University of Pennsylvania Law Review* 1361, 1396.

[45] In relation to the constituent rights, blame arises from a failure to be guided by the duty not to affect the constituent rights of other humans. Analogously, in relation to posited rights, blame would arise from a failure to be guided by a posited duty. Posited duties are discussed in greater detail in section 3.3.5.

[46] NE Simmonds, 'Introduction' in WN Hohfeld, *Fundamental Legal Conceptions as Applied in Judicial Reasoning* (Aldershot, Ashgate Publishing, 2001) xv–xvi.

defensive actions as being immune to blame allows us to accommodate our intuition that Anne should be free to interfere with Brian's actions so as to protect her own locomotive. A posited immunity then seems the best way to account for the blamelessness of actions in defence of posited rights. Of course, since we are considering posited rights and a posited structure of norms to support them, there is nothing to prevent a liberal state from stipulatively fashioning the normative space for defensive action as a Hohfeldian authority, liberty or, indeed, claim right. However, if it is an immunity and not an authority, a liberty or a claim right that exempts a person from moral blame for defensive actions that affect the constituent rights of others, then even in respect of posited rights, an immunity is most likely to capture our intuitions. I therefore proceed on that basis and will let the intuitive plausibility of the resulting framework reflect on the appropriateness of my assumption.

Note that an immunity for posited rights would have to be limited inasmuch as it cannot purport to apply to any actions affecting the human constituent elements (which are also constituent rights). This is because as discussed in section 3.1, human constituent elements are logically prior to the rules of a moral criminal law. No such rule can legitimately authorise, or exempt from normative evaluation, any interference with human constituent elements. I will take it as understood in the discussion that follows that morally, no action affecting the constituent rights of a person can be made immune to criminal blame by a posited immunity. In section 4.1, I will argue that this posited immunity is the norm that underlies the paradigmatic form of criminal law justifications.

We next consider whether, like the existential immunity, a posited immunity for defensive action can be triggered without fault. Consider a posited right to property. D can protect her car against a threat caused by a storm, even though there is no fault involved. If the threat to D's car arises because T has a seizure and D's defensive action will not harm T in any way, then surely D can still protect her car, although the threat arose without fault. In fact, even if D's defensive action has a minor negative effect on T's posited rights (for instance, if D must temporarily restrain T), we would probably still not begrudge D her defence of her car. These examples suggest that fault is not necessary, but a contrary result is reached by theorists who rely on a theory of forfeiture to explain the legitimate defence of a right.[47] The forfeiture theory focuses on the right infringed by legitimate defensive action and attempts to explain why the person suffering this infringement suffers no wrong.[48] However packaged, the term 'forfeiture' carries with it punitive

---

[47] As explained in section 3.3.1, this is because forfeiture is generally used to explain the consequences generated by thinking of the appropriate defence of a right as a liberty or a claim right rather than as an immunity.

[48] Thomson, 'Self-Defense' 302–03; J Gardner and F Tanguay-Renaud, 'Desert and Avoidability in Self-Defense' (2011) 122 *Ethics* 111, 114; J McMahan, 'Self-Defense and the Problem of the Innocent Attacker' (1994) 104 *Ethics* 252, 259; S Uniacke, *Permissible Killing* (Cambridge, Cambridge University Press, 1994) 194; S Uniacke, 'In Defense of Permissible Killing: A Response to Two Critics' (2000) 19 *Law and Philosophy* 627, 628; F Leverick, *Killing in Self-Defence* (Oxford, Oxford University Press, 2006) 62–63, 67; F Leverick, 'Defending Self-Defence' (2007) 27 *OJLS* 563, 571–73.

undertones[49] and suggests some element of fault on the part of the person suffering the defensive action. It is this element of fault (or something akin to it) that is offered to explain to the person suffering the defensive action why she must put up with it without complaint.[50] However, if we are trying to explain why D (who defends her right) is not blameworthy, then our analysis should focus on what D may do to defend her right without incurring blame rather than on the desert of T (who suffers the defensive action). T may or may not deserve to suffer, but that is incidental at best to the question of what immunity for defensive action accompanies the grant of a right to D. It is because the forfeiture theory misses the point so profoundly that it has been subject to so much criticism.[51]

This is not to say that T's role in creating the threat to D's posited right has no significance. D cannot, for instance, defend her car against a storm by riding roughshod over T's property, even if we think that T's property is less valuable than D's car. Defining rights to be at the mercy of anyone who needs to appropriate them in defence of a 'superior' right would empty the term 'right' of much of its normative content and, unsurprisingly, no modern liberal state adopts such a radical stipulation of a posited right. An analogy with the rule in relation to constituent rights suggests that the best way to account for the intuition that T's involvement in creating the threat is normatively significant is to make T's rights (in principle) defeasible only if T authors the threat. This is compatible with the arguments made in section 3.1 and allows adequate licence for a person to protect her posited rights without devaluing the concept of a right by defining it to be subject to untrammelled act-utilitarianism. A posited immunity then permits intrusions into the posited rights only of persons who author a threat to the right being protected.

3.3.2 The State's Monopoly of Force[52]

Before considering the extent to which a posited immunity can authorise an incursion into the rights of others, it is necessary to contextualise the discussion.

[49] S Uniacke, *Permissible Killing* 194–95; S Uniacke, 'In Defense of Permissible Killing'; McMahan, 'Self-Defense' 259; A Grabczynska and KK Ferzan, 'Justifying Killing in Self-Defence' (2009) 99 *Journal of Criminal Law and Criminology* 235, 249.

[50] See, for instance, Gardner and Tanguay-Renaud, 'Desert and Avoidability'; Ferzan, 'Justifying Self-Defense' 734–35.

[51] See, for instance, Kadish, 'Respect for Life' 883–84; J Horder, 'Redrawing the Boundaries of Self-Defence' (1995) 58 *MLR* 431, 437–38; T Kasachkoff, 'Killing in Self-Defense: An Unquestionable or Problematic Defense?' (1998) 17 *Law and Philosophy* 509, 515–19; T Kasachkoff, 'Comment and Reply to Suzanne Uniacke's "A Response to Two Critics"' (2000) 19 *Law and Philosophy* 635; R Segev, 'Fairness, Responsibility and Self-Defence' (2005) 45 *Santa Clara Law Review* 383, 439–43; Grabczynska and Ferzan, 'Justifying Killing' 242–49; A du Bois-Pedain, 'Book Reviews—Self-Defence in Criminal Law by Boaz Sangero and Killing in Self-Defence by Fiona Leverick' (2009) 68 *Cambridge Law Journal* 227, 229.

[52] I have explained the central ideas in this section appear in greater detail in M Dsouza, 'Retreat, Submission, and the Private Use of Force' (2015) 35 *OJLS* 727. What appears here is a narrower sketch of the contours of a state's monopoly of force, which includes only ideas relevant to this study.

In particular, it is necessary to note how our normative expectations as to the scope of private access to force in defence of a right change when we move from considering constituent rights to considering posited rights. As was discussed in sections 3.1 and 3.2, when dealing with constituent rights, the state essentially recognises the limits of its powers and clothes these limits in the trappings of rights. On the other hand, when positing rights, the state creates entirely new rights by exercising its political powers. This difference is significant because it means that in respect of posited rights, the state does not merely clothe a pre-existing normative structure in its authority—it fashions the normative structure from scratch and so has much greater say in its design.

In the modern world, the state takes on the role of the primary 'enforcer' of rights and therefore assumes unto itself a monopoly over the legitimate use of force in its jurisdiction, so that an individual subject to its jurisdiction is only permitted to use force in an emergency.[53] The state stakes out the boundaries of its monopoly of force by making certain uses of force presumptively criminal, such that criminal liability will follow from them unless the agent can offer some defence. Other uses of force fall outside the boundaries of this monopoly. For instance, some argue that consent negates the actus reus of an offence and, when effective consent is given, the use of force is not presumptively criminal.[54] On that view, the state's monopoly of force does not extend to the consensual use of certain types of force. Other types of force treated as being outside the bounds of the state's monopoly of force include most instances of the purely private use of force against one's own rights or property. These propositions are consistent with the liberal view that the core domain of the criminal law is public or other-regarding conduct. Conduct that does not affect others or affects them with their consent is not the business of people outside the bounds of the private arrangement, and so cannot be the subject of legitimate liberal guidance.[55]

Even when a particular use of force is treated as being presumptively criminal (and, as such, is treated as falling within the ordinary bounds of the state's monopoly), the state identifies certain exceptions to its monopoly within which it permits an individual to use force. These include exceptions for force used in:

(a) the justified private defence of the person or property of either the self or others;[56]

---

[53] This idea traces back to Max Weber's famous essay entitled 'Politics as a Vocation' and is almost universally accepted as a foundational principle of state amongst modern liberal states. See also R Nozick, *Anarchy, State, and Utopia* (New York, Basic Books, 1974) 23, 117–18.

[54] RA Duff, *Answering for Crime* (Oxford, Hart Publishing, 2007) 208–10; M Dsouza, 'Undermining Prima Facie Consent in the Criminal Law' (2014) 33 *Law and Philosophy* 489, 494–97; and M Dsouza, 'The Power to Consent and the Criminal Law' (2013) ssrn.com/abstract=2225267 at 15. See also in this connection F Tanguay-Renaud, 'Individual Emergencies and the Rule of Criminal Law' in F Tanguay-Renaud and J Stribopoulos (eds), *Rethinking Criminal Law: New Canadian Perspectives in the Philosophy of Domestic, Transnational, and International Criminal Law* (Oxford, Hart Publishing, 2012) especially at 42.

[55] See in this context the discussion in sections 2.1 and 3.1.

[56] See in this regard GP Fletcher, *Rethinking Criminal Law* (Boston, Little Brown & Company, 1978) 867, who explains that it is implicit in the modern Anglo-American conception of defensive force that

(b) the prevention of crime; and

(c) making a citizen's arrest.

For the present purposes, the most important of these exceptions is the first, and the very fact that it is seen as an exception to the state's monopoly of force is significant in itself. This means that any theory for explaining the justified use of force in private defence must conform to the intuited expectation that such force be an exception to the state's monopoly.

To understand how being an exception to the monopoly of force affects the immunity posited for force used in defence of a posited right, we need more detail about this monopoly of force. An argument about the exact specifications of the extent of the state's monopoly of force[57] and its defeating conditions belongs in the realm of political philosophy, and lies outside the scope of this study. For narrative convenience, and for the purposes of this study, I will adopt a view of the monopoly of force that is couched in such broad terms as to hopefully be acceptable to most readers, especially those with a fairly liberal view of the state. As per this account, the state's monopoly of force is as extensive as is permitted in a moral, rule-of-law state. It extends to all presumptively criminal uses of force. Thus, whenever an instance of the use of force would, in the absence of a defence, lead to a criminal conviction for the person deploying the force, that use of force is covered by the state's monopoly of force. So, for instance, force used in private defence would be presumptively criminal, as would be force used in response to duress. Both uses of force presumptively violate the state's monopoly of force.

Furthermore, on the account of the state's monopoly of force adopted here, private access to force ordinarily monopolised by the state is permitted only exceptionally. When the state permits private access to force, it allows an individual limited access to its own power to use force. As such, the state cannot permit a private actor to use force that it was not itself authorised to use. At its highest, the exception to the state's monopoly may permit the individual to 'stand in' for the state,[58] and even in those circumstances, she would be subject to all restrictions

---

access to such force is derivative of the state's monopoly of force. See also WRP Kaufman, 'Self-Defense, Imminence, and the Battered Woman' (2007) 10 *New Criminal Law Review* 342, 354–60; and M Baron, 'Self Defence: The Imminence Requirement' in L Green and B Leiter (eds), *Oxford Studies in Philosophy of Law: Volume 1* (Oxford, Oxford University Press, 2011) 256.

[57] I take no stand as to the source of the state's monopoly in this study. But note that even if the state receives its monopoly from its citizens, on any plausible account this entrustment cannot be a revocable delegation—it must (at least in effect) be an irrevocable transfer. No credible version of the state's monopoly of force would allow a person to unilaterally revoke the monopoly whenever convenient. Even if such a revocation is theoretically possible (say, by way of a revolution), that possibility can be discounted in the ordinary course of political affairs.

[58] See, for instance, M Thorburn, 'Criminal Law as Public Law' in RA Duff and S Green (eds), *Philosophical Foundations of Criminal Law* (Oxford, Oxford University Press, 2011); M Thorburn, 'Justifications, Powers, and Authority' (2008) 117 *Yale Law Journal* 1070, 1126–28; VF Nourse, 'Reconceptualizing Criminal Law Defenses' (2003) 151 *University of Pennsylvania Law Review* 1691, 1713, 1725; Fletcher, *Rethinking Criminal Law* 867; Y Lee, 'The Defense of Necessity and Powers of the Government' (2009) 3 *Criminal Law and Philosophy* 133, 142–44; Ferzan, 'Self-Defense and the State' 476–78. See also *R v Jones (Margaret)* [2007] 1 AC 136, 174–76.

that apply to the state in its use of force. Therefore, if the state would not have been able to legitimately use force to intervene, then no private individual (including the holder of a right under threat) can legitimately[59] use force either. This is not to suggest that the individual must, or may, always use force exactly as the state would use it—it is competent for the state to delegate a lesser power to intervene than it itself has. However, if in a given situation, the state's own authority to use force is constrained by principles of moral and political philosophy, it cannot permit an individual who derives her authority to use force from the state to exercise that authority free of the constraints that limit its own use of force.

I make no assertion that these assumptions are either empirically correct or necessitated by philosophical principle—they are merely plausible stipulations that emerge from the existing literature on the subject and that I have found useful for the purposes of this study. The reader may prefer to substitute these with alternative stipulations, but should bear in mind that such changes will have knock-on effects on the stipulation of the conditions that trigger a person's entitlement to use force in defence of a posited right. In particular, they will affect the rules about the pre-emptive use of force and whether retreat is a precondition for the legitimate use of force.

The stipulations relating to the state's monopoly of force that I have assumed mean that an individual is not ordinarily at liberty to use force. She is only permitted to use force to defend against threats to her rights and even then only in an emergency—when there is no other way to dispel the threat. Uncontroversially, one alternative to privately using force may be to invite the state to deal with the threat where feasible, since it is primarily the state's responsibility to protect the rights of its subjects. There may be other alternatives as well. I will refer to this general precondition for legitimate access to private force as the 'Requirement' consideration. It ensures that private force is not used when there are alternative, less invasive ways of protecting the interest threatened.

When a threatened interest cannot be safeguarded without the private resort to force, it is, in principle, legitimate to privately use force. However, even then, since the agent derives her authority to use force from the state, she may not use force that is unavailable to the state. In other words, if the state would, for whatever reason, not have been permitted to intervene to protect the right threatened, then no private individual (including the holder of the right) can legitimately be permitted by the state to use force to protect it. I refer to this precondition for the legitimacy of private force as the 'Derivative Force' consideration. The Derivative Force consideration encapsulates at least two separate limiting subprinciples. These are:

(a)   parsimoniousness:[60] only the minimum effective force must be used; and

---

[59] Though it remains a possibility that a person illegitimately using force may be excused from criminal liability.

[60] I borrow this term from punishment theory. See generally N Morris, 'The Future of Imprisonment: Toward a Punitive Philosophy' (1974) 72 *Michigan Law Review* 1161, 1162–64. The concept to which it refers is well established in the context of defensive force as well. See Fletcher, *Rethinking Criminal Law* 870; and art 2(2) of the European Convention on Human Rights.

(b) non-disproportionality: the defensive force must not be of disproportionately greater magnitude than the threat.

Note that both these constraints also apply to the state itself when it uses force
to ward off a threat to an individual.[61] Parsimoniousness restricts the force
deployed to the least amount of force sufficient to mount an effective defence,
thereby ensuring that an appropriate amount of respect is accorded to the rights
of the individuals (including the aggressor) concerned. When such force is
being used privately, the requirement for parsimoniousness also minimises the
breadth of the exception to the state's monopoly of force. The requirement for
non-disproportionality secures that the force used to repel threats does not itself
generate inequity. Unsurprisingly, these Derivative Force constraints address the
sorts of concerns that are more apposite when defining state policy than when
guiding individual choices to use force.

The requirement consideration then encapsulates the necessary and sufficient
conditions for a private agent's in-principle access to legitimate force, and the
Derivative Force consideration limits the amount of force that may be delegated to
the said private agent, as well as the manner in which this force may be deployed.
Any limitation on a private individual's access to legitimate force or her subsequent deployment of it that flows from the state's general monopoly of force slots
into one of these two categories and, between them, these two categories encapsu-
late all the principled conditions[62] that must be met in order for a private use of
force to be dubbed 'justified'.

---

[61] I have deliberately chosen to avoid the terminology used in much of the academic discourse on
this subject. Usually, the terms used are 'necessity' and 'proportionality'. Necessity is generally understood to encompass the conditions that I label as 'requirement' and 'parsimony', and 'proportional-
ity' is generally used to refer to what I call 'non-disproportionality'. See, for instance, AJ Ashworth,
'Self-Defence and the Right to Life' (1975) 34 *Cambridge Law Journal* 282, 284–85; M Kremnitzer,
'Proportionality and the Psychotic Aggressor: Another View' (1983) 18 *Israel Law Review* 178, 178–79;
B Sangero, *Self-Defence in Criminal Law* (Oxford, Hart Publishing, 2006) 144, 151–52. See also S Lazar,
'Necessity in Self-Defense and War' (2012) 40 *Philosophy & Public Affairs* 3, who seems to include parsimoniousness (at 5) as well as some elements of non-disproportionality (at 5–6) in his understanding
of necessity. Writers who refer to the 'proportionality' constraint do not object to the use of defensive
force that is disproportionately *less* than the threat faced—their objection is to excessive defensive
force. I prefer the term 'non-disproportionality' because it is slightly better at conveying this idea. As is
obvious, the different terminologies refer to exactly the same overall set of ideas. However, I believe that
extant academic discourse apportions these ideas between 'necessity' and 'proportionality' in a manner
that is potentially misleading and obscures the conceptual connections between some of the principles
and considerations at work.
[62] Some writers argue that other factors relating to how the threat situation arose are also relevant.
Specifically, they argue that D's access to legitimate force is subject to additional conditions (not compatible with the requirement and Derivative Force considerations) if either: (a) D was herself responsible for creating the threat situation; or (b) if the person threatening D acts innocently or is not a
morally responsible agent. See, for instance, Sangero, *Self-Defence in Criminal Law* 203–04; Ashworth,
'Self-Defence' 300–01; Fletcher, *Rethinking Criminal Law* 865. Condition (a) is doubtful—it usually
relies on some theory of the forfeiture of rights, and the problems of the forfeiture theory are well cata-
logued. See n 48 above. A better way to reach the same conclusion as reached by condition (a) would
be to let D attract independent criminal liability for her fault for creating the threat situation (as well as
for any morally intrinsic consequences). As to (b), I will argue in sections 8.2, 8.2.2 and 8.2.3 that the

I think that this is a plausible description of the limitations we normatively expect to be placed on the scope of the posited immunity allowing for the defence of a right. These limitations can of course be explicitly set in place while defining each posited right. But I think that is unnecessary—a state that claims a monopoly of force can plausibly be understood to implicitly set the limitations described in place when positing a right, on the basis that it does not intend to dilute its monopoly by positing the right. The limitations described are needed to support the state's position as the primary enforcer of rights, and they flow from its political claim to a monopoly of force. Moreover, such a definitional stipulation is entirely compatible with the arguments made in section 3.1 about the extent to which individuals are existentially immune from guidance and blame in respect of defensive action taken against those who pose a direct threat to their constituent rights. This is so because this stipulation of the state's monopoly does not have any effect in relation to constituent rights. Those rights are fundamentally recognitions of the logical limits of state power and are therefore superior to the moral state's claimed monopoly of force. A state that recognises the logical priority of the ontology of its addressees over its own norms must, in relation to constituent rights, accept the structure of norms described in sections 3.1 and 3.2, including the existential justification, as it is.[63] Significantly, this means that a person behaving in a constituently human manner may use force to protect her constituent rights without considering whether recourse to state protection is available. For the reasons outlined in section 3.2.1, I believe that this proposition is quite defensible.

3.3.3 The Limits of Posited Immunities for the Defence of Posited Rights

Whereas the existential immunity for action taken in defence of a constituent right is internally limited in terms of what responses it exempts from moral evaluation because it includes only actions that are constituently human behaviour, no analogous internal factor limits a posited immunity. However, it is clear that a posited immunity would only be intuitively plausible if it did not purport to give a right-holder carte blanche to take any steps she pleased in order to defend her right. Modern legal systems limit the actions permitted in defence of a right by expressly or implicitly (as part of the monopolies of force that they claim) stipulating some sort of proportionality constraint, usually requiring that a defensive action not cause excessive harm or harm disproportionate to the harm

apparent culpability of the person authoring the threat does have some limited relevance, but only in a manner that feeds into the Derivative Force consideration.

[63] Ferzan, 'Self-Defense' 470–72 reaches a similar conclusion, although her argument proceeds on very different lines. If nothing else, this suggests that the argument being made herein has at least some intuitive appeal.

threatened.[64] Because posited rights are created by the exercise of our rational faculties, it is also entirely appropriate to use our rational faculties to rank posited rights (in terms of their relative value) and interferences with them (in terms of their relative severity). A proportionality constraint is therefore compatible with the structure of norms argued for in relation to constituent rights. Although fleshing out this proportionality constraint in terms of straightforward act-utilitarianism would be compatible with the arguments made hitherto (as long as it never authorised the overriding of constituent rights), an approach that does less violence to the notion of a right[65] would have greater intuitive plausibility in a liberal state, and so I will explore more nuanced versions of the proportionality constraint. In what follows, I examine the principles that govern derivative access to force in a state that adopts a stipulation of its monopoly of force along the lines described in section 3.3.2.

Recall that an individual's derivative access to force is limited by the parsimoniousness and non-disproportionality constraints. I consider first the non-disproportionality constraint. Brudner suggests that rights have a certain logical order of priority and suggests that rights are overridden by other rights that are logically prior to them.[66] He argues that as humans, we define our lives and reality by reference to our actions, which in turn are logically predicated on our capacity for purposiveness—our 'moral personality'. (This moral personality stems from what I call 'purposive agency' in this study.) For Brudner, therefore, our capacity for purposiveness is the central value by reference to which we should assess the relative priority of rights—the importance of rights depends on how crucial they are for giving practical confirmation to a person's capacity for purposiveness. The right to freedom from physical constraint is a human right because a person's self-ownership is the condition for objectively expressing any purposiveness. Conversely, property rights are rights of the person, because property manifests the instrumental value of things relative to persons, who are in turn confirmed as bearers of intrinsic value. Therefore, personality is logically prior to property as that by which the right of property is originally constituted, and personality is the conceptual limit of the right of property in the sense that the latter must yield to the former as the basis of its own existence. In a conflict between these rights, personality must be preferred both for its own sake and for the sake of property. On that basis, Brudner argues that a property-owner who prefers (by resisting a taking) his property to another's life commits a legal wrong, because this choice undermines the conceptual basis of property.[67]

---

[64] See, for instance, in England and Wales, s 76(5A) and (6) of the Criminal Justice and Immigration Act 2008.

[65] See Brudner, 'A Theory of Necessity' 341–44 for a brief description of the more obvious problems with act-utilitarian theories as applied to rights. For a more detailed critique, see B Williams, 'A Critique of Utilitarianism' in B Williams and JJC Smart, *Utilitarianism: For and against* (Cambridge, Cambridge University Press, 1973).

[66] Brudner, 'A Theory of Necessity' 362.

[67] ibid.

Brudner's assertion that moral agency is necessarily the central ordering value by reference to which rights must be ordered is intuited, but plausible, and so I will adopt it for the present purposes. However, I disagree with Brudner's deduction from it that a person who resists the taking of a lower right by someone trying to protect a higher right commits a legal wrong. Even if there is a hierarchy of rights, it does not necessarily follow that the superiority of one right imposes upon the holder of an inferior right any duty to submit to the taking of the inferior right. It is equally plausible that the consequence of this hierarchy is simply that the holder of the inferior right is not entitled to (one or more forms of) legal redress against a taking of her right for the protection of a superior right, though she may well take appropriate steps to protect her rights. For Brudner, the point of his hierarchical structure is that while the holder of an inferior right must submit to its taking, she is nevertheless entitled to (civil) compensation for the loss caused to her.[68] He points to the decision in the tort case of *Vincent v Lake Erie Transport Co*[69] to corroborate his argument. In *Vincent*, the Supreme Court of Minnesota, by a majority of two to one, awarded compensation to a dock-owner whose dock suffered damage after a ship's captain decided to keep his vessel moored to the dock after unloading the ship's cargo in order to avoid losing the ship in a storm, despite holding that the captain's actions were necessary. However, conceptually Lewis J's dissent is much more persuasive than the majority opinion. Lewis J pointed out that once it was found that the ship was lawfully in position when the storm broke and that the master was not at fault in leaving it there during the storm, there was simply no basis for tort liability. Liability in tort is generally premised on fault, whether arising from poor norm-reasoning or poor functional reasoning, and only in exceptional cases is no-fault liability imposed. Intuitively too, there is something incongruous about directing a person to pay compensation for her justified actions. A person acting with justification adopts a course of action that is available to her without any condition (ex ante or ex post) that she be willing or able to make civil compensation. It seems odd to tell an impecunious person that she is justified in defending her legal interests in an emergency, but must then pay through her nose or face civil prosecution for debt recovery if she exercises that option. I present a fuller argument about the consequences that I think ought to follow from a justified action in sections 3.3.4 and 8.2.2, but at this stage, I simply avoid assuming that a necessary corollary of ordering rights by reference to their importance for moral personality is that the holder of an inferior right must submit to a taking of that right for the protection of a superior right.

If we use Brudner's suggestion that the abstract values of rights be determined by arranging rights in order of their importance to moral personality, the most important right would be the right to possess purposive agency in the first place. This is consistent with my treatment of purposive agency as a constituent human

---

[68] ibid. See also J Quong, 'Killing in Self-Defense' (2009) 119 *Ethics* 507, 513.
[69] *Vincent v Lake Erie Transport Co* 109 Minn 456 (1910).

element, logically prior to normative guidance. However, for the sake of clarity, it is preferable to restrict this right-ordering exercise to posited rights and treat constituent rights like the right to purposive agency as being conceptually prior to all posited rights. In terms of the argument that Brudner makes, posited rights can be divided into two broad categories. The more important set of rights allow a person to objectively express her purposiveness and includes enabling rights that 'give practical confirmation to the person's self-certainty of [the] final worth [of her purposiveness]', such as the right to freedom from physical constraint, the right against assault and the right to freedom of expression. Subsidiary to these are rights to things that are expressions of human purposiveness. These are essentially property rights. Property rights, being logically subordinate to enabling rights, ought, in general, to yield to them. Brudner stops here and says that no matter how great the interference with property rights and how minor the alternative interference with enabling rights, a property right cannot override an enabling right.[70] It is easy to show, with appropriately constructed hypotheticals, that this result is implausible, and I will not defend it.

Instead, I propose that in trying to determine what defensive actions are appropriate, we also take into account the degrees to which the threat and the necessary defensive actions interfere with the posited rights that they respectively affect. Neither the abstract values of the competing rights nor the degrees of interference with them would individually settle the question of whether a defensive measure is a disproportionate response to a threat. Both would have to be considered and a cumulative view taken. Of course, this does not provide much by way of precise prospective guidance, but I think that any theory that claims to be able to do that lays itself open to challenge on the basis of intuitions generated by appropriately constructed hypotheticals. In fact, the law works quite well with conceptual place-markers such as 'proportionate',[71] and most liberal legal systems refer to such evaluative or partly evaluative concepts even while providing ex ante conduct guidance. Clearly, therefore, such a stipulation is at least intuitively plausible.

The second limiting constraint that applies in identifying immune responses is the parsimoniousness constraint—the insistence that the response adopted must be the minimum response that would effectively defend the right against the threat. Parsimoniousness accounts for the general consensus that where more than one effective response is not disproportionate to the threat faced, a state that

---

[70] Brudner, 'A Theory of Necessity' 362 puts it thus: 'the sole consideration admissible for overriding final rights relates to the preservation of their logical ground ... personality is logically prior to property as that by which the right of property is originally constituted. It is also, therefore, the conceptual limit of the right of property in the sense that the latter must yield to the former as to the basis of its own existence. Hence in any conflict between the right of property in a particular thing and values (such as life) indispensable to moral agency, the more essential value must be preferred both for its own sake and for the sake of property'.

[71] See, for instance, in England and Wales, s 76(5A) ('not grossly disproportionate') and s 76(6) ('not disproportionate') of the Criminal Justice and Immigration Act 2008.

respects and values rights must provide an immunity only for the least invasive response.[72]

3.3.4 Is There a Duty to Submit to Appropriate Defence of a Posited Right?

Although some theorists think that a person suffering appropriate defensive action should be under a duty to submit to it,[73] an analogy with the structure of norms accompanying a constituent right suggests that there should be no such duty for posited rights either. If the posited immunity is really just an immunity and not a claim right, then, by definition, it does not imply the presence of a corresponding duty in others. Of course, since we are in the realm of posited norms, a state is entitled to posit a duty to submit to such action. However, the argument for such a duty traces to the characterisation of the normative space for appropriate defensive action as a claim right. I resisted that proposition and I likewise resist its sequitur about the duty to submit.

In any event, I have not encountered any convincing explanation of why such a duty is needed or useful. The practical efficacy of imposing a duty to submit to defensive action is probably minimal—it seems unlikely that the mere imposition of a duty to submit to defensive action will change the behaviour of those who would not anyway have been moved by the threatened person's predicament. Usually, therefore, the imposition of such a duty would have to be accompanied by the threat of a substantial penalty for non-compliance with it. If defensive action is available against threats to rights authored without fault, then it seems perverse to penalise a right-holder for protecting her rights against an undeserved infringement (especially given that the person threatening her rights may well be doing exactly that herself). If, on the other hand, defensive action is only available against fault-based threats to rights, then, as discussed earlier, this unduly restricts the availability of the entitlement to take defensive action. One might avoid both these challenges by stipulating that the duty to submit applies only where the original threat was authored with fault arising from poor functional reasoning. But this

---

[72] *cf* Alexander, 'Lesser Evils' 618–20, who argues that all non-disproportionate responses should be exonerated from moral blame because this would incentivise the reduction of the overall disutility in the world. I disagree because I share neither Alexander's commitment to thoroughgoing consequentialism nor his faith in the efficacy of and/or need for incentives to encourage behaviour that reduces the level of overall disutility in the world. Moreover, Alexander's views are very much the minority opinion. In any event, denying an immunity from blame to non-parsimonious defensive action does not preclude the state from completely or partially excusing the agent from blame.

[73] See, for instance, PH Robinson, 'Criminal Law Defences: A Systematic Analysis' (1982) 82 *Columbia Law Review* 200, 273–85; PH Robinson, 'The Bomb Thief and the Theory of Justification Defenses' (1997) *Criminal Law Forum* 387, 404–05; K Greenawalt, 'The Perplexing Borders of Justification and Excuse' (1984) 84 *Columbia Law Review* 1897, 1925; Fletcher, *Rethinking Criminal Law* 760–62; Gardner and Tanguay-Renaud, 'Desert and Avoidability' 113; McMahan, 'Self-Defense' 257, 263. See also generally DN Husak, 'Conflicts of Justification' (1999) 18 *Law and Philosophy* 41, especially 56–66.

limited stipulation is unlikely to satisfy the proponents of the duty and, further-more, it is inelegant and reeks of unprincipled ad hocery. In any event, the positive case for criminal liability for purely functional blame itself remains equivocal at best. No doubt some states may nevertheless choose to posit some duty to sub-mit, but they may equally choose to let the ex post regime of civil compensation address liability for any losses caused. I do not think that such a duty is necessary to ensure the intuitive plausibility and justice of the overall system, and all things considered, because of the incoherence and complexity that would be introduced into the system by introducing a duty to submit, I prefer to avoid doing so. Instead, I treat the entitlement to take appropriate defensive action strictly as an immunity from norm-blame.

I will spend some time drawing out the consequences of not having a posited duty to submit to defensive action in Chapter 8, but one issue calls for immedi-ate clarification: if there is no duty to submit to an immune action, then what *should* ideally happen when a person acts under a posited immunity? Consider the following example: Betty has (deliberately or inadvertently) locked Anita in her (Betty's) shop and, in order to protect her right to liberty, Anita must break Betty's shop window. Betty, who happens to be monitoring the live feed from her shop's CCTV cameras, sees Anita about to throw a shelf through her window. If Betty is not required to submit to Anita's action, then what steps can she take to protect her window and how, ideally, should the situation be resolved? I address the second question first—the situation may be resolved either by Anita succeed-ing in securing her liberty by breaking Betty's shop window or by Betty succeed-ing in preventing Anita from doing so by taking appropriate (by which I mean non-disproportionate and parsimonious) steps. Both Anita and Betty would be claiming an immunity from norm-blame for actions taken to protect their posited rights (although Betty may incur norm-blame based on prior fault if she delib-erately locked Anita in). The structure of norms supporting a right is not meant to answer the question: 'What should happen?' Instead, it answers the question: 'What may the right-holder do?' The answer to this question may well be different for different people with different rights at stake in the same conflict of rights, and this is not, in any manner, problematic.[74] As to what a third person chancing upon the scene can do, that depends on the general duties and authorities generated by a posited right, and so I will examine that issue after I have set out my views on how the duties and authorities generated by a posited right operate.

The other question has more bite. If Anita's action (breaking Betty's shop win-dow) is an appropriate response to the threat posed to her right to liberty by Betty (or things over which Betty has rights), does this not mean that any move by Betty to protect her shop window will be inappropriate because it will prevent Anita from protecting her right to liberty? The error in this proposition lies in the iden-tification of the interests being compared at each stage. Since we are examining the

---

[74] See also in this connection M Baron, 'Justifications and Excuses' (2005) 2 *Ohio State Journal of Criminal Law* 387, 403–05.

internal consistency of a theory that does not impose on a person a duty to submit to immune action, we may take it that Betty has no duty to submit to Anita's action. If so, then in evaluating the proportionality (and thus the appropriateness) of Betty's proposed responses to Anita's immune action, the fact that it will cause the Anita to fail to defend her (Anita's) rights cannot be a consideration. Instead, Betty need only consider whether, and to what extent, her proposed defensive action will itself affect (as opposed to prevent a defence of) Anita's rights. Admittedly, sometimes the distinction between affecting Anita's rights and preventing a defence of them will be gossamer thin, but that is a problem that pervades the criminal law's distinction between acts and omissions, and it is not something that affects the arguments made here uniquely. I leave that general problem to be addressed some other day.

To return to our example, then, when deciding on the appropriateness of her planned defensive action—breaking Betty's window—Anita would compare the effects of her proposed action (ie, the permanent damage to Betty's property) to the threat she suffers (ie, the temporary deprivation of her liberty). However, because Betty's proposed defensive action is different from that of Anita's, Betty's analysis will not relate to the same rights. Betty must consider only the interferences with other people's rights that her proposed defensive action will cause rather than those that they will prevent from being avoided. Even on this analysis, a situation in which Betty can only stop Anita by triggering a circuit that would deliver an electric shock (capable of causing pain but not serious injury) to Anita when she touches the shelf would be evaluated differently from one in which Betty can stop Anita by deploying additional metal shutters on the inside of the window. In the first case, Betty's action might be judged to be a disproportionate interference with Anita's right not to be hurt or subjected to physical discomfort, whereas in the second, it would not be disproportionate, since it would not affect any of Anita's rights at all. From this we can conclude that the elimination of the duty to submit to defensive action does not make the proposed system of norms supporting a posited right internally contradictory. In fact, it reinforces the concept of a right by creating an across-the-board general exemption from norm-blame for any right-holder who takes appropriate steps to defend her rights against a threat.

3.3.5 Posited Duties and Authorities

In analysing the norms that support posited rights and posited immunities, direct analogues of the duty and authority that support constituent rights are good starting points. The direct analogue of the duty not to affect the constituent rights of others would be a posited duty requiring each person not to affect the posited rights of others. This duty would be violated by any person who adverts to the duty and nevertheless chooses to behave contrary to the norm's guidance. Like the duty for constituent rights, the posited duty would underlie doctrinal criminal law rules proscribing the infliction of harm to the rights of others. Of course, it is possible, in the exercise of human rationality, to do away with the advertence condition for wrongdoing in respect of posited duties, and indeed most jurisdictions have some negligence-based criminal liability. Nevertheless, the arguments made in relation to constituent rights as to why advertence is a sine qua non for wrongdoing are equally valid for posited rights. As in relation to constituent rights, so also in relation to posited rights—the criminal law's norms are meant to influence conduct. Someone who advertently chooses her behaviour by reference to the norms complies with them, and someone who advertently chooses not to obey them, violates them. Whether the ideal outcome occurs should be irrelevant to that inquiry. Therefore, when proposing a model structure of norms to support a posited right, I would retain the advertence requirement even for posited duties, leaving liability for the inadvertent harming to be addressed by normative systems that do not claim as close a connection to morality as the criminal law (for instance, systems of tort liability). At any rate, if we must have criminal liability for negligence, then, as I have explained in section 2.2.3 above, this can be introduced by positing situation-specific norms directing people to meet certain quality standards in respect of their functional reasoning and criminally blaming people who fail to be guided by such secondary norms.

Posited duties fill in at least some of the normative blanks that were previously the domain of unrestricted purposive agency. Previously, all actions that did not violate the duty not to affect the constituent rights of others and did not fall within the existential immunity (either directly or through the authority to intervene) were both normatively unrestrained and normatively unsupported. Accordingly, they attracted neither moral approbation nor moral reprobation. Posited duties supply additional restraints on a person's exercise of her constituent purposive agency and, where these restraints are flouted, the violator commits a legal wrong. However, posited duties cannot restrict the scope of existentially immune actions because existential immunities are prior to moral rules. Hence, despite her posited duties, a person acting under her existential immunity may use, damage or destroy the posited rights of any other person, whether the latter is the source of the threat to her constituent rights or not, without attracting blame. This does not apply to non-existentially immune actions in defence of constituent rights—actions by which D uses a non-threatening human instrumentally may well attract criminal blame if the state posits a duty to not use other humans instrumentally, even if the agent was acting to protect her constituent rights.

A posited authority would be very similar to its counterpart for constituent rights and would also underlie doctrinal criminal law rules permitting a person to commit a prima facie offence in defence of the posited rights of another. However, there is one minor difference. Actions that fall within the ambit of the existential immunity are external to moral normativity and so are not subject to normative judgment at all. Hence, by their very nature, such actions can never be a violation of the duty not to affect the constituent rights of others, and no authority to intervene can arise in respect of them. Yet, a person whose actions answer to a posited immunity may well be violating her posited duty and thereby technically committing a 'wrong' (though she would be immune to blame consequent upon it). If the posited authority corresponded exactly to its counterpart for constituent rights, then it would arise on these facts and would, in principle, authorise onlookers to intervene against the 'wrongdoer'. Consider the following scenario: Andy is about to damage Bob's car using his cricket bat. Bob exercises his posited immunity and attempts to snatch Andy's bat away from him and destroy it (assuming that both actions are absolutely necessary to prevent Andy from damaging Bob's car). In doing so, Bob violates his posited duty not to threaten Andy's right to his bat, even though he is immune to any blaming judgment for doing so. Andy, of course, is under no duty to submit to Bob's immune action and can take appropriate action to retain his bat. If the posited authority was an exact analogue of the authority for constituent rights, then Charles, who has been watching everything, could access Andy's posited immunity, and prevent Bob from wresting the bat away from Andy.

Had the bat and the car been replaced by constituent rights, this result would not have followed. Charles would only have been permitted to intervene *against* Andy, because only Andy would have violated his duty not to affect the constituent rights of others. Presumably, we would want a similar result even when the rights in question are posited. This may be achieved by stipulating that the posited authority will arise only when a person violates a posited duty while not being immune to a blaming judgment for such violation. Once it arose, however, the posited authority would function in the same way as the authority for constituent rights, and it would grant an onlooker access to the posited immunity (if any) of the person suffering the wrongful action. Furthermore, as in the case of the authority for constituent rights, the onlooker would only have access to the directly affected person's posited immunity in a derivative capacity. Hence, if the onlooker believed that the directly affected person had chosen to submit to the threatened wrongful action, she (the onlooker) would not be permitted to intervene.

This set of posited norms supporting a posited right would work in much the same way as the set of norms supporting constituent rights and would tend to produce results that share much of the intuitive plausibility of those produced by the norms supporting constituent rights.

3.4 The Criminal Law's Underlying Conduct Rule System

With a plausible structure of posited norms in place to support posited rights, we can now return to one of the propositions with which I began this project, viz that subject to certain caveats and limitations, the criminal law at core endorses and enforces moral norms.[75] I have argued in this chapter that the moral contours of

---

[75] See the text accompanying n 2 in the Introduction above.

the criminal law are defined by the human constituent elements and the constituent rights that correspond to them. A system of criminal law that endorses and enforces the set of norms that support constituent rights, and a compatible set of norms that support posited rights would therefore also, at its core, endorse and enforce moral norms. In the following chapters I will refer to the composite of these sets of norms supporting constituent and posited rights as the criminal law's underlying conduct rule system—rules that a liberal moral criminal law system will inevitably have at its core. To recap, this set includes the following:

1. Rules that recognise all constituent rights.
2. Rules that set in place, or at least do not purport to disturb, the set of immunities, duties and authorities described in sections 3.1 and 3.2, for all constituent rights.
3. Rules that put in place for all posited rights, however chosen, a set of supporting norms that is compatible with the set of norms accompanying constituent rights.

This description of the criminal law's underlying conduct rule system sets it up as a standard external to the words of the criminal law provisions, by reference to which one may determine the appropriate manner in which to behave. It encapsulates all the conduct guidance in a liberal moral criminal legal system, irrespective of how the draftsperson frames the actual doctrinal provisions thereof. Although any compatible (and internally coherent) set of norms supporting posited rights can be part of such a criminal law's underlying conduct rule structure, in the rest of this study I will be relying upon the set of posited norms sketched in this chapter. I do so because this set of posited norms has been modelled on the set of norms supporting constituent rights, and so it is likely to share any intuitive plausibility that the moral set of norms may have and generate a familiar and intuitively appealing criminal law system. Using this stipulation of the conduct rule system underlying a liberal and moral criminal law, I will, in the subsequent chapters, attempt to map the perplexing borders of justifications and rationale-based excuses.

Part III

Translating Theory into Doctrine

4

The Theoretical Framework of Rationale-Based Defences

I started my study by rejecting the wrongness hypothesis, suggesting that both justifications and rationale-based excuses are defences arising from an evaluation of the agent's reasons for acting, and arguing that this should be viewed as negating the agent's blameworthiness on the basis of the quality of her reasoning. But the rejection of the wrongness hypothesis for justifications means that the accompanying account of excuses being based on factors that negate the culpability of the agent cannot now be set up as the basis of the distinction between justifications and excuses. Excuses do negate the culpability of the agent, but so do justifications. What then sets justifications apart from rationale-based excuses? In this chapter, I set out my conception of the paradigm forms of justifications and excuses, and explain how they fit into a useful model of the criminal law. I also consider and situate a rationale-based defence that does not conform to these paradigm forms—the defence of necessity. This chapter is therefore about explaining how different types of rationale-based defences interact with and complement each other.

4.1 Rationale-Based Defences and the Conduct Rule/Decision Rule Distinction

In Chapter 3, I argued that the conduct rule system that characterises the criminal justice system includes, and is closely linked to, moral norms that exist prior to posited law. Thereafter, I set out my view of the structure of the morally derived conduct rules that animates the core of the criminal law. But whatever the exact content of this conduct rule system, as a matter of empirical observation of modern criminal justice systems, we can see that even if an agent's norm-rationality conforms to the guidance offered by it (ie, the criminal law's underlying conduct rule system), this does not necessarily mean that she avoids violating an offence definition. Sometimes, she may have violated an offence definition and may have done so for reasons that accord with the normative basis of the criminal law. For instance, causing bodily injury to another person is proscribed by various offence definitions. A person (D) violates one or more of these offence definitions when she deliberately injures another person (V). However, she may have done so in order to defend herself against a threat from V to her life. Thus, her reasons for violating the offence stipulation accord with the normative basis of the criminal law.

This oddity arises, in part, because by its nature, the entirety of the criminal law's conduct guidance in relation to a particular action seems too complex to be captured in a set of offence definitions. Therefore, offence definitions typically track the exceptions to the default position of universal unfettered freedom to act as one pleases. These exceptions are usually mapped by the duty not to affect the constituent elements of others and posited duties akin to it. However, when offence definitions do so, what remains is that portion of the conduct rule system that stems from existentially immune actions, the derivative authority to defend another person against a threat to her constituent rights, and their respective posited analogues.[1] Since these immunities and authorities exempt only specific persons from norm-based evaluation and operate only in respect of actions taken for specific reasons,[2] it is clear that a person claiming to invoke these immunities and authorities must submit her reasons for acting to the evaluation of the judge. In other words, such a person claims a rationale-based defence based on the normative guidance provided ex ante by the pre-legal immunity and authority, and posited immunities and authorities akin to them. She argues, that is, that she acted as she was permitted to act by conduct rules that form part of and underlie the criminal law.

Yet we also know that when a judge takes note of a claim to a supervening defence, she does so to assess the defendant's personal blameworthiness after the event. At the stage of evaluating conduct, rationale-based defences function purely as decision rules. Hence, the defendant's claim to a rationale-based

---

[1] Although for my purposes it is sufficient merely to observe this phenomenon as an empirical fact and to suggest that it is because the content of the available guidance is too complex to be reduced to a comprehensive offence stipulation, it has also been argued that this phenomenon is linked to the very nature of rules and of the exceptions to them. See in this connection L Duarte d'Almeida, *Allowing for Exceptions: A Theory of Defences and Defeasibility in Law* (Oxford, Oxford University Press, 2015) 77. Duarte d'Almeida argues for the 'irreducibility thesis', which (in the context of the criminal law) is the claim that exceptions to criminal law rules (ie, what I call rationale-based defences) cannot be restated in the form of conditions for the application of the rule (ie, the offence stipulation) itself. This means that the manner in which the rules that comprise the criminal law's underlying system of normative guidance are assigned to the categories of 'offence stipulation' and 'rationale-based defence' is not merely a matter of the arbitrary drafting choices made by a particular draftsperson. Offence stipulations include all conditions that must affirmatively be ascertained to exist in order to support a conviction, whereas rationale-based defences are all the conditions that, while not inconsistent with the conditions of the offence stipulation, must be *not ascertained* in order for a conviction to stand. See also the subsequently retracted paper by Hart that Duarte d'Almeida seeks to reinvigorate in his monograph: HLA Hart, 'The Ascription of Responsibility and Rights' (1948) 49 *Proceedings of the Aristotelian Society* 171.

[2] Immunities protect the person whose entitlements are threatened against blame arising out of certain actions taken to protect one's entitlements, and authorities allow a participant in the moral system to intervene when a person wrongfully threatens another's entitlements by accessing the immunities of the person threatened and taking blame-immune action to protect that person's entitlements.

defence to a crime involving norm-blame (ie, blame for not following the conduct guiding rules of the criminal law) can only be adjudicated by evaluating her norm-reasoning within the parameters of the facts as perceived by her. Similarly, her claim to a rationale-based defence to a crime involving functional blame (ie, blame for failing to notice facts that ought to have been noticed and failing to draw conclusions that ought to have been drawn based on those facts) can only be adjudicated by evaluating her functional reasoning by reference to standards of care that she ought to have met in exercising her functional capacities.

This means that rationale-based defences can function both as conduct rules (at the ex ante stage) and decision rules (at the ex post stage). But do both rationale-based excuses and justifications offer conduct guidance? Although some rationale-based defences that we traditionally recognise fit the contours of a claim to an immunity norm or an authority norm and therefore also guide conduct,[3] many others do not. For instance, we are intuitively reluctant to punish a person who, while being threatened at gunpoint, injures or steals from a non-threatening third party. But even though the threat is to the agent's constituent elements, because her actions are not directed at repelling the threat itself, they cannot fall under any existential immunity or any authority norm.[4] Similarly, in the facts of the extraordinary case of *R v Dudley and Stephens*,[5] while we may have sympathy for the plight of Dudley and Stephens, their killing of Parker would not be existentially immune from blame because Parker was not threatening them. Defences, if any, granted to the defendants in such cases do not correspond to any prospective conduct guidance available in the criminal law. Moreover, when allowing such defences, the courts do not say to the general public 'You are permitted to injure or steal from an innocent person if you are being threatened at gunpoint' and it does not say 'You are permitted to murder and cannibalise an innocent human when you are likely to starve if you do not'. Perhaps defences, the grant of which does not supply prospective conduct guidance, ought to be treated as being categorically different from defences that do supply conduct guidance.

Independently, we also know that there is a general consensus as to the normative (or conduct-guiding) content of excuses and justifications. As they are generally understood, rationale-based excuses are not meant as normative guides for how people should conduct themselves. They address only the judge and are meant to guide only her actions.[6] The judge is directed to exercise her evaluative judgment as to the extent (if any) to which the agent's reasoning merits exculpation from blame. Excuses are not intended to be a legitimate consideration in

---

[3] For instance, the defence of property (posited immunity), the defence of others and at least some instances of prevention of crime (authority norms).

[4] See in this connection the arguments made in sections 3.1 and 3.2.1.

[5] *R v Dudley and Stephens* (1884–85) LR 14 QBD 273.

[6] This statement is true of all excuses, although I confine myself in this section to rationale-based excuses.

the agent's reasoning when deciding on the appropriate course of action. They are therefore purely decision rules.[7] On the other hand, justifications are usually seen as being capable of guiding conduct,[8] albeit that they also have elements of decision rules.[9] It is generally accepted that justifications ex ante and contingently permit certain conduct by recognising that it is appropriate and, ex post, require the decision-makers evaluating the agent's conduct to verify that the specified contingencies in fact arose and that the permission to use defensive force granted was not exceeded. Hence, the law permits a person to plan her actions on the basis that she will be entitled to a justificatory defence.

Putting these two propositions together suggests that it might be appropriate to treat rationale-based defences containing guidance for conduct as justifications,[10] and rationale-based defences devoid of conduct-guidance as rationale-based excuses. Although there is no preordained sense in which the words 'justification' and 'excuse' must necessarily be used, a model of rationale-based defences as per which justifications are defences that fit the contours of a claim to an immunity norm or an authority norm, and rationale-based excuses are rationale-based defences that do not but nevertheless exculpate seems at least plausible.[11] The rest of this chapter will be dedicated to exploring this hypothesis in greater detail.

---

[7] M Thorburn, 'Justifications, Powers, and Authority' (2008) 117 *Yale Law Journal* 1070, 1095. See also K Greenawalt, 'The Perplexing Borders of Justification and Excuse' (1984) 84 *Columbia Law Review* 1897, 1899–900. When I say that excuses are purely decision rules, I mean that they are meant to offer no guidance to the defendant. They do of course offer some guidance to lawyers or other constituencies in the practice of the law.

[8] See, for instance, H Stewart, 'The Role of Reasonableness in Self-Defence' (2003) 16 *Canadian Journal of Law and Jurisprudence* 317, 333–36, who argues that justifications are conduct rules. See also J Gardner, 'Justifications and Reasons' in AP Simester and ATH Smith (eds), *Harm and Culpability* (Oxford, Clarendon Press, 1996) 124, who, while expressly rejecting the claim that justifications are conduct rules, concedes that justifications do tell the agent ex ante what conduct is permissible. His reasons for denying that justifications are conduct rules are conceptual—Gardner seems to work with a narrow view of what a conduct rule is, as per which it must necessarily provide imperative guidance (ie, 'Do this' or 'Don't do that'). See in this connection M Plaxton, 'John Gardner's Transatlantic Shadow' (2013) 39 *Queen's Law Journal* 329, 332. Without commenting substantively on that proposition, it suffices for me to say that the conception of conduct rules with which I work in this book also includes permissive guidance of the form 'You may do this'. Also in this context, consider the slightly ambivalent views of GP Fletcher, 'The Nature of Justification' in S Shute, J Gardner and J Horder (eds), *Action and Value in Criminal Law* (Oxford, Clarendon Press, 1993). In this (at 177), he comes close to suggesting that justification has strong guidance elements, because it is conduct that is not wrong, in the sense of being a violation of the law in the ideal sense of *Recht*. However (at 180), he treats justifications as decision rules. This may be because justifications are both conduct and decision rules.

[9] See also Thorburn, 'Justifications, Powers, and Authority' 1096–97, who makes the same initial assertion before suggesting that we abandon this language altogether.

[10] A similar treatment is suggested by J Hruschka, 'Justifications and Excuses: A Systematic Approach' (2005) 2 *Ohio State Journal of Criminal Law* 407, 413. See also J Hruschka, 'Imputation' (1986) 3 *Brigham Young University Law Review* 669, 701–02.

[11] See, for instance, MN Berman, 'Justification and Excuse, Law and Morality' (2003) 53 *Duke Law Journal* 1, 32–38, who makes a very similar argument, although he reaches slightly different conclusions and treats necessity, rather than the justified defence of rights in terms of immunity and authority norms, as the paradigmatic form of a justification.

4.2 The Normative Content of Justifications

Let us start with justifications. As I previously mentioned, justifications are usually seen as being conduct rules, albeit that they also function as decision rules. I also noted that the conduct guidance contained in the duty not to affect the constituent elements of others and posited duties akin to it is typically encapsulated in offence definitions. This leaves the conduct guidance stemming from existentially immune actions, the derivative authority to defend another person against a threat to her constituent rights, and their respective posited analogues. I argue that this conduct guidance is contained in justifications. This account of justifications can straightforwardly be used to explain the contours of justificatory claims like self-defence, the defence of others, the defence of one's property and the defence of the property of others.

Self-defence, in cases where the threat is to constituent rights, is a claim that one acted in conformity with the conduct rule that tracks the existential immunity from moral and criminal guidance applicable to constituently human acts of self-preservation, as described in section 3.1. A defendant who says that she acted in the defence of the constituent rights of others argues that she was acting in accordance with the conduct rule that tracks the authority to intervene described in section 3.2.2.

Where the threat concerned is not to constituent rights, but nevertheless to the person, self-defence is a claim that one acted as was permitted in terms of conduct rules that track the posited immunity described in sections 3.3.1–3.3.4. A defendant who says that she acted in the defence of someone else's non-constituent rights to the person argues that she was acting in accordance with the conduct rule that tracks the authority to intervene described in section 3.3.5.

Similarly, the defence of one's own property is permitted in terms of conduct rules that track the posited immunity described in sections 3.3.1–3.3.4, and the defence of the property of another is permitted in terms of conduct rules that track the posited authority described in section 3.3.5.

In Chapter 8, I will demonstrate that the model of paradigmatic justification that flows from these propositions is plausible in its scope as well as in the results that it generates.

4.3 Do Rationale-Based Excuses Have Normative Content?

In section 4.1, I said that it is generally agreed that rationale-based excuses are not meant to be normative guides for how people should conduct themselves. In the context of excuses to offences involving norm-blame, Duff disagrees. He says that the judicial grant of certain excusing defences (especially duress) in particular circumstances does have an inevitable guiding effect insofar as although the judge does not 'permit' what the defendant did, she does express the judgment that in the circumstances, society could not demand more of the defendant as a citizen.[12] I accept one part of Duff's analysis, but take issue with another.

First, the part of Duff's argument with which I agree. When Duff says that the judicial grant of an excuse like duress expresses the judgment that society could not demand more of the defendant as a citizen, one immediately asks: more what? Since he adopts a 'reasons' approach to supervening defences, for him the answer seems to be more (or better) norm-reasoning, ie, compliance with conduct rules (which he, along with Fletcher and Robinson, calls 'rules for citizens'). It is also instructive that the conduct rules to which Duff refers seem to be traced to society rather than to the criminal law specifically—but more on that later. In referring to norm-reasoning as the basis for an excuse, Duff correctly identifies the basis for the grant of a rationale-based excuse as a factor intrinsic to the defendant—her rationale for having acted in those circumstances—rather than the set of external circumstances that the defendant faces.[13] Hence, if the defendant committed the prima facie offence because in the circumstances, she thought she had good reasons to do so, then even if she was aware of and comforted by the fact that a court had previously excused a person acting for similar reasons in similar circumstances, that would have no bearing on whether she should be excused from criminal liability. This would be true even if in committing the prima facie offence, the defendant committed an act that she was in any case tempted to commit, provided that this temptation was not the reason that the defendant acted and that her actual rationale for acting was the belief that it was the appropriate thing to do. It is important to note that in the analysis above, to the extent that she is excused, the defendant is not guided by precedent at all—she merely reacts to the circumstances and her rational assessment of the necessary response thereto. If, however, the defendant was keen to commit the prima facie offence in any case and acted not because she was rationally convinced that that was the most appropriate thing to have done, but because she thought she could fulfil her secret desires and avoid punishment for it, given that in circumstances that were outwardly identical, another person was previously excused, then no excuse should be granted.[14]

---

[12] RA Duff, 'Rule-Violations and Wrongdoings' in S Shute and AP Simester (eds), *Criminal Law Theory: Doctrines of the General Part* (Oxford, Oxford University Press, 2002) 61–68, especially from 65 onwards. See also Y Lee, 'The Defense of Necessity and Powers of the Government' (2009) 3 *Criminal Law and Philosophy* 133, 137–38.

[13] For the time being, I may state that I broadly accept John Gardner's identification of the gist of an excuse as being that a person lived up to the standards of character which were expected of her. See J Gardner, 'The Gist of Excuses' (1998) 1 *Buffalo Criminal Law Review* 575. When translated into terms I use in my analysis, this means that a person should be excused if her norm-reasoning, even if inadequate by the criminal law's standards, accorded with the standards normatively expected of a person faced with the same perceived circumstances in the particular society to which she belongs.

[14] I qualify this statement in section 6.2, once I have developed my conception of a rationale-based excuse in greater detail.

In these circumstances too, the previous grant of the excuse should not be permitted to guide conduct. Of course, it is likely to be difficult to establish the defendant's reasons for acting as distinct from the circumstances in which she acted, but the heuristics we adopt for evidentiary convenience should not be understood as legitimate dilutions of the underlying principles. In this study, it is only the underlying principles with which I am concerned.

However, Duff's conclusion that the prior grant of a rationale-based excuse has normative significance for a person contemplating the commission of a prima facie offence is problematic. For Duff, the grant or refusal of a rationale-based excuse informs the citizen about what the law can demand of her, on pain of condemnation. He then says that if the law is to respect and address citizens as responsible agents, it must not deceive them and must make it clear to them what the law demands of them, and what is liable to happen to them if they act contrary to those demands. He therefore concludes that it should be made clear in the law's conduct rule system that when the pressure imposed is onerous enough, a citizen may well give in to duress and yet avoid liability. In other words, he says that rationale-based excuses do have a conduct-guiding role.

The flaw in Duff's argument is that it makes too little of a distinction that Duff himself makes between conduct that is required, conduct that is permitted and conduct that is tolerated. Duff says that the grant of a rationale-based excuse answers the (citizen's) question 'What *must* I do (in order to avoid condemnation)?' rather than the alternative questions 'What *should* I do?' or 'What am I *permitted* to do?' He then expressly accepts that these questions have different answers and also accepts that even the grant of an excuse will not change the answer to the latter questions. In addition, he accepts that a citizen relying on the answer to the former question as one of her reasons for committing a prima facie offence ought not to be granted a defence, since her claim to the defence lacks moral merit.[15] If that is the case, then even according to Duff, the grant of a rationale-based excuse does not provide guidance as to what the citizen should do, or even as to what she is permitted to do. He must then be of the view that the set of conduct rules includes rules that tell a citizen what she should do, rules that tell her what she may do *and* rules that tell her what she will get away with doing. Whereas I have no objection to the law's conduct guidance answering the first two of these inquiries, I doubt very much that the law should provide ex ante guidance as to the last inquiry. The grant of a rationale-based excuse fundamentally affirms that the defendant's act was undesirable. Why then should the law provide guidance that operates to favour its commission? Duff's answer seems to be that this is what a system that respects and addresses its citizens as responsible agents would do—it would make a full disclosure and trust the citizen, as a responsible agent, to make the appropriate choice. He criticises Dan-Cohen's concept of 'selective transmission' and says that the concealment of the fact that citizens will not be convicted

---

[15] Duff, 'Rule-Violations' 66–68.

if they give in to (sufficiently serious) duress amounts to deceit. Yet he maintains that a person who acts based on this guidance ought not to be excused.[16] If so, then all Duff seems to be arguing for is the disclosure of the existence of rationale-based excuses and the facts on which they were previously granted.[17] A mere disclosure of this sort would not amount to guidance or, if it were taken to be guidance in favour of acting, the guidance provided (such as it is) would actually be incapable of being followed without being rendered false. Duff's argument is therefore internally incoherent—he argues for the provision of guidance by which one cannot choose to be guided. The better view therefore remains that rationale-based excuses are not meant to provide normative guidance and that they are purely decision rules.

Separately, where the criminal law blames for poor functional reasoning, it is uncontroversial that to the extent that it also makes an excuse available, the excuse has no normative quality. The grant of an excuse in relation to such crimes is not meant to guide other people to display the levels of carelessness, objective recklessness or otherwise poor functional reasoning displayed by the defendant.

I will attempt in Chapter 6 to explain the source of exculpation in rationale-based excuses consistently with the arguments made herein and to show that the resulting model has a plausible coverage and generates intuitively appealing outcomes.

4.4 The Normative Content of the Non-paradigmatic 'Necessity' Justification

The suggestion as to the nature of a paradigmatic justification proposed in section 4.2 cannot accommodate a defence of purely lesser-evils necessity. For someone who believes that necessity is exclusively an excusatory defence, this

---

[16] ibid 67.

[17] Duff seems to be fighting a straw man version of Dan-Cohen's argument on this point. Dan-Cohen does not argue for the non-disclosure of the existence of rationale-based excuses as a means of discouraging undesirable behaviour. He merely points out that these excuses refer to standards that are by their very nature difficult to exhaustively communicate to the public in advance as a conduct rule. These standards are evaluative and imprecise, and can only effectively be applied by persons who have been specially trained or instructed on how to do so. Dan-Cohen expressly shrinks from endorsing any actual effort to segregate the communications to the officialdom and to the citizenry—he merely argues that actual practice can be analysed as achieving, to a limited extent, the sort of selective communication that would be desirable in the acoustically separated world he describes in his thought experiment. See M Dan-Cohen, 'Decision Rules and Conduct Rules: On Acoustic Separation in Criminal Law' (1984) 97 *Harvard Law Review* 625, 636–37. Neither Dan-Cohen nor any other proponent of the view that rationale-based excuses are not meant to guide conduct argues for the concealment of the existence of the defence, or even of the cases in which it has been granted. The only point that they make is that rationale-based excuses are incapable of providing very useful conduct guidance because they rely on concepts that cannot be communicated effectively to people who have not been specially trained.

presents no problem in itself—it might still be possible to explain necessity as an excuse. But for most contemporary theorists, necessity (or at least some subset of necessity) is a rationale-based justificatory defence. Alexander, in fact, considers (one form of) necessity as the paradigm form of a justification.[18] He discusses the classic example of a person (D) averting the destruction of 1,000 houses in a forest fire by burning down a blameless person's (V's) house at the edge of the city, thereby creating a firebreak, and argues that D would be justified.[19] Under the quality of reasoning model as set out hitherto, D would not be justified because she would not be acting in terms of any permissive conduct rule underlying the criminal law. She might (as we will see presently) be excused, but, of course, one of the central arguments of this book is that the concepts of justification and excuse are not interchangeable. Yet, the weight of the general opinion seems to favour Alexander's conclusion, albeit that if the houses in the firebreak example are replaced with humans, then opinions as to the appropriateness of D's actions would seem to evince considerably less unanimity.[20]

To take the position that necessity in the firebreak case is not a justificatory defence would then be implausibly revisionist. Yet, a justificatory defence of necessity cannot be explained in the same way as the other justificatory defences I have mentioned. As such, it cannot automatically claim to possess the features that we associate with the justifications that I have identified as being paradigmatic. To construct a plausible account of justificatory necessity as a supervening defence, we therefore first need to identify the features that the resulting model of necessity should be able to accommodate in order to be conform to our intuitions.

From the way that necessity has been explained by various theorists, the intuitive consensus seems to be that necessity should occupy a space higher than a mere excuse. It should be as similar to a paradigmatic justification as possible. It should therefore have the same consequences as an exemption from norm-blame (which is what a justification recognises). Nevertheless, we would expect the defence of necessity to also apply to situations in which the rights of a non-threatening person are affected by the agent. We also know that the need for a necessity defence (at least in cases of the firebreak variety) is often explained by reference to its overall benefit to the system and society, rather than as a concession to the difficult situation in which the individual concerned finds herself.[21] In other words, the

---

[18] L Alexander, 'Lesser Evils: A Closer Look at the Paradigmatic Justification' (2005) 24 *Law and Philosophy* 611.

[19] ibid 630. Similar situations are also discussed by Greenawalt, 'The Perplexing Borders' 1908–09 and DN Husak, 'On the Supposed Priority of Justification to Excuse' (2005) 24 *Law and Philosophy* 557, 570, and all agree that D should be considered justified.

[20] As is evidenced by the continued response that the insightful study of such an example by JM Taurek ('Should the Numbers Count?' (1977) 6 *Philosophy & Public Affairs* 293) continues to draw. See, for instance, N Hsieh, A Strudler and D Wasserman, 'The Numbers Problem' (2006) 34 *Philosophy & Public Affairs* 352; R Lawler, 'Taurek, Numbers and Probabilities' (2006) 9 *Ethical Theory and Moral Practice* 149; and W Lübbe, 'Taurek's No Worse Claim' (2008) 36 *Philosophy & Public Affairs* 69.

[21] Alexander, 'Lesser Evils' 631–32. See also PH Robinson, 'A Theory of Justification: Societal Harm as a Prerequisite for Criminal Liability' (1975) 23 *UCLA Law Review* 266; Greenawalt, 'The Perplexing Borders' 1908–09; and Husak, 'Supposed Priority' 570.

broad consensus is that in these cases, the necessity defence ought only to be made available for norm-reasoning we wish to positively encourage (rather than merely tolerate). We therefore expect there to be normative conduct-guiding content in this sort of necessity and, as a corollary, we would expect a person whose actions are justified by this sort of necessity not to attract norm-blame.

This is the sort of necessity that I will attempt in Chapter 7 to accommodate in my model of rationale-based defences in the criminal law.

4.5 In Summary

To sum up, then, we expect justifications, both paradigmatic ones and necessity, to have normative content—ie, to contain conduct guidance by reference to which the general public can plan their lives so as to avoid attracting criminal law norm-blame. We do not expect rationale-based excuses to contain the same conduct guidance.

The source of exculpation and the normative content of paradigmatic justifications is fairly easy to identify (and, indeed, I did identify these in section 4.2). However, I still need to show that the resulting model of paradigmatic justification is plausible in its scope and the results it generates. Thereafter, I need to explain exculpation in rationale-based excuses and necessity in a manner that is consistent with the expectations described in sections 4.3 and 4.4 above, and to show that this model generates results that are plausible in terms of coverage and outcome. If I can achieve these tasks, then the distinction between justifications and rationale-based excuses tentatively proposed at the beginning of this chapter begins to show promise. I will attempt to undertake these tasks in Chapters 5, 6 and 7.

5

The Contours of Paradigmatic Justifications

I suggested in Chapter 4 that the paradigmatic form of a justification is one in which the defendant is immune to norm-blame because her norm-reasoning complies with the conduct rule system underlying the criminal law. Inasmuch as it allows for the exculpation only of persons exercising the immunities and authorities of the criminal law's underlying system of norms, this conception of the paradigm justification is fairly narrow.[1] It accommodates only self-defence, the defence of others, the defence of one's property and the defence of the property of others. I will explain how understanding these justifications in terms of the theoretical arguments made herein modifies the options available to the various classes of interested agents in Chapter 8. A more immediate concern is how this view of the paradigm justification maps onto the conduct and decision rules of a practically useful model of liberal criminal law. What does this view have to say about how a justification should be drafted and applied? How does it limit the scope of (paradigm forms of) justification? In this chapter, I address these and related questions.

5.1 The (Irrelevance of the) Framing of a Paradigmatic Justification

Tying our conception of a paradigmatic justification to the content of the system of normative guidance underlying the criminal law generates one important efficiency. I have previously argued that the mere circumstance of being in

---

[1] Not everyone accepts this as the paradigm form of a justification. See, for instance, L Alexander, 'Lesser Evils: A Closer Look at the Paradigmatic Justification' (2005) 24 *Law and Philosophy* 611, in which 'lesser evils' is taken to be the paradigmatic form of a justification. This leads Alexander into conclusions that we find intuitively unsettling. See also §3.02(1) of the Model Penal Code; M Thorburn, 'Criminal Law as Public Law' in RA Duff and S Green (eds), *Philosophical Foundations of Criminal Law* (Oxford, Oxford University Press, 2011) 36; PH Robinson, 'Criminal Law Defences: A Systematic Analysis' (1982) 82 *Columbia Law Review* 200, 214; E Colvin, 'Exculpatory Defences in Criminal Law' (1990) 10 *OJLS* 381, 387.

violation of a conduct norm does not automatically generate norm-blame, since norm-blame depends on the evaluation of the agent's attitude towards the normative guidance.[2] The same also applies to the generation of approval for conduct on the basis of a norm—entitlement, that is, to a justificatory defence. The mere circumstance of fortuitously having acted so as to find oneself in compliance with a justificatory conduct norm (assuming it to have been stated in objective terms) should not entitle the agent to a justificatory defence.[3] Instead, in order to be entitled to a justificatory defence, the agent should have been motivated by a permissive conduct norm drawn from the system of norms underlying the criminal law.

Although there is some academic writing that suggests disagreement with this proposition,[4] there is strong doctrinal support for it in the classic case on the point, *Dadson*.[5] In this case, a constable (D) saw V stealing wood from a copse and called for him to stop. Instead, V attempted to flee, whereupon D fired at and injured V. D was brought to trial on the charge of wounding with intent to do grievous bodily harm. As the law stood at the time, although the theft of this wood would ordinarily have been a misdemeanour, since V had previously been convicted of similar offences, his theft on this occasion was a felony. Furthermore, a constable was permitted to shoot in order to prevent the commission of a felony, but was not permitted to do so to prevent the commission of a misdemeanour. D was unaware of V's prior convictions and was therefore unaware that he was legally entitled to shoot at V. The question before the court was thus whether D was entitled to claim a justificatory defence on the basis that, even though he did not know it, he acted in a manner that was permissible as per the conduct guidance of the criminal law. The answer was a resounding 'No', and this answer has become fairly well entrenched in doctrinal orthodoxy ever since.[6]

On that view of how a justification should be applied, it is irrelevant whether the justification is framed in objective terms ('You can do X when Y') or subjective terms ('You can do what you believe to be X when you believe that Y') when stipulating its normative content. It must be understood by reference to the defendant's subjective perception of the facts. The same conclusion also follows from the fact that at the ex post stage of a criminal trial, justifications function purely as

---

[2] See section 2.2.2.

[3] See also L Alexander and KK Ferzan, 'Results Don't Matter' in PH Robinson, SP Garvey and KK Ferzan (eds), *Criminal Law Conversations* (Oxford, Oxford University Press, 2009) 150.

[4] PH Robinson, 'Competing Theories of Justification: Deeds versus Reasons' in AP Simester and ATH Smith (eds), *Harm and Culpability* (Oxford, Clarendon Press, 1996) 45; PH Robinson, 'A Theory of Justification: Societal Harm as a Prerequisite for Criminal Liability' (1975) 23 *UCLA Law Review* 266. See also G Williams, *Criminal Law: The General Part* (London, Stevens & Sons, 1961) 25.

[5] *The Queen v Dadson* (1850) 4 Cox CC 358.

[6] See, for instance, RL Christopher 'Unknowing Justification and the Logical Necessity of the Dadson Principle in Self-Defence' (1995) 15 *OJLS* 229; AP Simester, JR Spencer et al, *Simester and Sullivan's Criminal Law: Theory and Doctrine* (Oxford, Hart Publishing, 2016) 695; D Ormerod and K Laird, *Smith and Hogan's Criminal Law* (Oxford, Oxford University Press, 2015) 58–59, 448–49. The same position also obtains in German law. See in this connection A Reed, M Bohlander et al (eds) *Defences in Criminal Law: Domestic and Comparative Perspectives* (Farnham, Ashgate, 2014) 227–28.

decision rules. As decision rules dealing with the apportionment of norm-blame, their applicability to the facts must be assessed from within the parameters of the facts as perceived by the defendant, irrespective of whether they are framed by reference to objective facts or to subjective perceptions of facts.[7]

In its own way, the relative conceptual independence of justifications from the draftsperson's language is reassuring. There would be little point in trying to identifying a philosophy of justification if the manner in which any given justification was actually applied depended on the vagaries of the draftsperson. However, since the system of normative guidance that underlies the criminal law enjoys a degree of independence from the language employed by the draftsperson, justifications tied to that underlying system of normative guidance also enjoy that relative independence.

5.2 The Scope of the Paradigm Justification

By adopting a view of paradigmatic justifications that depends solely on establishing that the defendant's norm-reasoning complied with the conduct rule system underlying the criminal law, I have limited the applicability of paradigm justifications to assessments of norm-reasoning.[8] The possibility of 'justifying' poor functional reasoning is excluded because the system of norms underlying the core of criminal law does not guide functional reasoning.[9] Thus, where the criminal law censures for functional blame, the absence of norm-blame does not itself exonerate the defendant. Moreover, where the same action may attract liability for both offences predicated on norm-blame and offences predicated on functional blame, the defendant's perfect norm-reasoning will ground a justificatory defence to charges predicated on poor norm-reasoning, but will not protect her against charges predicated on poor functional-reasoning. That said, as argued in sections 2.2.2 and 2.2.3, ideally poor functional reasoning should not found criminal liability.

Excluding any assessment of the defendant's functional reasoning has further significance as well. On this view of a paradigm justification, the quality of the defendant's functional reasoning is completely extraneous to her entitlement to a justification. Hence, even a person who assaults another in the honest but unreasonable belief that certain facts exist that would make her act one of warranted self-defence would be justified on this view. I therefore argue in support of the principle established in the much-criticised case of *Beckford v R*.[10]

---

[7] See section 2.2.4.

[8] However, this does not imply that only justifications can protect against blame based on poor norm-reasoning. I will argue in Ch 6 that norm-blame can be excused as well as justified.

[9] See section 2.2.2.

[10] *Beckford v R* [1988] AC 130. See also the text accompanying n 25 in Ch 2 above.

In *Beckford*, the defendant, a policeman, was sent to a house to investigate a report of a dangerous gunman terrorising someone there and, on arrival, he saw the (eventual) victim running away with what appeared to be a gun. He chased the victim and shot him dead. At the time of the shooting, the victim was unarmed, on his knees with his hands in the air, begging not to be shot. The defendant claimed to have believed that his life was in danger and claimed to have acted in self-defence. The Privy Council reversed the defendant's conviction, holding that a genuine mistake as to whether the use of force in self-defence was required could ground a defence, irrespective of how unreasonable the mistake was. Although whether a mistake was genuinely made is a matter of fact to be determined based on the evidence, if it is found that the defendant did make, or might have made, a genuine mistake in perceiving the circumstantial facts, then the appropriate blame that she deserves is functional blame (which should ideally be non-criminal) and not the morally loaded blame signalled by a murder (or any criminal) conviction.[11]

The English law of self-defence has a further refinement. It applies different decision rules to the evaluation of a defendant's assessment of the need for defensive action and to her assessment of what defensive action was appropriate. In respect of the former, *Beckford* is authority for the proposition that the courts have only to examine whether the defendant genuinely believed that defensive action is necessary. However, in respect of the latter, the courts must examine whether her assessment of the defensive action to take was reasonable in the circumstances as she perceived them.[12] A person's choice of defensive action may be inappropriate either because she has erred as to the normative guidance governing the types of responses that are appropriate when faced with such a threat,[13] or because she has erred as to the situational facts, resulting in her response actually being more heavy-handed than she intended.[14] In the former case, under English law, the defendant cannot claim a defence,[15] whereas in the latter case, a defence is available so long as the mistake is reasonable.[16] According to the conception

---

[11] For a commentary critical of the judgment in *Beckford*, see AP Simester, 'Mistakes in Defence' (1992) 12 *OJLS* 295. Most of Simester's criticisms are doctrinal, and since I am not concerned with whether the decision is doctrinally sound, I need not comment on them here. However, Simester also argues that it is philosophically sound to require that a person who claims a supervening defence must take adequate care to ensure at least that any mistakes she makes in perceiving the circumstances necessitating defensive action are reasonable mistakes. I have already addressed and rejected that point of view in section 2.2.5.

[12] Criminal Justice and Immigration Act 2008, s 76.

[13] For instance, where an agent believes that it is alright to shoot at someone stealing apples from her yard because that is the only way to stop the thief, she commits an error as to normative standards. This example comes from a 1920 decision of the German Supreme Court as discussed by GP Fletcher, *Rethinking Criminal Law* (Boston, Little Brown & Company, 1978) 871.

[14] Consider, for instance, D, who, when warding off an assault, correctly believes that she is entitled to push the attacker T away, but fails to notice that the floor is wet. If the floor had been dry, the amount of force employed by D would have been proportionate. However, because the floor is wet and slippery, the same force turns out to be excessive, and D's push causes V to fall and suffer serious injury. This is a modification of the facts in *R v Scarlett* [1993] 4 All ER 629.

[15] See *R v Owino* [1996] 2 Cr App R 128.

[16] Criminal Justice and Immigration Act 2008, s 76(3) and (7).

of justification that I defend, the English law's conclusion in the former case is correct, since the defendant deserves norm-blame for her mistake as to the content of the norms.[17] However, English law deals with the latter case differently from the model of justification that I defend. On my model, where an agent responds excessively to a threat only because she honestly, though not reasonably, miscalculates the amount of force she is actually using, she makes an error ascribable to poor functional reasoning and not to poor norm-reasoning. Accordingly, while she may deserve functional blame, she does not deserve norm-blame, and so she should not suffer a criminal conviction. She should be granted a defence of justification because her error of functional reasoning, no matter how unreasonable it was, was not an error that calls for norm-blame.

Despite its overall adoption of the reasonableness standard, the English law does betray a lot of sympathy for this position. Section 76(7) of the Criminal Justice and Immigration Act 2008 says that in assessing the proportionality of defensive action taken, it must be borne in mind that 'a person acting for a legitimate purpose may not be able to weigh to a nicety the exact measure of any necessary action' and, further, that 'the evidence of a person's having only done what the person honestly and instinctively thought was necessary for a legitimate purpose constitutes strong evidence that only reasonable action was taken by that person for that purpose'. Moreover, in the case of *Scarlett*,[18] decided prior to the passing of the 2008 Act, the Court of Appeal held that a pub landlord who evicted a rowdy customer using force that was objectively found to have been excessive would only have committed assault (and consequently rendered himself liable to a possible conviction for manslaughter for the customer's resulting death) if he had intended his response to be excessive or had been reckless as to whether it was excessive.[19] This case has sometimes been taken to hold that a defendant who acts under an unreasonable mistake as to the normative standards governing the proportionality of permissible responses is nevertheless entitled to a justification defence.[20] The judgment itself is equivocally worded, and so there is certainly enough to justify such a reading. However, it need not necessarily be read in that manner.[21] The judgment records that the defendant 'had given clear evidence that he had only intended to use sufficient force to remove the deceased from

---

[17] I assume the existence of a meta-rule in the criminal legal system deeming all subjects to be aware of all conduct norms. See the text accompanying n 27 in Ch 2 above.

[18] *Scarlett* (n 14). See also the text accompanying n 24 in Ch 2 above.

[19] Incidentally, this is also the position under German law. See Reed, Bohlander et al, *Defences in Criminal Law* 231.

[20] Simester, Spencer et al, *Simester and Sullivan's Criminal Law* 704–05.

[21] In fact, in *Owino*, the Court of Appeal made it clear that in its view, such a reading of *Scarlett* would be mistaken. It explained that the court in *Scarlett* 'was not saying, in our view (and indeed if [it] had said it, it would be contrary to authority) … that the belief, however ill-founded, of the defendant that the degree of force he was using was reasonable, will enable him to do what he did … if that argument was correct, then it would justify, for example, the shooting of someone who was merely threatening to throw a punch, on the basis that the defendant honestly believed, although unreasonably and mistakenly, that it was justifiable for him to use that degree of force. That clearly is not, and cannot be, the law'. *Owino* (n 15) 134.

the bar, an act he was lawfully entitled to do'.[22] Hence, the defendant was clearly not claiming to have been under any misapprehension as to the extent of his normative entitlement to use force, and no submissions to this effect were made by the prosecution. Since the jury nevertheless found that the amount of force actually used was objectively excessive, it must have concluded that the defendant had applied excessive force by mistake or unfortunate happenstance. If so, then the judgment in *Scarlett* can be reconciled with the ruling in *Owino* by reading (down) *Scarlett* to operate only in relation to mistakes of functional reasoning resulting in the use of defensive force that, objectively considered, was excessive. In such cases, the flaw (if any) is in the defendant's functional reasoning and not her norm-reasoning, and therefore the defendant attracts functional blame rather than criminal norm-blame. The defendant's entitlement to raise a justification defence to any conviction that implies norm-blame remains unaffected. Such a reading of the principles stated in *Scarlett* and *Owino* would support the model of justification that I defend.

However, the ruling in *R v Martin (Anthony)*[23] is not so easily reconciled with the model of justification that I propose. In that case, the defendant shot at burglars who had broken into his house at night, killing one and seriously injuring another. The court ruled that expert evidence to the effect that the defendant suffered from paranoid personality disorder which might have heightened his perception of the risk he faced from burglars was irrelevant to the determination of the appropriateness of his response to the threat. Instead, it reduced the defendant's murder conviction to a conviction for voluntary manslaughter owing to diminished responsibility. Whilst this ruling may have been doctrinally sound, its moral appropriateness is questionable. If the defendant genuinely suffered from a condition that heightened his perception of a risk to himself, then surely that is evidence to support the his claim that he genuinely thought the risk to himself was so great as to merit the use of lethal force in response. This is not an error of norm-reasoning—the defendant was not claiming (or, at least, did not have to claim) that in all cases of burglary, the use of lethal defensive force is normatively appropriate. The defendant made an error as to how much threat *these* burglars posed to him. Undoubtedly, if the burglars had posed a sufficient threat, the defendant would have been normatively entitled to use lethal force to defend himself. Therefore, the evidence excluded was relevant to establish that the defendant's error was not one of norm-reasoning, but was instead one of functional reasoning. The partial defence of diminished responsibility is premised on a preliminary finding that the defendant is guilty of murder, and that finding is then discounted in view of the defendant's mental condition. The preliminary finding is therefore that the defendant displayed poor norm-reasoning. That finding has no basis—although the defendant's paranoid personality disorder affected the quality of his functional

---

[22] *Scarlett* (n 14) 636–37.
[23] *R v Martin (Anthony)* [2003] QB 1.

reasoning, there was no evidence to establish that his norm-reasoning was poor. The defendant deserved a finding that reflected this fact. In a legal system that adopted the model of justification that I defend, evidence of such a defendant's paranoid personality disorder would be relevant to support a successful plea of justification, though it would not necessarily preclude a finding of liability for poor functional reasoning[24] or an order requiring the defendant to undergo treatment. At worst, on these facts, the defendant ought to have been convicted of a suitably framed involuntary manslaughter offence.[25] This seems to me a fairer way of labelling the defendant in terms of what it was that he did wrong.

To conclude, then, a person's entitlement to a paradigmatic justification depends entirely on the quality of her norm-reasoning. This must be assessed within the parameters of the facts as honestly perceived by the defendant. Insofar as the defendant is found to be justified in acting as she did, her norm-reasoning conforms to the normative guidance contained within (and underlying) the criminal law. Since a justified agent acts entirely without any fault in her norm-reasoning, no fault-based consequences, whether criminal or civil, can flow from her norm-reasoning. Of course, even a person who is justified in terms of her norm-reasoning may have exhibited deficient functional reasoning. In such cases, she may incur fault-predicated liability on the basis of her poor functional reasoning.[26] As I have previously stated, I think that, ideally, this liability should be confined to civil liability.[27]

5.3 Partial Justifications?

One suggestion that is sometimes made is that there are some defences that are partially justifications—provocation being the most commonly cited candidate

---

[24] The English House of Lords decision in *Ashley v Chief Constable of Sussex Police* [2008] UKHL 25 demonstrates that the courts accept that non-criminal liability arising out of poor functional reasoning may survive a successful plea of self-defence. In that case, the court affirmed the imposition of tortious liability for the poor functional reasoning displayed by a police officer who unreasonably concluded that a situation requiring lethal defensive force had arisen, even though the officer had successfully pleaded self-defence in criminal proceedings.

[25] For instance, gross negligence manslaughter, in which (as per current English doctrine) the manslaughter conviction is premised entirely upon the defendant's poor functional reasoning. Even in respect of this charge, a defendant should be entitled to produce evidence of her paranoid personality disorder to moderate the standard of functional reasoning by reference to which she should be judged. Indeed, it is possible that by doing so, she would escape criminal liability altogether. But if the defendant's actions are indeed attributable entirely to a mental condition, then that should not seem like a perverse result. The facts in *Martin (Anthony)*, unfortunate as they are, arguably call for treatment and not punishment.

[26] See, for instance, *Ashley v Chief Constable of Sussex Police* [2008] UKHL 25.

[27] See section 2.2.5.

for this category of defences.[28] Although this position has not gained significant academic support, it is useful to consider the compatibility of the concept with the view of paradigmatic justification that I have adopted. I can do so quite briefly.

I previously made the point that a justificatory conduct norm does not detract from the range of behaviour in which an autonomous being may engage, but instead recognises an exception to a general conduct norm that has already proscribed certain conduct.[29] One implication of this proposition is that conduct that does not quite meet the standards necessary to qualify unreservedly for the protection of the justificatory norm continues to be proscribed under the primary moral conduct norm enshrined in the offence definition. Hence, on this account of the defence, a paradigmatic justification is an all-or-nothing concept. Conduct is either justified or not justified—it cannot be partly justified.[30] Consequentially, a provoked, disproportionate or premature reaction to a threat is not (paradigmatically) justified, even partially. Gratifyingly, this result is in line with the orthodoxy on this issue[31] and therefore suggests that the argument on the nature of justifications made herein conforms to doctrinal expectations.

5.4 Collateral and Accidental Harm

Consider the following two related examples:

> Case 1: accidental harm—D is justifiably defending herself against an attack by T. She aims a blow at T, who ducks at the last moment, as a result of which, D hits bystander V. Or, perhaps, D hits T, but in doing so, she also accidentally hits V's priceless vase, breaking it. On the model of paradigmatic justification defended herein, is D justified in respect of the harm caused to the person or property of V?
>
> Case 2: collateral harm—D, in order to justifiably defend herself against an attack by T in a pub, picks up the nearest hard object—one of the pub landlord V's beer mugs—and smashes it on T's shoulder.[32] Again, on the model of paradigmatic justification defended herein, is D justified in respect of the harm caused to V's property?

---

[28] MN Berman and IP Farrell, 'Provocation Manslaughter as Partial Justification and Partial Excuse' (2011) 52 *William and Mary Law Review* 1027; AJ Ashworth, 'The Doctrine of Provocation' (1976) 35 *Cambridge Law Review* 292, 307.

[29] See sections 2.1 and 5.1.

[30] The rulings in *Palmer v The Queen* [1971] AC 814 and *R v Clegg* [1995] 1 AC 482 support this proposition. See also in this connection S Eldar and E Laist, 'The Misguided Concept of Partial Justification' (2014) 20 *Legal Theory* 157.

[31] ibid. This is also the position in French law. See Reed, Bohlander et al, *Defences in Criminal Law* 215.

[32] This example is adapted from an example frequently used in textbooks on German criminal law and described in Reed, Bohlander et al, *Defences in Criminal Law* 230–31.

The first thing to be said in respect of these cases is that despite superficial similarities, they are, at least potentially, quite different. In the accidental harm case, the initial temptation is to argue that D is not criminally liable in respect of the harm done to either V's person or her property, because she does not meet the requirements for committing a prima facie offence against V. Specifically, she lacks the mens rea to harm V or her property. However, one may be hesitant to accept this intuition, because many jurisdictions have doctrines of transferred malice or transferred intention, as per which the defendant's intention to do a particular type of harm to one person transfers to the person accidentally harmed instead.[33] That said, I think that abandoning this initial intuition would be premature at this stage. Even apart from the fact that the doctrine of transferred malice is a limited doctrine,[34] its relevance in the domain of legal philosophy is questionable. It is widely accepted that the doctrine of transferred malice is a deeming doctrine. In other words, it is not the logical corollary of principled arguments about the nature of the criminal law; rather, it is a legal fiction.[35] If that is true, then there is no reason to believe that it evidences some underlying philosophical truth about the presence of all the elements of a prima facie offence against V. Hence, the existence of this doctrine need have no necessary effect on the structure of the philosophical analysis of the accidental harm case. Perhaps the knee-jerk response to this scenario is correct after all—it certainly generates an intuitively plausible liability outcome.

However, there is at least one explanation of the doctrine of transferred intention that eschews the notion that it is a legal fiction. Sometimes called the 'impersonality' doctrine, this is the argument that, properly understood, the mens rea for (many) offences is unconnected to the intended identity of the victim. Hence, when a person has been killed due to D's actions, in the manner that D intended

---

[33] See, for instance, in respect of England and Wales, AJ Ashworth and J Horder, *Principles of Criminal Law* (Oxford, Oxford University Press, 2013) 189–91; Ormerod and Laird, *Smith and Hogan's Criminal Law* 150–53; Simester, Spencer et al, *Simester and Sullivan's Criminal Law* 173–75.

[34] For instance, malice does not seem to transfer when the actus reus of the crime apparently committed is categorically different from the actus reus of the crime intended. See *The Queen v Pembliton* (1872–75) LR 2 CCR 119. In addition, there is some authority to suggest that this doctrine does not permit a 'double transfer' of intention. Hence, when D's stabbed a pregnant V1 in the abdomen and caused her to go into labour prematurely, he was of course liable for the injuries caused to V1. However, he was not guilty of murdering the baby, V2, who died some four months after being born, due to complications arising from her grossly premature birth. This is because reaching that result would require D's intention to cause serious injury to be transferred twice—first from V1 to her unborn foetus and then again from the foetus to the living V2. See *Attorney General's Reference (No 3 of 1994)* [1996] 2 WLR 412. See also Ashworth and Horder, *Principles of Criminal Law* 190–91; Simester, Spencer et al, *Simester and Sullivan's Criminal Law* 174–75; Ormerod and Laird, *Smith and Hogan's Criminal Law* 150–53.

[35] DN Husak, 'Transferred Intent' (1996) 10 *Notre Dame Journal of Law Ethics & Public Policy* 65, 83–86. See also WL Prosser, 'Transferred Intent' (1967) 47 *Texas Law Review* 650; AM Dilloff, 'Transferred Intent: An Inquiry into the Nature of Criminal Culpability' (1997) 1 *Buffalo Criminal Law Review* 501, 504, 506; M Bohlander, 'Transferred Malice and Transferred Defenses' (2010) 13 *New Criminal Law Review* 555, 581; Reed, Bohlander et al, *Defences in Criminal Law* 51.

that she be killed, that is enough to establish that D has prima facie committed murder. That D intended for the victim to be someone else goes to motive and not intention, and is irrelevant in establishing the prima facie offence.[36] The same argument applies mutatis mutandis in respect of offences other than murder.[37] If one accepts this view, then one must concede that even in the accidental harm case, a prima facie offence has been committed against V, and so D does need to offer a rationale-based defence in order to avoid criminal liability.

Even on this view, though, the arguments made in section 2.2.2 about the nature of criminal blameworthiness suggest that in the accidental harm case, D is not criminally blameworthy in respect of the harm caused to V or V's property. If, as was argued there, criminal blame depends on a failure to be guided by the norm-guidance offered by the criminal law, then a person who exhibits fealty to the norm-guidance offered by the criminal law is criminally blameless. Given that D was justified in aiming a blow at T, her aiming of the blow at T must have been in accordance with the criminal law's normative conduct guidance. The fact that the (normatively permitted) blow accidentally harmed V or V's property instead does not support any finding of inadequate commitment to being guided by the criminal law's conduct norms. The important thing to note here is that while the consequences of D's conduct may provide the law with a basis for making a blaming judgment (ie, something for which to blame), D's blame*worthiness* depends on whether the conduct in which she chooses to engage conforms to the normative guidance available to her; it does not depend on the consequences of that conduct. Since D's chosen conduct was permissible, she was not norm-blameworthy. In other words, she is justified.[38] As such, at least insofar as criminal liability is

---

[36] See in this connection J Horder, 'Transferred Malice and the Remoteness of Unexpected Outcomes from Intentions' [1996] *Crim LR* 383; Bohlander, 'Transferred Malice' 556.

[37] Although for the present purposes I do not need to express any settled view in favour of either of these approaches to parsing the doctrine of transferred intent, I confess that my preference is for the explanation offered by the impersonality doctrine. While this may not always reflect the doctrinal law in a given jurisdiction, it does seem to me to be a more philosophically appealing explanation for why we think that D ought to, in certain types of cases, to be held criminally liable when she accidentally harms someone other than her intended victim.

[38] *Pace* Bohlander, 'Transferred Malice', 557–58, who argues that since rationale-based defences are 'relational', they only apply in respect of harm caused to particular persons. Thus, he says, D may exercise self-defence only against her attacker and no one else—the notion of a generic self-defence being 'patently absurd'. Hence, Bohlander does not think that a rationale-based defence can be 'transferred' in the manner that I suggest. I think that Bohlander's conclusion is premised on a failure to distinguish between the different roles played by a justificatory rule at the different stages of the criminal law. True, the ex ante conduct guidance provided by a justificatory criminal law rule such as the rule on self-defence is relational. In fact, it is also a key requirement of the view of paradigmatic justification that I propose that the prima facie criminal act be directed towards the source of the threat to agent's interests. However, this does not mean that at the subsequent stage of evaluating the agent's criminal blameworthiness, the fact that someone else's interests were harmed excludes the availability of the justification. If D intended to harm only T (ie, the person authoring the threat)'s interests, then she selected her behaviour in accordance with the normative guidance in the justificatory rule and is therefore not blameworthy. In other words, D can be justified even if the outcomes intended to be encouraged by the justificatory conduct norm do not occur.

reserved for the norm-blameworthy, she cannot be held criminally liable for the inadvertent harm caused to V.[39] To the extent that the criminal law also blames for poor functional reasoning, it might be possible to hold D liable for the harm caused to V if that harm can be traced to some deficiency in D's functional reasoning.

Whereas on the first analysis of the accidental harm case, D is not criminally liable because she does not satisfy the elements of any prima facie offence, on this second analysis, D is not (ordinarily) criminally liable because she is justified. My own tentative preference is for the second analysis, but irrespective of which analysis is preferred, one reaches the same intuitively plausible liability outcome, viz that D is not criminally liable for the harm caused to V or her interests in the accidental harm case.

Let us now consider the collateral harm case. In this case, D does intend to use V's beer mug and will be aware of the substantial risk of harm to the mug in using it as a defensive weapon. Without getting into the intricacies of whether D can be said to have obliquely intended harm to the mug or whether she was merely reckless as to the possibility of such harm, let us assume that given her deliberate use of the beer mug, she satisfies the mens rea of some offence relating to the damage to the mug. The question is whether she can now claim a justification in respect of this offence. This must be answered separately in relation to cases in which T's threat is to V's constituent rights, and in relation to cases in which T's threat is to D's posited rights.

Where the threat is to D's constituent rights, and D is invoking her existential justification to respond to it, then on the terms of the existential justification, as described in section 3.2.1, she is immune from norm-blame in respect of the damage done to V's property. V's property rights, being posited, are logically subsequent to D's existential justification and cannot qualify it. As such, D's justification also extends to the damage done to V's beer mug.

On the other hand, where the threat is to D's posited rights, then even if she is justified in respect of her response vis-a-vis T, she cannot claim a paradigmatic justification in respect of the damage she causes to V's beer mug, since no part of the threat to which she was responding emanated from V or V's property. It might be possible for D to lay claim to a non-paradigmatic justificatory defence of necessity. Alternatively, D may be exculpated under a rationale-based excusatory defence such as duress of circumstances. The evaluation of these possibilities will have to wait until after Chapters 6 and 7, in which I will describe the outlines of rationale-based excuses and justificatory necessity. For the time being, though, it

---

[39] Incidentally, the same conclusion is reached in doctrine as well by way of another deeming fiction—the fiction that: 'When the fault is transferred, any defence which D might have had is transferred with it.' See Ashworth and Horder, *Principles of Criminal Law* 190. See also Bohlander, 'Transferred Malice' 557; Simester, Spencer et al, *Simester and Sullivan's Criminal Law* 174; Ormerod and Laird, *Smith and Hogan's Criminal Law* 593.

suffices to note the existence of these possibilities.[40] It is also conceivable[41] that D may not be exculpated either by the defence of necessity or by any rationale-based excuse. In those circumstances, D would continue to be criminally liable in respect of the damage done to V's property.

5.5 The Unjustifiable

The line I have adopted on the definition and nature of a justification leads me to one necessary boundary implication. In section 3.1, it was noted that actions involving the instrumental use of a person that also cause harm to the used person's constituent elements remain subject to moral and criminal guidance, and are not existentially immune to moral and criminal blame. Such actions would not be justified even if done in defence of one's own constituent rights. Furthermore, since such actions harm another person's constituent elements, they cannot be justified under a posited immunity either. In other words, the instrumental use of a person is always unjustifiable when it affects the constituent elements of the person used. To my mind, by definition, crimes such as (at least some instances of) torture,[42] genocide, slavery and at least some forms of serious sexual offences require the intention to treat humans as non-human—either as faceless members of a collective or as instruments in a larger purpose. They also involve harm to the victim's constituent elements. As such, the commission of these crimes can never be justified in a moral criminal law.[43]

This position directly contradicts the usual line of arguments to the effect that torture (including those forms in which the victim's constituent elements are harmed for instrumental purposes) may, in some special circumstances, be justified or legally permitted.[44] These arguments tend to assume that in principle,

---

[40] This is also essentially the position in both German and Swedish law. See Reed, Bohlander et al, *Defences in Criminal Law* 230–31 (in relation to German law) and 306 (in relation to Swedish law).

[41] Albeit unlikely on the present facts. Perhaps it would be easier to imagine such a case if V's property were something significantly more valuable than a beer mug and the harm that D was seeking to avoid was minimal.

[42] The definition of torture is widely debated, and both principles and political considerations affect the exact terms used in any definition. I do not want to enter into that debate here. However, on any plausible comprehensive account of torture, at least some forms of torture would involve both harming the victim's constituent elements and treating her as a mere instrument. For the present purposes, I restrict my arguments on torture to these instances, without suggesting as a corollary that any other forms of torture that exist are permissible.

[43] Note, however, that this does not rule out the possibility that a rationale-based excuse might be available.

[44] A Dershowitz, *Why Terrorism Works: Understanding the Threat, Responding to the Challenge* (New Haven, Yale University Press, 2002) 149–63; RA Posner, 'Torture, Terrorism, and Interrogation' in *Torture: A Collection* (Oxford, Oxford University Press, 2004) 293–94; W Brugger, 'May Government Ever Use Torture? Two Responses from German Law' (2000) 48 *American Journal of Comparative Law* 661, 676–78; A Raviv, 'Torture and Justification: Defending the Indefensible' (2004) 13 *George Mason Law Review* 135, 156–78.

the state has the power to authorise even such forms of torture,[45] and then focus on *when* the state may exercise this power, an issue which is addressed by reference to consequentialist reasoning.[46] My response to these lines of argument is to reject the notion that any moral state has the in-principle authority to perform (at least) the specified forms of torture, or even to interfere at all with a person's constituent elements for reasons external to an existential immunity. The constituent elements are logically prior to the authority of any moral state, and consequentialist considerations are simply incapable of overriding the logically superior proscription against forms of torture or dehumanising behaviour that affect human constituent elements. And if that result arguably deprives the state of one of its potential responses to extant or anticipated threats, so be it.

---

[45] Usually, this assumption is not made explicit. However, it underlies the political philosophy of persons who argue that the state has the authority to legitimately affect any person's constituent rights for reasons external to those that fall under the existential immunity. This underlying assumption also permeates other areas of moral-legal discourse. See, for instance, MH Kramer, *The Ethics of Capital Punishment: A Philosophical Investigation of Evil and its Consequences* (Oxford, Oxford University Press, 2011), who assumes the state's in-principle authority to take life for non-existential immunity reasons in making his argument as to the permissibility of the death penalty. In a powerful essay ('The Justification of Punishment and the Justification of Political Authority' (1986) 5 *Law and Philosophy* 393), M Philips makes the same point as is made in the main text about the assumption that the state has the authority to punish at all. See also, in the same context, C Brettschneider, 'The Rights of the Guilty: Punishment and Political Legitimacy' (2007) 35 *Political Theory* 175, 182–86.

[46] Pro-torture arguments generally tend to be consequentialist at core, as O Gross, 'Are Torture Warrants Warranted? Pragmatic Absolutism and Official Disobedience' (2004) 88 *Minnesota Law Review* 1481, 1497 observes. See, for instance, Dershowitz, *Why Terrorism Works* 144; Posner, 'Torture, Terrorism, and Interrogation' 293–94; Raviv, 'Torture and Justification' 156–78 and GE Jones, 'On the Permissibility of Torture' (1980) 6 *Journal of Medical Ethics* 1111–13.

6

Rationale-Based Excuses

We can now turn our attention to rationale-based excuses. Instead of treating rationale-based excuses as a catch-all category for defences that do not fit into the principled categories of rationale-based defences that I describe, in this chapter I will attempt to set out an independent explanatory framework for rationale-based excuses. In doing so, I will argue that rationale-based excuses are much more flexible than paradigmatic justifications in terms of the conduct to which they apply and the extent to which they protect from liability, and hence their stipulations may be very different in different jurisdictions. Nevertheless, I will argue that rationale-based excuses are united by the underlying principled basis for the protection from liability that they offer.

6.1 Why Rationale-Based Excuses Excuse

John Gardner's proposal as to the gist of excuses, being based on a 'reasons' view of the criminal law, is a useful starting point for developing a theory of excuses that fits into a system of defences founded on the quality of reasoning hypothesis. Gardner argues that the gist of excuses is neither the Humean view that one's actions did not evidence one's character nor 'that one had no capacity to conform, in one's actions, to the standards of character which were demanded of one. On the contrary ... the gist of an excuse is that one lived up to those standards'.[1] The agent shows that she manifested 'as much resilience, or loyalty, or thoroughness, or presence of mind as a person in her situation should have manifested'. He further explains that '[t]he character standards which are relevant ... are not standards of our own characters, nor even the standards of most people's characters, but rather the standards to which our characters should, minimally, conform' and clarifies that these standards can, in appropriate cases, be adjusted to account for the special role played by the agent in the context of her actions.[2] I read

---

[1] J Gardner, 'The Gist of Excuses' (1998) 1 *Buffalo Criminal Law Review* 575, 598. See also RA Duff, 'Choice, Character, and Criminal Liability' (1993) 12 *Law and Philosophy* 345, 358–59.
[2] Gardner, 'The Gist of Excuses' 584–87, 592–94. See also AP Simester, 'On Justifications and Excuses' in L Zedner and JV Roberts (eds), *Principles and Values in Criminal Law and Criminal Justice* (Oxford, Oxford University Press, 2012) 100.

Gardner as suggesting that there are normative standards of character that we (as a society) expect of moral agents fulfilling a particular role, and that in order to be excused, the agent must meet these standards. According to him, then, a person may be excused for committing an act that there were undefeated reasons to avoid when her reasons for doing so demonstrated that she was either not morally deficient (as in the case of the so-called 'putatively justified' agent) or not deficient in terms of character traits (as adjusted, if appropriate, for the role performed by the agent).

In addition to resilience, loyalty, thoroughness and presence of mind, Gardner also considers things like fortitude and self-restraint as traits that define the standards of character expected of us. It should be noted that, generally, criminal law conduct rules do not focus on providing guidance relatable to these features, although they may do so peripherally. The criminal law does not tell us how courageous or how loyal we should be. It does, in some situations, tell us how much self-restraint we must show or how thorough we must be. Yet, as a system of normative guidance, the criminal law focuses on telling us what conduct shows us to be morally deficient rather than what conduct shows us to have deficient character traits.

The model of justification proposed in this book treats any person who demonstrates that her norm-reasoning complied with the criminal law's morally derived norms as being justified. Gardner, on the other hand, would treat some such persons—for instance, putatively justified actors—as being merely excused or, where the putatively justified actors also exhibited poor functional reasoning, not even excused. But even though some elements of his theory of excuses are incompatible with the norm-reasoning view of justifications, Gardner's approach to excuses has considerable intuitive appeal and does suggest a compatible model of rationale-based excuses.

We need excuses in the domain of norm-reasoning because situations inevitably arise in which although the criminal law's guiding norms direct the agent to do something, society cannot demand it of the agent. This is because we accept that sometimes the criminal law's guidance is too demanding and that in those circumstances, it is unreasonable for us to require that the agent obey it or be criminally condemned. We might applaud one who nevertheless acts in terms of the criminal law's morally derived norms, but we cannot blame one who does not, since we hesitate to say that a person in her position ought to have displayed moral fortitude amounting to heroism.[3] On considering the norm-reasoning of such a defendant, we conclude that it did not conform to the conduct rule system underlying the criminal law, but nevertheless feel that it conformed to the standards that we as a society normatively expect from ourselves when performing the same role as the agent in the same circumstances.

This suggests that there exists a second normative system in addition to the morally derived criminal law conduct rule system, which also plays a role in

---

[3] I use this characterisation of what is expected from the gold-standard person in society in the same sense as Gardner does in 'The Gist of Excuses'.

guiding the behaviour of individuals. This second normative system provides us with guidance as to how society (and not just the conduct rules of the criminal law) expects and wants us to behave—it tracks societally appropriate reasoning rather than reasoning that is appropriate according to the criminal law's conduct rules, and it is influenced by all the normative guidance deemed relevant within a particular society. Societal conduct norms may come into being through the organic process of societal interaction, unlike the criminal law's conduct norms, which must formally and authoritatively be inducted into (or recognised as part of) the criminal legal system. Criminal law conduct norms guide their subjects as to what behaviour is legally required or permissible, whereas societal norms guide their subjects as to what behaviour is societally required or permissible. Conformity with the societal normative system may not ensure compliance with the conduct rules of the criminal law, but it will influence ex post criminal law decisions on the imposition of liability. To be clear, in any civilised society, criminal law norms play a strong guiding role as to what is societally expected from a person. However, in a system that identifies societally appropriate conduct, criminal law norms are not decisive and must be weighed against additional factors such as prudential and consequentialist concerns, socially acceptable concessions to the human tendency for self-preference, etc.

Clearly, a societal normative system may generate normative guidance that differs from that given by the criminal law conduct rule system. Consider, for instance, a person threatened with the death of all the people in her village if she does not kill one innocent bystander. The morally derived norms underlying the criminal legal system may still proscribe killing the bystander, but a system of norms that tracks societally appropriate reasoning might provide contrary guidance. In this situation, if the person did kill the bystander, she would not be justified under the criminal law. However, saying that killing the bystander was unjustified does not preclude us from admitting nevertheless that it was conduct normatively underwritten by society.

Where such a case arises, there is a strong normative argument for excusing a person who heeds the contrary guidance of the system of societal norms, because if we, as a society of moral agents, would in the same circumstances normatively expect ourselves to do the same thing as the agent, then she has shown herself to be no more evil than is the societal benchmark. The logical space for an excuse is therefore best described by Cohen's astute observation that 'being in a position to utter a well-grounded [moral] truth does not suffice for being in a good position to condemn'.[4] It would be hypocritical for persons belonging to such a society to condemn the agent as evil, and to do so would convey the false impression that the agent deserves to be singled out to bear such a morally loaded label. As Cohen puts it:

> We can distinguish three ways in which a person may seek to silence, or to blunt the edge of, a critic's condemnation. First, she may seek to show that she did not, in fact, perform

---

[4] GA Cohen, 'Casting the First Stone: Who Can, and Who Can't, Condemn the Terrorists?' (2003) 58 *Royal Institute of Philosophy Supplement* 113, 121.

the action under criticism. Second, and without denying that she performed that action, she may claim that the action does not warrant moral condemnation, because there was an adequate justification for it, or at least a legitimate excuse for performing it. Third, while not denying that the action was performed, and that it is to be condemned (which is not to say: while agreeing that it is to be condemned), she can seek to discredit her critic's assertion of her standing as a good faith condemner of the relevant action.[5]

Cohen would treat an excuse as a factor that operates prior to an examination of the critic's standing to condemn, and this position is very defensible within his framework, especially since he does not confine himself to rationale-based excuses. However, in the context of this study, I believe that rationale-based excuses can be seen as operating by discrediting the implicit assertion by the critic (in this context, the legal system as the conduit through which society expresses moral condemnation) of its own standing as a good faith condemner.

Cohen further says:

I should make clear what I am not claiming, when I say that a critic may be disabled from condemning, and, therefore, in the relevant sense, may be unable to condemn, the agent under judgment. I do not mean that the critic cannot be speaking the truth when she condemns the agent: it is central to the interest of the phenomenon under exploration here that she might well be speaking the truth. Nor do I mean that the critic should be forbidden, under whatever sanction, to make the relevant utterance. Whether there ought to be a legal prohibition, even whether there is a moral prohibition, on the utterance, is a somewhat separate matter. What I mean is that there are facts about the critic that compromise her utterance considered as, what it purports to be, a condemnation: the focus is on that intended role, or illocutionary force, of the utterance.[6]

Like Cohen, I make no imperative claim that there *should* be an excuse defence made available in every case in which the condemner society lacks the standing to condemn the defendant without indulging in hypocrisy. It is up to the wisdom of the legislative and judicial authorities in each jurisdiction to appropriately define the sets of cases in which they grant an excuse, and the mere fact that a jurisdiction has committed itself to a morally distinctive criminal legal system would not commit it to recognising any rationale-based excuses whatsoever. That said, a system of rationale-based excuses that is sensitive to the society's standing to criticise the defendant is logically coherent and intuitively plausible. Such a system would also be immune to the challenge that it is hypocritical for being based on society's pretence to virtue that it does not possess.[7]

---

[5] ibid 119.

[6] ibid 119–20.

[7] For a discussion of this kind of hypocrisy, see R Crisp and C Cowton, 'Hypocrisy and Moral Seriousness' (1994) 31 *American Philosophical Quarterly* 343, 343–44. See also RJ Wallace, 'Hypocrisy, Moral Address, and the Equal Standing of Persons' (2010) 38 *Philosophy & Public Affairs* 307, who discusses the incoherence of hypocritical blame. Wallace goes further and argues that the right against being blamed hypocritically is a moral right. His argument stems from a fuller understanding of morality than the limited one I use here—he argues that each agent has a moral interest in protection from social opprobrium.

This approach to theorising a rationale-based excuse is novel. Most existing theories of excuse either operate within the parameters of the wrongness hypothesis and suggest that excuses negate criminal blameworthiness[8] or attempt to explain irresponsibility excuses and rationale-based excuses jointly as cases involving the negation of (actual or effective) responsibility.[9] On the view of a paradigm rationale-based excuse proposed here, the defendant's desert of blame in terms of the criminal law's underlying morally derived system of norms is unaffected by granting her a rationale-based excuse. She continues to be morally at fault, and so fault-based civil consequences may still follow from the defendant's conduct, depending on the content of the applicable civil law. The rationale-based excuse that I propose protects the defendant from criminal liability by first denying the agent's blameworthiness in terms of societal norms and then suggesting that it would be hypocritical for a society with those norms to single out the defendant for criminal liability, even if the agent has no grounds to argue that the criminal conviction was undeserved in terms of the criminal law's norms. In other words, it denies the agent's societal blameworthiness and the criminal law's assertion of standing as a good faith condemner of the agent's actions.

That said, many existing theories of excuse can be co-opted into this framework for approaching rationale based-excuses, in that they may explain the reasons for which an agent's societal blameworthiness is denied. Hence, it would be perfectly plausible to explain why an agent's societal blameworthiness was negated in terms of her will being overpowered by threats made by others or the circumstances in which she found herself. This means that despite being novel, the approach to rationale-based excuses defended here is compatible with most familiar accounts of rationale-based excuses and generates recognisable results. For instance, like more traditional accounts of rationale-based excuse, this approach can also explain why standard rationale-based excuses like duress or excessive self-defence might excuse a defendant from criminal liability. I will not express a preference for any particular detailed account of rationale-based excuses here—no such preference flows inevitably from the arguments that I have made hitherto. However, with some minor tweaks, most mainstream accounts of rationale-based excuse can comfortably slot into this analysis. Some of the outcomes generated would be different of course. For instance, because of the altered demarcation of the border between justifications and excuses defended in Chapter 5, putative self-defence, which is often classified as an excuse in mainstream accounts of rationale-based excuses, would be a justification instead. Nevertheless, on the whole, the explanation of exculpation in rationale-based defences proposed here provides a clear

---

[8] See, for instance, MN Berman, 'Justification and Excuse, Law and Morality' (2003) 53 *Duke Law Journal* 1, 4; MS Moore, *Placing Blame: A Theory of the Criminal Law* (Oxford, Oxford University Press, 2010) 674; J Horder, *Excusing Crime* (Oxford, Oxford University Press, 2004) 8–9.

[9] See, for instance, DN Husak, 'On the Supposed Priority of Justification to Excuse' (2005) 24 *Law and Philosophy* 557, 560, 573; JL Austin, 'A Plea for Excuses' (1956–57) LVII *Proceedings of the Aristotelian Society* 1, 3.

and defensible account of the underlying principles without necessitating a radical rethink of the existing approaches to rationale-based excuses.

Within the criminal law, an excuse is a decision rule, and decision rules are capable of admitting considerations external to the guidance contained in the criminal law's system of conduct rules. In my view, the fact that the defendant has shown herself to be no worse than the jurisdictional society normatively requires and expects her to be supplies the basis for a decision rule in the criminal law that excuses the defendant from criminal liability.

6.2 'Bootstrapping'

In an area of little agreement, if there is one relatively uncontroversial issue, it is what is called the 'bootstrapping' question. To understand this question, consider the following case:

> D commits a prima facie offence 'φ'. When questioned, she admits that one of her reasons for committing φ was that the courts have previously found committing φ to be excusable in the circumstances in which D found herself.

The bootstrapping question is whether, if D relies on the existence of a rationale-based excuse to the charge of committing φ as one of her reasons for committing φ, she continues to be entitled to claim the defence. Theorists working within a reasons conception of supervening defences agree that because excuses supply rules for adjudication and not rules for guidance of conduct, they exclude an agent from relying on the previous grant of an excuse for committing φ in similar circumstances. As Simester puts it: 'D had better not choose to φ *because* she thinks she has an excuse.'[10]

Unfortunately, I cannot join in the chorus of agreement on this issue—at least not wholeheartedly. The conception of rationale-based excuse for which I have argued means that although bootstrapping is unlikely, it is not *conceptually* ruled out. The fact that the previous grant of an excuse is not meant to guide conduct means only that it cannot create a conduct rule within the criminal law and therefore that it cannot be the basis of a justification. There is no conceptual reason why this also excludes the possibility that it might found a rationale-based excuse. In theory, it is possible for there to be a convention according to which it is societally permissible to rely upon the previous grant of a rationale-based excuse when choosing one's actions. In other words, in the same way that convention

---

[10] Simester, 'On Justifications and Excuses' 108. The same proposition is made by Gardner, 'The Gist of Excuses' 597, who asserts that: 'To attempt to benefit from a legal excuse by being guided by it is to forfeit that excuse.' See also M Dan-Cohen, 'Decision Rules and Conduct Rules: On Acoustic Separation in Criminal Law' (1984) 97 *Harvard Law Review* 625, 671. Gardner and Simester have conceptions of rationale-based excuses that are, in all aspects relevant to this point, similar to the model defended in this study.

might make it societally acceptable to steal a car in order to avoid being shot dead, convention might also make it societally acceptable to rely on the previous grant by the criminal courts of a rationale-based excuse for doing φ as a reason in favour of doing φ again in similar external circumstances. If such a convention did exist, then in principle, it too could supply the basis for a decision rule in the criminal law permitting the grant of a rationale-based excuse.

That said, I am unaware of any society in which such a convention exists. It is not generally considered a societally acceptable reason to commit φ that a rationale-based excuse was previously granted to someone who committed φ in outwardly identical circumstances.[11] Moreover, as previously stated, even if such a convention did exist, the law-making authorities and the judiciary would be under no obligation to adopt a rationale-based excuse generating decision rule based on it. Perhaps it is the general societal consensus that one should not act in a morally blameworthy manner simply because one is likely to be excused from criminal liability that makes it incongruous for us to conceive of a rationale-based excuse that relies on bootstrapping.

6.3 The Flexibility of Rationale-Based Excuses

This conception of a rationale-based excuse leaves the contours of the defence very open-ended. All I have proposed here is a theory as to the source of the excusatory force of rationale-based excuses. This supplies a basis, though not a conclusive argument, for the grant of a rationale-based excuse in the sorts of cases in which they are usually granted. As such, in this section, instead of studying the limits set by this conception of rationale-based excuses, I will attempt to enumerate some of the possibilities and flexibilities it creates for states to shape their own rules on rationale-based excuses.

The explanation of rationale-based excuses in terms of hypocrisy relies on the existence of a societal framework of conduct-guiding norms. I do not intend to examine the necessary content of such a framework here—indeed, I am agnostic as to whether this framework of norms has *any* necessary content. That said, for the present purposes, I will assume that these societal norms are entirely context-dependent, in that any given society in any given era may have its own internal rules about what conduct is considered acceptable and appropriate. On that view, different societies may have different views about what conduct may be

---

[11] Perhaps when D2 commits φ in circumstances that are outwardly identical to those in which D1 was excused for committing φ, we intuitively think that D2 should also be excused. However, I doubt that this is because of a shared convention that D1's being excused gives D2 a reason to commit φ. More likely, it is because in the absence of contrary evidence, we assume that the outward circumstances affected D1 and D2 in the same way, motivating them to commit φ for identical or very similar reasons. If so, then D2's reasons would be as normatively acceptable as D1's reasons for acting.

excused, the relative values of various competing interests, the concessions that may legitimately be made to behaviours or weaknesses considered to be part and parcel of human nature, and so on. Hence, in principle, the forms of societal normative conduct guidance of different jurisdictions may bear little resemblance to one another. This naturally means that the exact contours of the rationale-based excuses that exist in different jurisdictions may also bear little resemblance to one another.

In fact, the foregoing analysis understates the amount of variations in detail that the hypocrisy-based conception of rationale-based excuses permits. The content of rationale-based excuses in any given jurisdiction is in fact one step removed from the content of the societal normative conduct guidance available in that jurisdiction. Whatever the societal normative conduct guidance in a jurisdiction, it is for the state (through its political, executive, legislative or judicial limbs) to identify the elements thereof that are accepted into the criminal law decision rules of that jurisdiction. Hence, even if there is, for example, a clear societal consensus that one can be excused for cannibalising a non-threatening person because one was on the brink of starvation while adrift on the high seas,[12] and there appeared to be no other way to survive, the state is not obliged to actually excuse a person who does so. It is for the state to stipulate the minutiae of the conditions subject to which the defence is made available, and it does so by way of posited law. Its decisions in this regard may be influenced by factors in addition to its general commitment to avoiding hypocrisy. These may include considerations of a political, social or ethical nature.

So, for instance, in respect of the defence of duress, each state can have rules about how imminent[13] or direct[14] the triggering threat must be in order for the defence to be available. It can also, for policy reasons, make the defence unavailable in respect of certain offences[15] or classes of persons.[16] Note, however, that nothing in this description of a rationale-based defence actually requires the creation of these restrictions on the availability of the defence. The mere fact that it is within the state's theoretical power to restrict the availability of a rationale-based defence does not make it appropriate for the state to do so. The policy considerations that influence the state's decision to make available or unavailable a rationale-based excuse defence to any particular offence or class of persons must be judged on their own merits. So, in principle, it would be perfectly appropriate for English law

---

[12] These facts are, of course, adapted from the case of *R v Dudley and Stephens* (1884–85) LR 14 QBD 273.

[13] *R v Hudson (Linda)* [1971] 2 QB 202.

[14] *R v Valderrama-Vega* [1985] Crim LR 220.

[15] For instance, it may, like the English courts, make the defence unavailable for the offence of murder (*R v Howe (Michael Anthony)* [1987] AC 417) or attempted murder (*R v Gotts (Benjamin)* [1992] 2 AC 412).

[16] See, for instance, *R v Hasan (Aytach)* [2005] 2 AC 467, where the House of Lords in England and Wales ruled that an individual who voluntarily associated with criminals could not claim the defence of duress when those criminals threatened him with violence and that he ought to have foreseen the risk of being subjected to compulsion by threats of violence.

to reverse its refusal to allow a rationale-based excuse defence to a charge of murder or attempted murder. It would also be appropriate for the English courts, if they so wished, to qualify their ruling in *Hasan (Atyach)* to ensure that a rationale-based excuse is available, in principle, to persons with abusive spouses in respect of threats made by the spouse.[17] Furthermore, since there is no principled basis for distinguishing between cases in which the defendant is directed to commit a nominated crime and cases in which she is not, the distinction that English law makes between duress by threats and duress of circumstances[18] is also not mandated by underlying moral-legal theory.

Similarly, this conception of rationale-based defences might also support the creation of rationale-based defences hitherto unknown in English law. Consider, for instance, the following excusatory defences that are available in German criminal law, but not in English criminal law:

1. Persons who commit a prima facie offence while labouring under a mistake of law may be excused from criminal liability if their mistake was unavoidable.[19] This defence would also make sense under the conception of rationale-based excuses set out here, even if the criminal law contained a posited meta-rule deeming individuals to be aware of all its conduct guidance.[20] If society accepts that it did not expect the mistaken defendant to have known the content of the criminal norm violated, then it would be hypocritical for that same society to claim the moral standing to criminally blame that defendant for not being guided by that norm.

2. German law excuses from criminal liability individuals who engage in 'excessive self-defence', provided certain conditions are satisfied. First, the excess involved must be intensive (ie, the defensive response was permissible in principle, but excessive in severity) rather than extensive (ie, no defensive response was permissible even in principle because the attack was not yet, or no longer, proximate enough to permit a response).[21] And, second, the excess must be attributable, at least in part, to the defendant's asthenic mental state (ie, states

---

[17] This was the concern voiced by Baroness Hale in her separate judgment in *Hasan (Aytach)* (n 16) 508–12.

[18] See in this connection AP Simester, JR Spencer et al, *Simester and Sullivan's Criminal Law: Theory and Doctrine* (Oxford, Hart Publishing, 2016) 760–71.

[19] A Reed, M Bohlander et al (eds), *Defences in Criminal Law: Domestic and Comparative Perspectives* (Farnham, Ashgate, 2014) 237–38.

[20] See the description of such a norm in n 27 in Ch 2 above.

[21] I employ a similar distinction in section 8.2.1 in the context of analysing the exact point at which justified defensive force becomes available to an agent. Incidentally, Irish law too contains a 'doctrine of excessive defence', which reduces murder to manslaughter in cases where the defendant was entitled to use a certain degree of force, but goes beyond what was necessary and justified, and kills as a result. See *People (Attorney General) v Dwyer* [1972] IR 416. See also Reed, Bohlander et al, *Defences in Criminal Law* 171, 174, 181. Similar defences also exist in Dutch law (art 41(2) of the Dutch Penal Code), in the law of New South Wales, South Australia, Western Australia and Victoria, and in Swedish law. See Reed, Bohlander et al, *Defences in Criminal Law* 255, 257–58, 260, 262–63 (in relation to Dutch law), 189 (in relation to Australian law) and 307 (in relation to Swedish law).

characterised by weaknesses such as fear, terror or confusion). Where instead the intensive excess is attributable to the defendant's sthenic mental state (ie, states such as rage, hate or indignation), no excuse is available.[22] Although the distinctions between intensive and extensive excesses, and between responses not attributable to asthenic states and responses attributable (at least in part) to asthenic states are not mandated by the theory of rationale-based excuses proposed here, they, or any permutation and combination thereof, are defensible in terms of it. These distinctions may be indicative of a societal consensus on the conditions under which society normatively expects its members to defend themselves in a manner considered excessive under criminal law. Alternatively, they may represent the conditions imposed by the state as a political decision, when agreeing to excuse certain classes of defendants whose conduct enjoys a broader societal approbation.

As in the case of evaluating norm-reasoning for justifications, norm-reasoning for excuses should ideally also be evaluated from within the agent's subjective perspective. Errors in functional reasoning should not affect our assessment of the agent's norm-reasoning. However, this is not a necessary corollary of the underlying theory, since there is no intrinsic entitlement to be excused even when one's norm-reasoning conforms to the societally expected standards of norm-reasoning in a particular jurisdiction. Therefore, the state may well demand that to avail of a rationale-based excuse in respect of her norm-reasoning, the defendant must also display an acceptable standard of functional reasoning. Hence, the arguments made in this book supply no philosophical support or objection to the English rule in respect of duress, according to which, when assessing the defendant's norm-reasoning, reference must be made to the defendant's *reasonable* belief as to the existence and extent of the threat in response to which she commits the prima facie offence.[23]

As a side-note, I think it is very likely that in most modern liberal societies, conduct that obeys the criminal law conduct norms would also meet societal normative standards. But even if this were not the case, an agent who proves that her conduct accords with the criminal law conduct norms will not attract any criminal law norm-blame and should not be required to also prove that her conduct conformed to societal norms (and was therefore excused) in order to avoid norm-blame predicated criminal censure. Therefore, to ensure that she avoids criminal punishment, a person may either comply with the criminal law's unambiguous moral guidance in favour of or against committing an act, or she may ignore it and risk punishment by committing the act, provided that she is convinced that her so acting, even though morally wrong, is societally appropriate and will be excused on that basis.

---

[22] Reed, Bohlander et al, *Defences in Criminal Law* 232.

[23] *R v Safi (Ali Ahmed)* [2003] EWCA Crim 1809. See also *Hasan (Aytach)* (n 16).

Because rationale-based excuses and justifications track different normative systems of conduct guidance, it is possible that a morally unjustified agent may be completely excused from norm-blame. Nevertheless, because excuses do not track exceptions to conduct rules, but instead function (in the criminal law) as pure decision rules militating against a conviction, they do not purport to make conduct morally 'permissible'. Hence, they need not be all-or-nothing concepts. Moreover, since the normative standard applicable to excuses is societally appropriate conduct rather than the more uncompromising standard of conduct that accords with the criminal law conduct norms, the rules for assessing whether an agent should be excused are more flexible than the rules for assessing whether she is justified. They can therefore admit a wider array of considerations relevant to the social evaluation of conduct. Accordingly, to the extent that it is accepted in society, these rules may make accommodations for a human tendency for self-preference, or feelings of concern for the troubled background or immediate circumstances of the defendant. Furthermore, if socially acceptable reasoning permits it, even defensive actions that affect the rights of persons other than those responsible (directly or through their entitlements) for authoring the threat may be excused. Of course, to the extent that the defensive action affects persons who do author the threat, some notion of contributory responsibility for the defensive action may also be allowed to limit the amount of criminal liability that accrues to the defendant. In addition, there is no conclusive reason to insist that considerations of non-disproportionality and parsimoniousness should apply as anything more than guiding, albeit strongly guiding, factors. In principle, then, an action that was not the minimum defensive action needed to protect a legally safeguarded interest can be excused to the extent that it was necessary, and a defensive action that was disproportionate to the threat posed can be excused to the extent that it would have been proportionate. Moreover, an agent who commits a prima facie offence for several reasons, only some of which merit lenience, can be granted an appropriate partial excuse. It is also conceivable that types of conduct that can never be justified may be excused if the consequentialist considerations in play are powerful enough to make the conduct socially appropriate. The actual contours of the excuse defence depend on posited law, but in principle, much greater flexibility is available when positing excusatory decision rules.

The situation is slightly different where the criminal law extends itself to blame for functional unreasonableness. In these offences, since there are no standards of functional reasoning predicated by the system of norms underlying the core of criminal law,[24] the defendant is judged by reference to posited standards of functional reasoning or, in the absence of those, by reference to societally appropriate standards of functional reasoning. The posited law may allow for rationale-based excuses to such offences as well, by permitting the defendant to show that

---

[24] See section 2.2.2.

her functional reasoning went some way towards reaching the expected standards. However, a complete rationale-based excuse to such an offence is unlikely to arise, if only because compliance with the standards necessary for a complete excuse would usually mean that the prima facie offence was not committed in the first place. It is theoretically possible for different posited and societal standards of functional reasoning to exist in respect of the same action, but in such cases, it is likely that the posited standard will be understood as overriding the societal standard. This is because, unconstrained by any requirement of conformity with an underlying moral core, the act of positing a standard for functional reasoning usually suggests an intention to override the societal standard.

To summarise, then, the hypocrisy-based conception of rationale-based excuses proposed here allows states to offer a wide variety of potential rationale-based excuses, with vastly different technical stipulations and preconditions. The heads of excusatory defence available in different jurisdictions may differ because of differences in the underlying societal system of normative conduct guidance and/or because different states reach different decisions as to which norms from that underlying system ought to form the basis for a rationale-based excuse. Furthermore, even when similar heads of defence are available, the contours that they assume may vary widely because these too depend on decisions that different states may take differently. Hence, states may make different decisions about a plethora of issues, including:

(a) which excusatory defences are available;
(b) to which offences they may apply;
(c) whether the defendant's desert of blame should be judged by reference to the facts that she actually perceived or by reference to the facts that she ought to have perceived;
(d) whether to make accommodations for human frailties such as fear, confusion, rage and the like;
(e) whether to allow for partial excuses; and
(f) whether to allow for excuses to offences involving functional blame.

The model of excuses described in this chapter is in many ways similar to John Gardner's model. It too accepts that when an unjustified agent's reasoning reveals no deficient character traits (within which term I include traits relating to both norm-reasoning and functional reasoning), she should be granted a rationale-based excuse, although it goes further and traces the underlying basis for that proposition to the notion of hypocrisy in blaming. However, because Gardner and I differ on how we draw the boundaries of a justification, we also differ on which conduct we label as being excused.

7

Supervening Justificatory Necessity

The overall model of supervening defences that one gets by combining the model of paradigmatic justifications set out in Chapter 5 and the model of rationale-based excuses set out in Chapter 6 is comprehensive in terms of its coverage, in that it offers rationale-based protection from criminal liability to a plausible and defensible range of defendants. Even so, some hard cases test the intuitive plausibility of the results generated by this model. For instance, consider an example that Alexander discusses:

> A forest fire is raging and is threatening to engulf a nearby village. D can avert the destruction of a thousand houses by this forest fire by burning down a house on the edge of the village in a controlled fire, thereby creating a firebreak. The house belongs to a blameless person (V), who does not consent to its destruction.[1]

Should D nevertheless burn down V's house, she would, at best, be excused under quality of reasoning model as set out hitherto. Yet this seems to run against the grain of the general opinion that D would actually be justified by reason of necessity. Parenthetically, however, note that if the houses in the firebreak example are replaced with humans, then opinions as to the appropriateness of D's actions would seem to evince considerably less unanimity.[2]

This chapter will explore the possibility of carving out an intuitively plausible and philosophically defensible niche for a justificatory supervening defence of necessity. The argument will not proceed by critiquing existing proposals as to the defence of necessity, whether derived from precedent or from philosophical writings. Instead, it will follow the methodology previously employed to derive and describe the norms underlying the core rules of the criminal law. I will start by identifying areas of broad consensus on what necessity should do and will then

---

[1] L Alexander, 'Lesser Evils: A Closer Look at the Paradigmatic Justification' (2005) 24 *Law and Philosophy* 611, 630. Similar situations are also discussed by K Greenawalt, 'The Perplexing Borders of Justification and Excuse' (1984) 84 *Columbia Law Review* 1897, 1908–09 and DN Husak, 'On the Supposed Priority of Justification to Excuse' (2005) 24 *Law and Philosophy* 557, 570, and all agree that D should be considered justified.

[2] As is evidenced by the continued response that the insightful study of such an example by JM Taurek ('Should the Numbers Count?' (1977) 6 *Philosophy & Public Affairs* 293) continues to draw. See, for instance, N Hsieh, A Strudler and D Wasserman, 'The Numbers Problem' (2006) 34 *Philosophy & Public Affairs* 352; R Lawler, 'Taurek, Numbers and Probabilities' (2006) 9 *Ethical Theory and Moral Practice* 149; and W Lübbe, 'Taurek's No Worse Claim' (2008) 36 *Philosophy & Public Affairs* 69.

examine the extent to which these goals can be achieved through principled argument. The model of necessity I will propose will therefore not aim to explain the existing rules on necessity in any jurisdiction—it will merely aim to be intuitively plausible and compatible with the model of justification and rationale-based excuse proposed so far.

7.1 Disambiguation

Before embarking on this endeavour, it is important to identify the exact sort of necessity with which I will primarily be concerned in this chapter, because the general label of 'necessity' has been applied to at least four different types of defensive claims.[3] These four variants are excusatory necessity (also known as duress of circumstances), self-defence, lesser evils necessity and best interests interventions. I am not concerned in this chapter with excusatory necessity, since I treat that defence as a rationale-based excuse and address it in Chapter 6. Nor am I concerned with necessity as self-defence—I address that form of the defence in section 3.2.1 and Chapter 5. This leaves us with lesser evils necessity and best interests interventions.

Lesser evils necessity is a defensive claim premised on a utilitarian weighing of the evils brought about, on the one hand, by not acting and, on the other, by acting as the agent did (or proposes to do). This form of the necessity defence was referred to and applied by Brooke LJ in *Re A*,[4] a case that I will discuss in some detail in the next few pages. Essentially, the exculpatory force of this defensive claim comes from the fact that if the agent does not act, an evil will inevitably occur, but by choosing to act, the agent avoids that evil, albeit by causing a much lesser evil. It is therefore argued that the agent's behaviour should be encouraged by the law and treated as justified.

Best interests interventions necessity claims are raised in cases involving the commission of an act that is prima facie an offence against V, in the best interests of V, in circumstances in which V is either incapable of consenting to the intervention or has no effective opportunity to do so.[5] This plea may be raised in a criminal trial arising out of an intervention made or (rather less conventionally for a criminal law 'defence') in proceedings seeking the court's prior permission to make the intervention concerned.

Stark distinguishes this form of necessity from lesser evils necessity by reference to the 'motivation of the harm doer'. He argues that in lesser evils necessity

---

[3] W Chan and AP Simester, 'Duress, Necessity: How Many Defences' (2005) 16 *King's College Law Journal* 121, 124–27. See also F Stark, 'Necessity and Nicklinson' [2013] *Crim LR* 949, 950, 952–63.

[4] *Re A* [2001] Fam 147. See also Stark, 'Necessity and Nicklinson' 957–59.

[5] See, for instance, *F v West Berkshire Health Authority* [1990] 2 AC 1; *Great Western Hospitals NHS Foundation Trust v AA, BB, CC, DD* [2014] EWHC 132 (Fam); Stark, 'Necessity and Nicklinson' 955–56.

cases, 'the defendant is motivated by the simple avoidance of the threatened consequence, whether this is done to protect one of his interests or the wider public interest'. Conversely, in best interests interventions cases, 'the harm doer is motivated completely by the person who is being harmed and seeks to further her interests, not those of anybody else'.[6] Stark's proposition is correct, but does not necessarily tell us the full story about the underlying theoretical distinction between these last two forms of necessity. Chan and Simester say that the rationale underlying best interests interventions necessity involves a form of paternalism, because the agent acts on behalf of another, in the perceived best interests of the latter, in circumstances in which there is no opportunity to consult with the beneficiary.[7] In other words, the agent makes a benevolent decision on behalf of the beneficiary. Chan and Simester refer to Lord Goff's dicta in *F v West Berkshire Health Authority*[8] to note that best interests interventions necessity is subject to two conditions, viz:

> First, D's action must be in the best interests of V; [and] secondly, V's right to refuse consent must not be overridden, a condition that is usually satisfied where V cannot be communicated with and the action is not contrary to V's known wishes.

Incidentally, this has some similarities with the argument I made in sections 3.2.2 and 3.3.5 that an authority norm can authorise an agent to act on behalf of another, provided that she (the agent) does not override any perceived autonomous decision by the direct victim to submit to a particular harm. However, the crucial distinction is that in best interests interventions cases, the person suffering the 'defensive' action has not violated any duty norm, and so does not create any authority norm in favour of other people permitting them to take the concerned 'defensive' action. In fact, she is the 'victim' both of the initial threat and the 'defensive' action taken to ward off that threat.

I will not be describing a model of necessity that explains or applies to best interests intervention necessity here. The reason is that I suspect that at its core, the exculpatory force of best interests interventions necessity is not adequately captured either by Chan and Simester's tentative suggestion of benevolent paternalism or Stark's related motivation-based hypothesis. Although I cannot expand on these views here, it seems to me that philosophically, this form of the necessity defence is actually not a supervening defence at all. Instead, I think that it is most likely a negation of the implicit actus reus element of non-consent present in victimising offences, by way of recognising a substituted consent.[9] This is perhaps why the courts insist that irrespective of the balance of interests involved, a person's competent refusal to consent to an intervention cannot be overridden in his

---

[6] Stark, 'Necessity and Nicklinson' 956.

[7] Chan and Simester, 'Duress, Necessity' 127.

[8] *F v West Berkshire Health Authority* [1990] 2 AC 1, 75–76.

[9] There is some support for this view in English cases, even though primary and delegated legislation in England and Wales prevents the courts from analysing most best interests interventions necessity cases in terms of substituted consent. Lord Templeman, for instance, spoke of the court using its

or her best interests.[10] Substituted consent is meant to supply consent where the victim is incapable of considering whether or not to consent—it is not meant to override a competent exercise of personal autonomy by which a person refuses to consent.

My position is that the circumstances identified by Lord Goff in *F* under which 'harmful' interventions made in the best interests of the victim/beneficiary are not criminal are better analysed as preconditions for the recognition of the authority to substitute the victim/beneficiary's consent, and conditions relating to how such authority to substitute consent may be exercised. If so, then best interests interventions necessity is not a supervening defence and it ought not to be analysed as one. The fact that the rationale behind the past or proposed intervention is relevant to any decision about whether to recognise the intervenor's claim to the authority to provide substituted consent for the victim/beneficiary should not lead to a category error about the nature of best interests interventions necessity.

My focus in the rest of this chapter will be lesser evils necessity. Although I will not attempt to comprehensively describe the contours of this defence, I will briefly touch upon the essential features and limits of a justificatory supervening lesser evils necessity defence that is compatible with the arguments made in this book. I will first identify the essential features that we associate with such a defence and will then identify the source of the exculpation it offers. Thereafter, I will examine how justificatory supervening necessity compares to paradigmatic justifications

wardship jurisdiction to authorise (or permit ex ante) such an intervention in respect of a girl under the age of 18 in *In Re B (A Minor) (Wardship: Sterilisation)* [1988] AC 199, 205–06. See also *F v West Berkshire Health Authority* (n 8) 51.

Similarly, in *F v West Berkshire Health Authority* (n 8), Lord Griffiths (at 70) described his insistence that the court's approval be sought before making any interventions in the best interests of a patient in terms of substituted consent. Lord Goff (at 77) explained that a doctor acting in the best interests of a patient who is unable to consent 'may... be treated as having the patient's consent to act'. He also agreed with Court of Appeal's dictum that doctors and others who have a caring responsibility towards an incompetent person V are required to exercise a 'right of choice' in relation to their treatment. Furthermore, both Lord Brandon (at 63, 65–66) and Lord Goff (at 82–83) suggested that it was unfortunate that the court's *parens patriae* jurisdiction had been legislatively limited so that it no longer extended to patients like the one they were considering, and that had this jurisdiction still existed, granting consent under it would have been the more appropriate way of disposing of the case. More support for this view may be found in cases from other jurisdictions, in which the court's *parens patriae* jurisdiction is not so limited. Courts in various jurisdictions in the US use substituted consent in such cases. For instance, see the case of *In Re Grady* (1981) 85 NJ 235, which has facts almost identical to those in *F v West Berkshire Health Authority* and which was disposed of in a similar manner, but by reference to substituted consent provided by a guardian to whom the state's authority as *parens patriae* was delegated (at 251, 258–67). The court in this case explicitly rejected the proposition that a standard of necessity needed to be met in order to legalise the proposed intervention (at 262–63). See also *Mohr v Williams* (1905) 95 Minn 261, 268–69; *Bennan v Parsonnet* (1912) 83 NJL 20, 23–26; *Ruby v Massey* 452 F Supp 361, 366–72. Canada also adopts a similar approach. See the judgments of the Supreme Court of Canada in *Re Eve* [1986] 2 SCR 388 and the British Columbia Court of Appeal in *Re K* [1985] 4 WWR 724. The same is also true in Australia. See *In Re Jane* (unreported) Family Court of Australia, 22 December 1988.

[10] *F v West Berkshire Health Authority* (n 8) 75–76. See also *St George's Healthcare NHS Trust v S* [1998] 3 All ER 673.

in its ability to offer prospective guidance and subsequent exculpation. In doing so, I will address the most common principled objections to offering a supervening justificatory defence of necessity and will describe the results that the proposed model of supervening justificatory necessity would generate on the facts of difficult cases.

7.2 The Defence We Expect

I now return to the task of setting out my proposal for a model of necessity as a rationale-based, supervening defence. Based on the manner in which necessity has been explained by various theorists, the intuitive consensus seems to be that necessity should occupy a space higher than a mere excuse.[11] It should be as similar to a paradigmatic justification as possible. It should therefore have the same consequences as an exemption from moral blame (which is what a justification recognises).

Nevertheless, necessity cannot fit the contours of the paradigm justification proposed herein. We would expect the defence of necessity to apply to situations in which the rights of a non-threatening person are affected by the agent, but as explained in section 3.3 and Chapter 5, paradigm justifications can only be exercised against the source of the threat. Necessity's exculpatory force must therefore stem from factors external to the underlying conduct rule system for criminal law identified in Chapter 3. We also know that the need for a necessity defence is often explained by reference to its overall benefit to the system and society, rather than as a concession to the difficult situation in which the individual concerned finds herself.[12] In other words, the broad consensus is that the necessity defence ought only to be made available for norm-reasoning we wish to positively encourage (rather than norm-reasoning we merely accept as being what we would also expect from ourselves) in the interests of society as a whole.

---

[11] See, for instance, A Brudner, 'A Theory of Necessity' (1987) 7 *OJLS* 339; Alexander, 'Lesser Evils'; MN Berman, 'Lesser Evils and Justification: A Less Close Look' (2005) 24 *Law and Philosophy* 681, 699–700; GP Fletcher, 'The Right Deed for the Wrong Reason: A Reply to Mr. Robinson' (1975) 23 *UCLA Law Review* 293; VF Nourse, 'Reconceptualizing Criminal Law Defenses' (2003) 151 *University of Pennsylvania Law Review* 1691, 1710–15; M Thorburn, 'The Constitution of Criminal Law: Justifications, Policing and the State's Fiduciary Duties' (2011) 5 *Criminal Law and Philosophy* 259.

[12] Necessity is described as the defence of lesser evils, and the evils are quantified by reference to a 'social harm calculus' rather than their effect on just the individual. See Berman, 'Lesser Evils and Justification' 693–94, 700–01; Alexander, 'Lesser Evils'; Brudner, 'A Theory of Necessity' 362–63; Chan and Simester, 'Duress, Necessity' 126; PH Robinson, 'Criminal Law Defences: A Systematic Analysis' (1982) 82 *Columbia Law Review* 200, 213–14. See also §3.02(1) of the Model Penal Code; and M Gur-Arye, 'Legitimating Official Brutality: Can the War against Terror Justify Torture?' (2003) dx.doi.org/10.2139/ssrn.391580, 38; M Gur-Arye, 'Can the War against Terror Justify the Use of Force in Interrogations?' in S Levinson (ed), *Torture: A Collection* (Oxford, Oxford University Press, 2004) 191.

7.3 Exculpation in Lesser Evils Necessity

Since we are referring to the interests of society as a whole, we may consider rationale-based excuses, which protect prima facie offenders from criminal liability on the basis of the societal appropriateness of their reasoning. It will be recalled that the societally appropriate reasoning standard is usually influenced by several consequentialist factors that are irrelevant to the conduct rule system of the criminal law. Although the model of necessity being set up here is one of necessity as a justification, necessity may be thought of as a special case of rationale-based excuse in which the reasons supporting protection from criminal liability are overwhelming. It applies to cases in which the defendant chooses to affect the rights of another (whether or not the victim was directly or indirectly responsible for the initial threat) for the reason that doing so is overwhelmingly the socially preferable alternative to abstention from such a choice.

An objective consequentialist determination of necessity would exclude from the identification of the overwhelmingly socially preferable course of action considerations of self-preference and the contributory responsibility for the threat (if any) of the person suffering the defensive action. It would focus only on the comparative utility of the consequences generated by each course of action. However, this is not a necessary feature of the defence. Depending on the prevalent views, some weight may be accorded to these and other similar factors, and the resulting conception of necessity would also be compatible with the model of rationale-based defences proposed herein, provided that the defence was made available only to persons displaying norm-reasoning that society wishes to positively encourage. One thing that does not matter is the source of the threat (except insofar as the appropriate weight, if any, for contributory responsibility is being considered). The threat may be human-authored or it may arise purely due to circumstances. There is no good philosophical reason for making the necessity defence available only when the threat is human-authored or only where it arose circumstantially.

In cases of necessity, even though the defendant does, as a matter of fact, commit moral wrongdoing,[13] the law may deem her not to have acted with any moral fault, such that no fault-predicated criminal or civil liability can arise on the basis of her norm-reasoning.

---

[13] AP Simester, 'Wrongs and Reasons' (2009) 72 *MLR* 648, 653–54 observes that necessity and paradigmatic justifications are distinct, and that the distinction has to do with moral wrongness. He says that while a justified action does not violate the victim's rights, a necessary action does. In line with the arguments made in Ch 2, I believe the focus needs to be on the actor's norm-reasoning rather than the victim's suffering. Accordingly, I think that a person who acts with justification attracts no norm-blame since she does not violate the criminal law's duty norms, whereas a person who claims a necessity defence does violate a duty norm and does attract norm-blame (but is deemed not to).

7.4 Justificatory Supervening Necessity and Paradigmatic Justifications

The identification of the exact threshold beyond which choosing to affect the rights of another becomes 'overwhelmingly the socially preferable alternative' is something that must be done independently by each society based on its own respective mores. However, any moral criminal legal system will not permit or exempt from moral evaluation any action that exceeds the boundaries set by morality. Therefore, no moral conception of necessity as a justification can confer legitimacy upon actions by which a person affects another's constituent rights if they are not existentially justified. In other words, the normative reach of necessity extends only to granting moral approbation to interferences with posited rights.

Another important way in which necessity arguably falls short of a justification has to do with its ability to provide prospective guidance or authorisation for conduct. Doctrinally, the UK has been reluctant to recognise a general justifying (and therefore conduct-guiding) defence of necessity, particularly in victimising offences, but also in non-victimising ones. The main concern is that allowing individuals to make evaluative judgments about the relative value of the rights and interests in play in a given situation, and to decide for themselves based on those evaluations whether they continue to be obliged by the primary guidance of the criminal law's offence stipulations, would undermine the authority of the state and of law.[14] It is thought that such evaluative assessments ought to be undertaken only by the state and that giving citizens a plenary power to make such assessments by providing a conduct guiding defence of necessity may pave the way towards anarchy. Dan-Cohen agrees[15] and notes that legislatures sometimes place such a high premium on ensuring that a necessity defence is not used as a conduct rule that they may choose to exclude the defence from their criminal codes altogether and use clemency powers to fill in the gap left by its exclusion. He refers to Macaulay's report on the drafting of the Indian Penal Code 1860 as one example of this tendency and the clemency powers exercised in the aftermath of the guilty verdict in *R v Dudley and Stephens*[16] as another. However, his primary argument against the adoption of a general justifying defence of necessity is a theoretical one.[17] For him, because the defence of necessity is by nature essentially a decision

---

[14] See, for instance, *Southwark London Borough Council v Williams* [1971] Ch 734, 744–47. See also AP Simester, JR Spencer et al, *Simester and Sullivan's Criminal Law: Theory and Doctrine* (Oxford, Hart Publishing, 2016) 822–23.

[15] M Dan-Cohen, 'Decision Rules and Conduct Rules: On Acoustic Separation in Criminal Law' (1984) 97 *Harvard Law Review* 625, 637–45.

[16] *R v Dudley and Stephens* (1884–85) LR 14 QBD 273.

[17] Dan-Cohen, 'Decision Rules and Conduct Rules' 637–45. See also Berman, 'Lesser Evils and Justification' 701; and the judgment of the Israeli Supreme Court in *Public Committee Against Torture in Israel v The State of Israel* HC 5100/94, 53(4) PD 817, which unequivocally held at para 36

rule, it is simply incapable of providing useful prospective conduct guidance for the public at large, because it has to be couched in terms that the general public is incapable of precisely parsing into useful conduct guidance.

As to the first objection to the recognition of general justifying defence of necessity, the experiences of civil law countries Germany,[18] France[19] and Sweden,[20] and of some states in common law Australia[21] suggest that anarchy is not an inevitable consequence of giving statutory form to the defence of necessity as a justification. The Model Penal Code too recommends that individuals be permitted to make their own evaluative assessments about whether the harm or evil sought to be prevented is greater than the harm or evil caused by the preventive action, and to act based on that assessment.[22] In fact, even the common law regularly asks individuals to make evaluative judgments about the reasonableness of some course of action or the proportionality of a defensive response, and yet the system works tolerably well. Dan-Cohen's theoretical point about the imprecision of the language that must inevitably be used to describe the ambit of the necessity defence stands—this defence is less given to precise formulaic guidance than a paradigmatic justification like self-defence. To some extent, therefore, a person relying on the defence of necessity would have to make a leap of faith and hope that her assessment of the relative weights of the rights in play is confirmed by the state upon ex post evaluation. Nevertheless, a person with a good grasp of the general pulse of her society's attitudes towards the threshold for necessity is likely to make assessments that will be confirmed. Even where she fails, she would have to fail catastrophically to not even merit an excusatory defence to criminal liability.

In fact, even in the common law, the courts have increasingly been attempting to provide prospective guidance as to the availability of the justificatory defence of necessity when possible. The English courts in particular have been inventive

---

that: 'The very nature of the [necessity] defense does not allow it to serve as the source of authorization [to undertake actions that might ex post facto be found to have been necessary].' The court went on to hold that: 'The "necessity defense" has the effect of allowing one who acts under the circumstances of "necessity" to escape criminal liability. The "necessity defense" does not possess any additional normative value. It cannot authorize the use of physical means to allow investigators to execute their duties in circumstances of necessity. The very fact that a particular act does not constitute a criminal act—due to the "necessity defense"—does not in itself authorize the act and the concomitant infringement of human rights. The rule of law, both as a formal and as a substantive principle, requires that an infringement of human rights be prescribed by statute. The lifting of criminal responsibility does not imply authorization to infringe a human right.'

[18] See §34 of the German Strafgesetzbuch, as translated by Professor Dr Michael Bohlander, available at www.gesetze-im-internet.de/englisch_stgb.

[19] See art 122-7 of the French Penal Code. See also A Reed, M Bohlander et al (eds), *Defences in Criminal Law: Domestic and Comparative Perspectives* (Farnham, Ashgate, 2014) 217.

[20] See c 24 s 4 of the Swedish Criminal Code. See also Reed, Bohlander et al, *Defences in Criminal Law* 308.

[21] Criminal Code (Commonwealth), s 10.3; Criminal Code 2002 (Australian Capital Territory), s 41; Criminal Code (Northern Territory), s 33; Criminal Code (Queensland), s 25; Criminal Code (Western Australia), s 25; Crimes Act 1958 (Victoria) s 322R. See also Reed, Bohlander et al, *Defences in Criminal Law* 189–90.

[22] Model Penal Code, §3.02.

in agreeing to consider specific cases and provide ex ante guidance as to whether a proposed response to a threat would be covered by the defence of necessity. In the landmark case of *F v West Berkshire Health Authority*,[23] the House of Lords ruled that the court could exercise its inherent jurisdiction to declare that it would be lawful to surgically sterilise a sexually active adult woman who was unable to consent to the operation because of a mental disability and who, for the same reason, would not have been able to cope with pregnancy. In effect, the House of Lords declared in advance that a doctor who performed the sterilisation would not commit a crime, thereby creating a case-specific conduct rule to guide the medical team's conduct.[24] A similar declaratory relief was granted in extraordinary case of *Re A*,[25] where the court exercised its inherent jurisdiction to declare that if doctors separated conjoined twins who would both die if not separated in order to save the life of one, they would not act unlawfully, despite their parents' refusal to consent.

7.5 Liability Outcomes in Cases of Potential Necessity

This willingness to provide ex ante guidance as to the prospective existence of a necessity defence for a proposed course of action demonstrated in *F v West Berkshire Health Authority* and *Re A* is certainly compatible with the arguments made in this study, and is probably to be welcomed, subject to practical considerations about the court's time. However, neither decision can be explained in terms of the (post-moral) conception of necessity set out in this chapter, because in both cases, the action being considered impinged upon the constituent elements of a human. If necessity is an exclusively post-moral concept, it can never permit incursions into the constituent elements.

The outcome in *F v West Berkshire Health Authority* at least can be explained in a manner consistent with the arguments made as to the moral basis of criminal law. This was a best interests intervention necessity case and, as tentatively suggested in section 7.1, it is probably best explained as a negation of the prima facie offence by way of substituted consent. Although the court expressly denied that it was either consenting on behalf of the mentally disabled woman, F, to the sterilisation, or ratifying her mother's consent on her behalf, this denial is attributable to

---

[23] This is a best interests intervention case, but it is analysed as a supervening necessity case in England and Wales because of the way in which applicable legislation has drastically curtailed the court's *parens patriae* jurisdiction. Therefore, it demonstrates that the courts in England and Wales are willing to provide ex ante guidance in relation to what they consider to be cases of supervening necessity.

[24] Along similar lines, see the case of *Great Western Hospitals NHS Foundation Trust* (n 5). In this case, the court used its inherent jurisdiction to permit doctors to perform an elective caesarean section on an adult patient who was temporarily unfit to consent (or refuse consent), but in respect of whom, because of a technicality, the court could not exercise jurisdiction under the Mental Capacity Act 2005.

[25] *Re A* (n 4).

the doctrinal constraints that fettered the court. Philosophically, the outcome can best be explained by reference to substituted consent.[26] When a person is incapable of exercising purposive agency, the absence of her consent cannot automatically be equated with either a refusal to consent or a denial of the opportunity to consent or refuse consent. The inability of a person to exercise purposive agency negates one assumption as to the constituent elements of a human that forms the basis of the moral limits of the criminal law identified in section 3.1. As such, the results generated on the basis of those limits cannot strictly be said to apply in their entirety to people who cannot exercise purposive agency (or, indeed, who lack or are significantly deficient in any of the other constituent human elements identified in section 3.1). For the sake of argumentative convenience (and disclaiming as unintended any pejorative connotation that doing so may imply), I refer to humans who have not yet developed or who lack or are deficient in any constituent human element as 'imperfect moral agents'.[27] In the category of imperfect moral agents, I include infants as well as some mentally and physically disabled persons. Given that in respect of such agents the basis for applying the entire moral framework of law is somewhat weakened, some amount of rationalisation of some of the standard rules for imperfect moral agents is desirable and would not be contrary to the moral framework of the law. In the case of persons who cannot exercise their purposive agency, the legal system may be adjusted by allowing another human or institution to make certain choices and decisions on behalf of and in the best interests of the imperfect moral agent. The result in *F v West Berkshire Health Authority* can be explained, without violence to the general model of criminal law defences set out in this study, as an instance of the court recognising the validity of substituted consent by F's mother to a procedure in the best interests of F. Arguably, in the absence or unfitness of a close relative like F's mother, the responsibility of consenting on behalf of F might have fallen upon the court as *parens patriae*.

The outcome in *Re A* cannot be explained so easily. The parents of the conjoined twins 'J' and 'M' refused to consent to the separation, and therefore the matter went to court. Any notion of the court (or anyone else) stepping in to consent on behalf of M, the twin who died due to the separation, is logically incoherent. Any party exercising M's purposive agency on her behalf would have to have acted in M's best interests, and not in the best interests of J or in the 'overall best interests' of J and M. It is difficult to accept (at least not consistently with the arguments made in section 3.1) that it was in M's best interests to die. In the unusual facts of *Re A*, many of the argumentative positions premised on the separateness

---

[26] See also the discussion of best interests interventions necessity cases in section 7.1. In *F v West Berkshire Health Authority* (n 8), both Lord Brandon (at 63, 65–66) and Lord Goff (at 82–83) expressed disappointment at the curtailment of court's *parens patriae* jurisdiction such that it no longer extended to patients like F, and suggested that had such jurisdiction existed, granting consent under it would have been a better way to dispose of the case.

[27] This is a term I borrow from MN Berman, 'Justification and Excuse, Law and Morality' (2003) 53 *Duke Law Journal* 1.

of individuals were inapplicable, because the twins were conjoined. As such, on these special facts, M was authoring a threat to J (although she was not doing so in a blameworthy manner) merely by existing. Therefore, J would, in principle, have been entitled to exercise her existential immunity against M and, in doing so, to cause M's death. Of course, J, being an infant, was in no position to do so, and thus it might be thought that her parents could do so on her behalf—perhaps they were impelled by what is arguably a constituently human behaviour: that of protecting their infant. But even then, since protecting their infant J would only have been possible by killing their infant M, that course of action would have also involved the defiance by the parents of the same constituently human behaviour. Had they chosen to kill M, they could not have been described as 'merely being true to what constitutes them as human', and hence their course of action would have remained within the realm of evaluation under a human morality and could have attracted moral (and consequentially criminal) blame.[28] As it happened, the parents of J and M refused to consent to the operation. Since no one believed that M had acted with fault in authoring the threat to J, no authority arose to permit third parties to intervene to protect J's constituent rights.[29] Therefore, the court could not have authorised the surgical separation in a manner consistent with the model of criminal law proposed here, either by way of substituted consent or as a third party defending a direct victim. This is not to say that had the doctors gone ahead, they could not have been excused under the model proposed in this study.[30] Clearly, saving the life of J in these circumstances would have been considered the appropriate course of action by most modern liberal societies. But if so, the correct course of action would have been to let the doctors decide their course of action according to their conscience and, if they decided to perform the separation operation in order to save J's life, to excuse them from criminal liability.

In summary, insofar as the courts in *F v West Berkshire Health Authority* and *Re A* understood themselves to be declaring that a rationale-based based defence would be available to doctors who performed the operations proposed in each case, they were in effect creating a case-specific conduct rule. Doing so is consistent with the concept of necessity set out in this chapter, although practical difficulties will limit the court's ability to do so in each case. Furthermore, the experience of some civil law jurisdictions suggests that legislating a lesser evils necessity defence is a viable option and might be able to provide useful prospective guidance without overly burdening judicial resources. However, neither *F v West Berkshire Health Authority* nor *Re A* is a good example of the defence of necessity as set out in this study. *F v West Berkshire Health Authority* is a best interests interventions necessity case

---

[28] See in this connection section 3.1, where a similar argument is made.

[29] Recall from the discussion in section 3.2.2 that the authority to intervene is predicated on the commission of a wrong relatable to the duty not to harm the constituent rights of others. Hence, in order for someone to claim the authority to intervene in this case, she would have to believe that M had (advertently) violated her duty not to harm J's constituent right to life.

[30] That option was not open to the doctors under British criminal law, which does not recognise any rationale-based excuse for causing death.

that is better analysed as a case involving the negation of an actus reus element, and the outcome in *Re A* simply cannot be reconciled with the model proposed herein. In my view, the ruling in terms of the availability of a justificatory defence (though not necessarily the eventual liability outcome) in *Re A* ought to be rejected. Along similar lines, the model of necessity proposed here supports the rejection of a justificatory necessity defence to the defendants in *Dudley and Stephens*[31] on the basis that the state cannot, by way of a deeming provision, confer legitimacy upon actions by which a person affects another's constituent rights in the absence of an existential justification. Once again, this is not to say that Dudley and Stephens could not, or should not, have been granted a rationale-based excuse for their actions, but that is a separate matter altogether.

The outcomes generated by this model of necessity in the *Re A* and *Dudley and Stephens* cases are at least intuitively plausible, even if some may disagree. Moreover, this model also generates plausible outcomes when applied to the facts of other cases that are discussed in the context of the English law of necessity. For instance, although the court in *R v Kitson*[32] refused to offer any defence to D on a charge of drink driving after he woke up in a driverless car that was rolling down a hill and took the wheel to steer it to safety despite being inebriated, there are good grounds for allowing D a defence of necessity on the model of necessity described here. This would be in line with common sense—in steering the car to safety, D prevented injury to himself, damage to the car and, possibly, damage to pedestrians and private property nearby. In doing so, he caused no harm, and so the 'evil' he chose to bring about was undoubtedly and overwhelmingly lesser than the evil he thereby averted. Similarly, this model of necessity would in principle also support the courts' willingness to make a justificatory necessity defence available to the defendants in the cases of *Pommell*[33] and *R v S Ltd and L Ltd*[34] (subject of course to their accounts of why they committed their respective

---

[31] *R v Dudley and Stephens* (1884–85) LR 14 QBD 273.

[32] *R v Kitson* (1955) 39 Cr App R 66.

[33] *R v Pommell* [1995] 2 Cr App R 607. In this case, early one morning, D was found by the police lying in bed with a loaded sub-machine gun in his hand. He claimed that late the previous night, he had confiscated it 'off a geezer who was going to do some people some damage with it' so as to prevent that from happening. He claimed that he had planned to hand it into the police, but was arrested before he had time to do so! D was convicted of a possession of firearms offence after the trial judge ruled that, even if one believed D, he had not gone to the police immediately and so, as a matter of law, the defence of necessity was unavailable to him. The Court of Appeal reversed the conviction, holding that in principle, the defence of necessity was available to D on his version of the facts, provided that his delay in approaching the police could be explained.

[34] *R v S Ltd and L Ltd* [2009] EWCA Crim 85. In this case, the Court of Appeal was considering an appeal on a procedural point in a case involving a private security firm charged with offences relating to deploying unlicensed security guards contrary to the Private Security Industry Act 2001. On its merits, the defendant firm had raised the defence of necessity, saying that it had acted because of fears of imminent terrorism on the premises for which it was responsible. The Court of Appeal held that it was possible to conceive of circumstances in which a continuing threat to a certain area, for example, the centre of London, was believed reasonably to be so imminent as to compel those responsible for the safety of that area to act in breach of the law. It accepted that in principle, a defence of necessity would be available to the offence charged in those circumstances.

prima facie offences being credible). It would also lend qualified support to the court's conclusion in the case of *Buckoke v Greater London Council*.[35] That was a civil case seeking an advance declaration that the common law defence of necessity that would protect from criminal liability the drivers of fire engines who crossed red lights to reach burning buildings quickly so as to minimise damage to property and, potentially, save lives. Although this advance declaration was refused, the Court of Appeal simultaneously stated that in practice, it would expect the police and the judicial system to effectively collude in letting off firefighters who crossed red lights in emergency cases. While the reluctance to issue advance generalised guidance is understandable in terms of English doctrine, as I argued in section 7.4, such advance guidance is not conceptually impossible—it may simply be incapable of offering the same level of specificity as other conduct rules. Even so, the Court of Appeal made it quite clear that should a firefighter somehow come to be prosecuted for a traffic offence in a case like this, it would expect the police, the prosecution and/or the magistrates not to punish her. That is the conclusion that would be reached under the model of necessity described here as well.

Like the model of rationale-based excuses described in Chapter 6, the model of supervening justificatory necessity outlined here is sensitive to the societal and political values of the jurisdiction in which it operates. Hence, it is conceivable that different jurisdictions might reach different conclusions about whether a justificatory necessity defence might be available in a case like *Southwark London Borough v Williams*.[36] Nevertheless this approach to theorising supervening justificatory necessity supplies us with the conceptual tools necessary to isolate the factors that are relevant in deciding whether or not a defence should be available. It also allows us to round off the discussion of the collateral harm example that was left inchoate in section 5.4. To recapitulate, the issue left open there was whether D, who justifiably defends herself against an attack by T in a pub by smashing the pub landlord V's beer mug on T's shoulder, can claim avail of any defence (other than a paradigmatic justification) in respect of the harm caused to V's property? Having set out models of rationale-based excuse and supervening justificatory necessity, it now appears that the answer depends on the extent to which D's decision to use V's property to defend herself accords with societal normative expectations and, if so, whether the state is willing to make that societal approbation the basis of a decision rule allowing a defence. The former will probably depend largely on a comparison of the evil that T threatened to visit on D and the evil visited on V by the damage to the beer mug. If the evil that D would have suffered had she not defended herself using the mug vastly outweighs the evil of the damage to the mug, then there is a basis for the state to acquit D on the basis of the supervening justificatory necessity of her actions.[37] If it did so, then there would be no basis to

---

[35] *Buckoke v Greater London Council* [1971] Ch 655.

[36] *Southwark London Borough Council v Williams* (n 14).

[37] This appears to be the likely position in German law as well. See Reed, Bohlander et al, *Defences in Criminal Law* 233–34.

hold D criminally liable and there would be no norm-blame-related basis to hold D liable in civil law either.[38] Of course, D might still suffer non-fault-predicated civil liability or, if her functional reasoning was in blameworthy, civil liability predicated on functional blame.

Even if the evil that D would have suffered had she not defended herself using the mug does not vastly outweigh the evil of the damage to the mug, it might still outweigh the evil of the damage to the mug sufficiently to generate societal normative approbation for D's decision to appropriate V's mug in service of her own defensive project. If so, then there is a basis for granting D a rationale-based excuse, although even if it did, this would not automatically exclude civil liability predicated on D's norm-blame and functional blame (if any).

One final general observation must be made before closing this chapter's discussion of the standard forms of rationale-based defences. The evaluation of the quality of a person's reasoning requires the identification of that person's reasons for acting. In most situations, there will be more than one operating reason for a person's actions, and several factors will weigh on a person's mind when deciding on an appropriate course of action. A practical course of action in such cases would be to identify the agent's dominant reason for acting. This is particularly important in the context of justifications, since they are all-or-nothing defences requiring us to judge an agent based on why she chose to commit a prima facie offence. Of course, it is difficult to be precise in identifying the dominant reason for an agent's action, but that is precisely what the courts and juries are asked to do in the exercise of their evaluative functions in a variety of contexts. In fact, a rule telling a decision-maker to use her judgment to identify the dominant motivation is the paradigmatic decision rule—it does not claim to offer precise formulaic guidance because it is addressed not to the general public, but rather to persons trained, or selected and specially instructed, to make evaluative decisions.

---

[38] Under German law, V would be able to require D to pay compensation for the damage to the beer mug. See §904 of the German Strafgesetzbuch, as translated by the Langenscheidt Translation Service, available at www.gesetze-im-internet.de/englisch_bgb. See also Reed, Bohlander et al, *Defences in Criminal Law* 233. As I argued previously, it seems perverse to effectively impose a price barrier to D's access to defensive force while conceding that it is necessary for D to employ such defensive force. The model of supervening justificatory necessity described here provides a principled basis for rejecting this stipulation, at least in the absence of any deficiencies in D's functional reasoning.

8

Mapping the Model's Implications

With a hypothesis about the paradigmatic forms of justification, excuse and necessity in place, it is now time to evaluate the intuitive appeal of the model proposed. To this end, in this chapter, I draw out some additional implications of adopting the model proposed so as to provide a more complete description of normative guidance provided by it to each of the affected constituencies. It is then up to the reader to decide for herself whether or not she finds the system intuitively appealing. Before I begin this project, however, it would be useful to flag up certain intuitions to which this model will avowedly not appeal. I do this by charting the evaluative assessments generated in different test cases by the model of justification that I defend.

8.1 The Tragic and the Fortuitous

If one accepts the arguments on the nature of justification made so far, then the following situations may arise in relation to a person 'D' who admits to having committed a prima facie offence (that is, having caused a stipulated actus reus with the corresponding mens rea) and then claims a supervening defence:

1. D does not deserve functional blame, and the objective facts are as she perceives them. However, she deserves norm-blame, and her conduct occasions the breach of another's rights.
2. D deserves functional blame and norm-blame. She fails to perceive the true facts, and her norm-reasoning based on the facts that she does perceive is poor. Her conduct occasions the breach of another's rights.
3. D is justified, but deserves functional blame for not perceiving the true facts. Her conduct may or may not occasion the breach of another's rights.
4. D is justified and deserves no functional blame. The objective facts are as she perceives them. Hence, her conduct does not occasion any actionable breach of another's rights.
5. D is justified and deserves no functional blame. Yet, because her perspective is inevitably limited, she does not perceive the true facts, and so her conduct occasions the undeserved breach of another's rights.

6. D deserves norm-blame and may or may not deserve functional blame as well. Yet, due to a fortuitous alignment of facts unknown to her, her conduct does not occasion an *undeserved* breach of any other person's rights.

Assuming that D is not claiming any excuse in any of these cases, we may examine whether she deserves a criminal conviction. The first two situations are straightforward cases in which D deserves criminal convictions that recognise her norm-blameworthiness and label her as a morally reprehensible person. In the third case, D should ideally not be convicted under the criminal justice system, but since she is nevertheless at fault, she can be made to bear the civil liability for the damage, if any, caused by her. The fourth case is straightforward: D has a complete defence to criminal liability and incurs no fault-predicated civil liability, not least because there is no actual (undeserved) damage done. The fifth and sixth cases set up intuitive challenges to the proposed model of rationale-based defences. In the fifth case, D deserves neither norm-blame nor functional blame, yet her conduct causes some person to suffer an undeserved breach of her (the latter's) rights. In the sixth case, D deserves norm-blame and, whether or not she deserves functional blame, the objective facts are such that she fortuitously does not violate the rights of any other person. What consequences should the system generate in these last two cases?

My response to the sixth case has been suggested by an argument previously made,[1] viz that the mere circumstance of fortuitously having acted so as to find oneself in compliance with a justificatory conduct norm (which is stated in objective terms) does not entitle D to a justificatory defence, and that in such cases, D continues to *deserve* criminal censure. That said, since the system's entitlement to award that particular censure has not arisen, it may well be that the censure is not awarded.

In the fifth case, the arguments made so far suggest that D should have a complete defence to criminal liability, as well as to any fault-based civil liability. She should be treated as if she committed no wrongdoing, even though a wrong occurred and she authored it. I stand by this result generated by the model. When one examines the commission of an offence, one examines whether the agent did the 'bad thing', in the transitive verb sense. A bad thing may have happened and the agent may have authored it, but if neither the agent's moral nor functional reasoning was flawed, the agent did not do the 'bad thing' (although she may have done the 'thing'). As Greenawalt puts it, '[a] person may distinguish his evaluation of the desirability of the act from his evaluation of the actor's conduct'.[2]

---

[1] See section 5.1.

[2] K Greenawalt, 'Distinguishing Justifications from Excuses' (1986) 49(3) *Law and Contemporary Problems* 89, 94. See also K Greenawalt, 'The Perplexing Borders of Justification and Excuse' (1984) 84 *Columbia Law Review* 1897, 1908); and BB Sendor, 'Mistakes of Fact: A Study in the Structure of Criminal Conduct' (1990) 25 *Wake Forest Law Review* 707, 759–60.

What then is the significance of the fact that the bad thing occurred? In arguing against what he calls the 'closure view of wrongdoing,'[3] John Gardner identifies the basis of that view as the optimistic presumption that the perfection of our rational facilities will lead to the perfection of our lives,[4] and challenges it. He argues that although it is usually the case that when we exhibit and act on perfect functional reasoning, the outcomes follow our intentions, sometimes there is a gap between the intended outcome and the actual outcome. This is because of the inherent limitations of human perspective—no human knows the 'objective truth' about things in the world, and each human has access only to her own subjective perception of this 'truth'. This gap may produce outcomes that are better or worse than the ones we intended. I will refer to the former as the fortuitous, while the latter corresponds closely to what John Gardner refers to as 'the tragic'. Alexander's example of the hateful radiologist,[5] for instance, is one in which fortuitous consequences ensue from a malicious act. Similarly, it is also possible to construct parallel examples of tragic cases, in which perspectival errors result in honest and reasonable claims to justification where objectively there was none.[6] If one accepts that defences are rationale-based, then there will be tragic or fortuitous circumstances that have no bearing on the blameworthiness of the agent causing them. These should be morally irrelevant to a justification or, indeed, a rationale-based excuse.

The adoption of this position leaves us with a subset of persons who are wronged by the actions of the agent, but who must be told that while their loss is tragic, the agent cannot legally be faulted for having caused it. They may of course have redress under arrangements that are not predicated on fault, such as contractual risk-apportionment arrangements, or statutory stipulations to the same effect in civil law (usually made for public policy purposes), or insurance arrangements. However, barring such exceptions, they have no entitlement to insist that the person who caused the loss should be punished and/or made to compensate them for the loss caused. This is unfortunate, but no more so than would be the imposition of liability of a nature that suggests fault upon a faultless person. On a related note, many states already make ad hoc ex gratia payments to victims of natural disasters and tragedies—they may consider making similar payments to

---

[3] See J Gardner, *Offences and Defences* (Oxford, Oxford University Press, 2007) 77, in his essay entitled 'In Defence of Defences'. Broadly speaking, this is the view that no action is wrong unless it is wrong all things considered. A justified action is not wrong and therefore it is not a 'wrong' that has to be justified, but only an action to which there is a rational objection.

[4] ibid 81.

[5] L Alexander, 'Lesser Evils: A Closer Look at the Paradigmatic Justification' (2005) 24 *Law and Philosophy* 611, 633. The radiologist maliciously administers a strong dose of radiation to a patient with the intention of causing cancer in him. Unbeknownst to both the patient and the doctor, the patient has a tumour at the site of the radiation, and the radiation extends the patient's life by 15 years.

[6] A simple one involves a person who kills an attacker in self-defence only to find out that the 'attacker' had been an actor who had been hired by her friends to 'prank' her for a TV show.

compensate victims of human-authored tragedies as well. This is certainly not mandated by the adoption of the model of rationale-based defences described, but would nevertheless mitigate the harshness of the tragedies it leaves unredressed.

In any event, it is clear that the model I propose will not satisfy (and does not claim to be able to satisfy) the intuitions of any person who believes that the creation of a sufficiently undesirable circumstance or consequence must necessarily generate a criminal law response so that the victim's loss does not go unredressed. I see the criminal law as a system aimed at condemning offenders for criminal wrongs rather than at redressing the losses of unfortunate victims. There is significant empirical overlap in these goals, but there is also a significant area of separation. To the extent that the author of an undeserved loss to a victim did not display poor reasoning, the model I defend unapologetically exonerates the author.

Having established that clearly, we can now begin to examine the plausibility of the answers suggested by the model of justification defended herein to several key questions about the rights and obligations of the various parties with interests in an emergent situation. I arrange these answers by the party concerned.

8.2 Implications for Persons Contemplating Defensive Action

Many of the questions that a person (D) contemplating defensive action may ask about how she should respond to a threat have already been answered in previous chapters. She knows by now that she will only be acting with justification if she believes that the force she intends to employ will affect only the rights of the individual (T) that she believes to be the source of the threat to her.[7] She knows that similar, but slightly different, rules apply depending on whether she (D) is protecting her constituent rights or her posited rights. Therefore, she knows that if she is protecting her constituent rights, she can use any means available to defend herself against the threat. She also knows that if she is protecting her posited rights, she can use only parsimonious and non-disproportionate means to do so, and cannot justifiably choose to harm any non-threatening party (unless such chosen 'collateral damage' falls under the special justifying defence of necessity).

---

[7] Strictly speaking, this statement needs to be qualified. A person who exercises her existential immunity to defend against a threat to a constituent human element will be existentially justified (or immune to moral blame for her actions) even if the exercise of her existential immunity involves harm to the posited rights of persons other than the threat. This is because posited rights are logically inferior to the existential immunity and therefore they cannot restrict the existential immunity in any way. However, as explained in section 3.1, when the seeming exercise of an existential immunity involves harm to the constituent elements of a non-threatening human, the actions involved are not truly immune from moral blame, because they cannot be described as the acts of a person who is 'merely being true to what constitutes her as a human'.

One question that remains to be answered is what steps, if any, she is required to take in order to avoid conflict without using defensive force. A related question is when, if ever, a person is not permitted to defend her rights.

There is dissonance amongst legal systems about whether a person is required to avoid conflict if possible instead of using defensive force. Some jurisdictions, especially in the US, do not expect a person to retreat in the face of certain attacks or from specified places.[8] Others, like England and Wales, treat retreat as an evidentiary factor in favour of the proposition that the use of defensive force was reasonable.[9] Still others, like Scotland, permit the use of force in defence only if the accused had no reasonable means of escape or retreat.[10]

In a state that claims a monopoly of force, whenever an individual's posited rights are threatened, the primary responsibility of protecting those rights rests with the state. The individual cannot use force to defend her rights unless the authority to use force is delegated to her by the state. Therefore, the principled answers to the questions posed in this section depend on the specification adopted by the state as to its monopoly of force.

Now, as explained in section 3.3.2, a moral state's stipulation of its monopoly of force cannot modify the operation of the norms relating to constituent rights described in section 3.2, because those norms are logically prior to posited norms, including a political stipulation by the state of its monopoly. Subject to these limits, a moral liberal state can adopt its own unique stipulation of its monopoly of force. Assuming that both types of states claim to be moral, one explanation for the difference between the rules of states that adopt the 'stand your ground' view and states that impose a duty to retreat before using force may be that they stipulate their monopolies of force differently. Perhaps the former states claim a narrower monopoly over the use of force or are more willing to delegate the authority to use force than the latter. But because I am not exploring issues of political philosophy

---

[8] North Carolina introduced provisions in 2011 to allow the use of deadly force without needing to retreat in response to the threat of death or great bodily harm to oneself or another, or unlawful and forceful entry into a dwelling, residence, workplace or vehicle (§14-51.3 and §14-51.2 of the North Carolina General Statutes). Florida introduced similar provisions in 2005 (§776.012, 776.013, 776.031 and 776.032 of the Florida Statutes). Illinois has similar provisions and additionally permits the use of deadly force without retreat to prevent the commission of a forcible felony (ss 7-1, 7-2 and 7-3 of the Illinois Criminal Code of 1961). So do Kentucky (§503.080 of the Kentucky Revised Statutes) and a few other American states. These are called 'stand your ground' laws and the rhetoric around many of them refers to the honour in not retreating in the face of criminal activity. In German law too, the traditional principle is that 'right must never yield to wrong' and therefore there is no requirement for a person to retreat in the face of a wrongful threat. This rule is moderated under special conditions by certain socio-ethical constraints requiring restraint, and possibly also a limited retreat, when the aggressor is not culpable or when the defender has given rise to the need for self-defence through her own unlawful acts. See in this connection GP Fletcher, *Rethinking Criminal Law* (Boston, Little Brown & Company, 1978) 865; M Kremnitzer, 'Proportionality and the Psychotic Aggressor: Another View' (1983) 18 *Israel Law Review* 178, 207; and A Eser, 'Justification and Excuse' (1976) 24 *American Journal of Comparative Law* 621, 632.

[9] Criminal Justice and Immigration Act 2008, s 76(6A). This was also the common law rule. See *R v Julien* [1969] 1 WLR 839; *R v Bird* (1985) 81 Cr App R 110; *Duffy v Chief Constable* [2007] EWHC 3169 (Admin).

[10] *McBrearty v HM Advocate* 1999 SLT 1333.

here, I find that explanation uninteresting. Instead, although I cannot defend any particular stipulation of the monopoly of force as the 'correct' one in this study, I will assume a moral liberal state with the stipulation described in section 3.3.2 and will describe the rule on retreat that would operate in such a state. In such a state, when the force that D is contemplating using would be presumptively criminal, D would only be permitted to use it subject to compliance with both the Requirement consideration and the Derivative Force consideration. Recall that in section 3.3.2, I had assigned the term 'Requirement' to the set of general preconditions for legitimate access to the private use of force in a state with a monopoly of force. These included the condition that the proposed use of force be directed against a threat to a right and the condition that recourse to the state's protection be unavailable. I had also used the term 'Derivative Force' to refer to the set of constraints on the private use of force that derive from, and mirror, the considerations that constrain the use of force by the state itself. With this background stipulation in place, we can examine whether, and to what extent, there is a 'duty to retreat'.

The first observation that must be made is that although theorists generally talk about the 'duty to retreat', what is being referred to, is not a duty at all. No jurisdiction imposes upon its subjects an imperative Hohfeldian duty to retreat; instead, where an actor uses defensive force instead of retreating to safety, some states withhold from her a rationale-based defence to the charge arising from the wilful use of that force.[11] Although this technical observation will be important as the argument unfolds, I will continue to use the term 'duty to retreat' here, because it is the familiar way of referring to the guidance favouring retreat. I will, however, use scare quotes with the term to emphasise that it is, in fact, a misnomer.

The principle traditionally identified as the basis for the 'duty to retreat' is necessity.[12] Necessity in this context is different from the defence described in Chapter 7. In this context, as generally used in academic discourse, the term 'necessity' refers to a combination of the constraints on the legitimate access to force that I call Requirement and parsimoniousness—the principle that only the minimum effective force must be used.[13] The argument from necessity is as follows: force

---

[11] B Sangero, *Self-Defence in Criminal Law* (Oxford, Hart Publishing, 2006), 195 picks up on this point. Unfortunately, he dismisses it as being insignificant, because he says that attacked people rarely opt to suffer the attack instead of retreating.

[12] JH Beale, 'Retreat from a Murderous Assault' (1903) 16 *Harvard Law Review* 567, 572–74; AJ Ashworth, 'Self-Defence and the Right to Life' (1975) 34 *Cambridge Law Journal* 282, 284, 293; AJ Ashworth, *Principles of Criminal Law* (Oxford, Oxford University Press, 2009) 120–24; F Leverick, 'Defending Self-Defence' (2007) 27 *OJLS* 563, 576–77; F Leverick, *Killing in Self-Defence* (Oxford, Oxford University Press, 2006) 69–86; Sangero, *Self-Defence* 193; Model Penal Code, §3.04(2)(b)(ii).

[13] See, for instance, Ashworth, 'Self-Defence' 284–85; Kremnitzer, 'Proportionality' 178–79; PH Robinson, *Criminal Law Defenses Volume 2* (Minnesota, West Publishing Co, 1984) 77; Sangero, *Self-Defence* 144, 151–52. Clubbing Requirement and parsimoniousness together has its appeal. For instance, just as one may say that the use of force is unnecessary if the threat can be averted by seeking state protection or retreat, we may say that the use of a particular amount of force is unnecessary if less force would have sufficed to repel the threat. But it may be due to the fact that the word 'necessary' (along with its variants) is flexible enough to apply to both these cases that valuable distinctions between these cases have been overlooked.

may be used in private defence provided that it is required and proportionate in the circumstances. Where the threat to a right can be avoided by retreat, the use of force is not necessary to protect that right.[14] Hence, if T threatens D's right and D can protect this right by retreating, then D does not legitimately need access to the use of force to defend the right.

Sangero challenges the identification of necessity (ie, Requirement + parsimoniousness) as the basis of the 'duty to retreat'. According to him, the duty stems instead from the proportionality constraint that restricts the amount of force that may be used in self-defence. Sangero points out that Beale's derivation of the 'duty to retreat' solely from necessity causes him to adopt the intuitively anomalous position that D must retreat from T if T intends to kill D, but may hold her ground and use defensive force—even deadly force—if T intends to rob D.[15] He further argues that although there is a general consensus that retreat is not required as an alternative to the use of moderate defensive force, a rule of retreat founded on Requirement or necessity may impose a 'duty to retreat' even in such cases.[16]

Sangero's distaste for Beale's conclusions is understandable, but he draws the wrong conclusions from it. Beale's suggestion that D must retreat from T's murderous assault, but can use deadly force to thwart T's attempt to steal is intuitively odd; however, it is odd not because the rule on retreat cannot derive from Requirement, but rather because Beale does not apply any proportionality constraint on the amount of force permissible. As Ashworth explains:

> An individual ought if possible to withdraw in the face of a threatened attack precisely because he is able to do so and therefore the use of force is not necessary for self-protection. But where property is threatened and that property cannot easily be moved, it is *ex hypothesi* necessary for the individual to stand his ground if he is to protect the property at all. How much force is reasonable in defence of particular property is the question of principle which then arises, and surely far less force is justifiable to protect property than to protect life or limb. A criminal whose offence merely concerns property has a stronger claim to retain his right to life and physical security than one whose endeavour involves violence.[17]

As regards Sangero's claim that the general consensus is that different rules apply in respect of lethal and non-lethal defensive force, this view, to the extent that it is held, probably derives from the special status of the right to life within Anglo-American and ECHR doctrinal jurisprudence, which necessitates special protection for an aggressor's life as compared to her other rights.[18] The distinction

---

[14] Ashworth, 'Self-Defence' 284–85; Sangero, *Self-Defence* 193–94.

[15] Sangero, *Self-Defence* 193–95. See also Beale, 'Retreat from a Murderous Assault' 572–74.

[16] Sangero, *Self-Defence* 193, 195. See also AP Simester, JR Spencer et al, *Simester and Sullivan's Criminal Law: Theory and Doctrine* (Oxford, Hart Publishing, 2016) 820–21, which points out that as a matter of doctrine, English law has different rules in respect of lethal and non-lethal defensive force.

[17] Ashworth, 'Self-Defence' 303.

[18] Sangero, *Self-Defence* 198–202 surveys the Anglo-American law on this point and reaches compatible conclusions. See also Simester, Spencer et al, *Simester and Sullivan's Criminal Law* 820–21.

between the rules applied may well have a strong doctrinal foundation,[19] but it is a mistake for Sangero to assume that it necessarily evidences the underlying philosophical principles behind the 'duty to retreat'. Although it is correct that having different rules in respect of lethal and non-lethal defensive force is not compatible with a 'duty to retreat' that derives from the necessity constraint on defensive force, Sangero's conclusion that the 'duty to retreat' is therefore not founded in the necessity constraint (or any part of it) is incorrect. There are no grounds for believing that the distinction between the rules in respect of lethal and non-lethal defensive force has its basis in philosophical principle, so it is at least possible that the dissonance Sangero identifies indicates that the distinction, rather than the principle, is philosophically incongruous.

Nevertheless, since Sangero's is the most detailed recent model of the 'duty to retreat', we may consider it on its own terms and use it as a platform upon which to construct a model of the 'duty to retreat' for the purposes of this study. Sangero draws up two tables in which he compares, first, the interests that compete in cases in which safe retreat is an option and, second, the competing interests in cases in which safe retreat is not an option. In cases where retreat is impossible, he argues that considerations such as the life (or, where the threat is a threat of injury, the interest in not being injured) of the person attacked, the social-legal order, the autonomy of the person attacked and the aggressor's guilt (Sangero does not treat actions taken to defend against innocent threats as instances of self-defence, preferring instead to treat them as instances of a separate necessity defence) favour the use of defensive force. However, the attacker's life (or where the defensive force required to repel the threat would be non-lethal, the attacker's interest in not being injured) and, where deadly force is needed to repel a non-lethal threat, the social-legal order operate against the use of force. Where retreat is possible, in the enumeration of the factors that favour the use of force, the attacked person's life/interest in not being injured is replaced by her interest in not being in danger, and her honour. Using the proportionality calculation that these tables represent, Sangero reaches conclusions about when the use of defensive force is appropriate.[20]

The more interesting table at this stage is the one relating to defensive force where retreat is possible. The fundamental flaw in Sangero's model is exposed in this statement that he makes:

> My opinion is that despite the possibility of safe retreat, defensive force is necessary, and in contrast to the accepted argument, the requirement of necessity is actually fulfilled. However, although *the interests necessitating defence do not include the life of the person attacked and his bodily integrity*—since these can be saved by means of a retreat—*they do*

---

[19] Admittedly, doctrinal law is influenced by philosophical principle, but because it is also influenced by a plethora of other factors, such as political will and the prevalent social mores, it is an unreliable guide to the philosophical principle underlying a legal norm. As is probably evident by now from the methods employed in this study, I prefer not to rely solely on doctrinal law to make points of philosophical principle.
[20] Sangero, *Self-Defence* 208–15.

include less central interests: the defence of the social-legal order, the freedom of action of the attacked person, and his honour. Consequently, the real question is no longer a question of necessity, but rather a question of proportionality: *whether the use of deadly defensive force for the defence of the social-legal order, freedom of action of the attacked person and his honour* meet the conditions of the proportionality requirement.[21] (Emphasis added)

Let us call the attacker T and the person contemplating retreat or the use of defensive force D. Let's say that T's attack is directed at a set of D's rights—'α'. In the extract above, Sangero treats D's life or bodily integrity as α, and Sangero takes himself to be explaining the scope of D's 'duty to retreat' from the threat to α. However, where it is possible to safely retreat from the threat to α, Sangero completely drops α from the proportionality calculation.[22] In its stead, he treats 'less central' interests like 'the defence of the social-legal order, the freedom of action of the attacked person, and his honour' as lending weight to D's claim to use defensive force. If we refer to these less central interests collectively as 'β', then Sangero is effectively asserting that D is entitled to β and that although T's threat is primarily aimed at α, she is simultaneously also threatening β. Since retreat from α is an option, Sangero excludes considerations arising from α and instead evaluates whether there is any proportionate way for D to protect β. If a non-disproportionate option exists, then D is permitted to stand her ground and defend β, but if no such option exists, D is directed[23] to submit to the loss of β. This is all very well, but it is surely misleading to describe this analysis as an analysis of the duty to retreat from a threat to α, and it is equally misleading to describe the 'stand your ground' guidance last recounted as guidance that it is unnecessary to retreat from a threat to α. By dropping α from the proportionality calculus, Sangero all but concedes the existence of a 'duty to retreat' from a threat to α because the defence of α does not require the use of force, while arguing that, nevertheless, β cannot be protected by retreat, and so force is needed to protect β. He then considers how much force would be proportionate in defending β. Ultimately, therefore, even on Sangero's view, the 'duty to retreat' depends on whether the use of force is *required* to protect either α or β, and with β being defined such that it cannot be protected by retreat, force is always required to protect it. It only remains to determine how much defensive force would be proportionate in order to defend β. Where no non-disproportionate defensive response to a threat to β exists,[24]

---

[21] ibid 194.

[22] Sangero might respond that the identity of the rights denoted by α would influence other factors that remain relevant, such as how serious T's threat to D's honour and to the social-legal order is, and how much guilt T carries. However, as I will argue, the legitimacy of these other factors in the proportionality calculus is itself less than certain.

[23] Like the direction in the 'duty to retreat', this direction is also a misnomer. There is no Hohfeldian 'duty to submit', just a disentitlement to a rationale-based defence to the charges resulting from the use of force if one does not submit. This disentitlement flows from the fact that even the parsimonious application of effective force would be disproportionate to the threat to β and therefore would not be justified.

[24] Sangero does contemplate such situations. See case 3 in respect of his Table 2(B) in Sangero, *Self-Defence* 208–09 and also his discussion of what is essentially the 'duty to submit' (at 215–17).

Sangero's guidance to D is more accurately transcribed as 'submit to the loss of β (and invoke state mechanisms for later redress)' than 'retreat from the threat to α'. When there is a proportionate defensive response to a threat to β,[25] Sangero's advice to D is more accurately transcribed as 'you may stand your ground and defend yourself against the threat to β' rather than 'you may stand your ground and defend yourself against the threat to α (or, α and β)'.

This demonstrates the importance of distinguishing the Requirement for defensive force from the proportionality of the contemplated force. Doing so gives due recognition to the primacy of the state in enforcing the law. It is for this reason that an explanation of the 'duty to retreat' in terms of Requirement (rather than proportionality) provides more plausible guidance. The 'duty to retreat' can be understood as arising when the threat posed to a right is inadequate to make a resort to force 'required', either because state protection is available or because the threat may be avoided without force. However, even when force is required to protect the right (that is, when there is no 'duty to retreat'), its use may not be justified if the amount of force required would be disproportionate to the threat.[26] The guidance generated in such cases is best labelled as guidance that it is more appropriate to submit to the threat.

If the duty to retreat does flow from the Requirement constraint, then the categorical distinction made in doctrinal law between the 'duty to retreat' in cases involving lethal and non-lethal defensive force cannot be explained on the basis of underlying philosophical principle. The severity of the most parsimonious (yet effective) defensive response to a threat has nothing to do with whether there is any way to avert the threat without using private force at all. Once it is established that force is required inasmuch as there is no way to protect the rights threatened without using private force, the determination of the amount of force permitted can (in philosophical principle) be dealt with under the same set of rules in relation to proportionality, irrespective of whether the most parsimonious effective response involves lethal force. Obviously, these rules would require a much higher threshold of proportionality to be met in order to justify the use of lethal force.

Even if we accept Sangero's model for what it really is—a theory of the proportionality analysis that D must undertake when considering her options when faced with a threat to β—there are problems with it. First, β may not always be worth as much as Sangero assumes that it is. In particular, it is a mistake to assume that the freedom of action of the attacked person is always a valid consideration. A person's freedom to act in a certain way may be a Hohfeldian liberty, or a Hohfeldian power or a Hohfeldian right. At least insofar as the 'freedom' may simply be a Hohfeldian liberty—the mere absence of any normative guidance against adopting the course of action—it seems doubtful that an individual can legitimately demand and receive state sanction to use force to secure the continued existence of a norm

---

[25] And, of course, does not involve submitting to the loss of α.

[26] I assume here that an existential justification cannot be invoked, since considerations of proportionality, or even access to state protection, have no application to those cases in my model.

vacuum. At the very least, Sangero ought to have made some normative argument in support of his conflation of the various types of 'freedoms' of action.

Second, Sangero's inclusion of T's guilt as a valid consideration is premised on his insistence that self-defence is available only against a culpable attacker.[27] This view is controversial, but even if it were correct, in his theory Sangero uses guilt as a purely binary factor. T's guilt in threatening D's interests indents the value of T's interests, such that when D's defensive actions affect T's interests, provided that T's interests are of a magnitude comparable to the interests threatened, D's actions fall within the purview of private defence. In the absence of guilt on the part of T, D may at best claim a necessity defence.[28] As such, it is a factor that qualifies a person as an aggressor rather than a cumulative factor in the proportionality calculus. To convert it into a factor that could play a meaningful role in a proportionality calculus, Sangero would have to treat guilt as a scalar factor, and that would bring it uncomfortably close to unfairly duplicating the work already done by the consideration of the harm to the social-legal order caused by the attacker's threat to β.[29] In any event, as is clear from sections 3.1 and 3.2.1, I argue that self-defence is available against even an innocent aggressor, provided that she authors the threat. Hence, the 'guilt' consideration is (at least) incompatible with the model of justification that I set out.

Third, in relation to the maintenance of the social-legal order, for Sangero this is *always* a factor in favour of the use of defensive force, because he insists that private defence is available only against a culpable aggressor. In Sangero's theory, a non-culpable aggressor does not threaten the social-legal order.[30] In passing, we may note that in a more secular model, which also explains the use of defensive force against non-culpable aggressors, the maintenance of the social-legal order may still be included as a possibly relevant factor, to be considered only if it applied on the facts. Sangero refers to the defence of prevention of crime as evidence that the protection of the social-legal order is an independent reason for the state to delegate force. For him, a person using defensive force against a culpable aggressor performs a 'policing action' because 'if the police were present at the time of the event, they would [also] have acted [in the same] way'. Moreover, the use of defensive force in these circumstances deters offenders, prevents offences and reassures subjects.[31]

Now Sangero treats self-defence as a justification and not an excuse. Therefore, he must believe that a person acting in self-defence acts non-criminally and is

---

[27] Sangero, *Self-Defence* 60.
[28] ibid 40–60.
[29] See in this connection the admission that Sangero (ibid 71) makes that for him, the weight attributable to the social-legal order stands in direct proportion to the weight of the interest endangered and to the guilt of the aggressor. Here Sangero uses the guilt of the aggressor as a scalar factor and determines the weight carried by the interest in maintaining the social-legal order by reference to it.
[30] ibid 55–56, 68–69.
[31] ibid 67–68.

within her rights—she does not violate the criminal law's underlying system of conduct norms and subsequently seek to be excused from criminal liability. If so, then Sangero needs to explain why he believes that a private individual should be generally empowered ex ante to perform police functions, deter crime, prevent offences or reassure other subjects. The maintenance of the social-legal order is not, at least in the first instance, an individual's responsibility—it is the responsibility of the state.[32] Modern states tend to characterise a private individual who takes on these functions as a vigilante and not an upstanding citizen.[33] Sangero's reliance on the defence of prevention of crime also needs closer attention. It is true that many modern states accept that an individual may take on the role of the state in the maintenance of the social-legal order when the state is unavailable, but this concession is limited. The individual may step in for the state only in respect of culpable threats to elements of the social-legal order that are considered to be core or foundational. For example, in England and Wales, section 3 of the Criminal Law Act 1967 allows an individual to use reasonable force in order to effect or assist an arrest or to prevent crime. However, section 24A of the Police and Criminal Evidence Act 1984 makes it clear that the power of private arrest may be exercised only in respect of indictable offences. Hence, at least in the context of the use of force to make an arrest, an individual's interest in the social-legal order is relevant only in respect of serious (and therefore indictable) crimes. The 'indictable crimes' restriction is essentially a proxy to identify crimes that present a threat to the more important elements of the social-legal order. Although there is no similar explicit statutory restriction limiting the use of force in order to prevent crime, this power too flows from the same underlying interest in the maintenance of the social-legal order. Therefore, it would be entirely appropriate for the English courts to adopt a similarly restricted view of the sorts of threats to the social-legal order that entitle an individual to use force to prevent crime. Moreover, given that the courts have hitherto had a very conservative attitude towards the prevention of crime defence,[34] this seems very probable indeed. So, for instance, it seems exceedingly

---

[32] Sangero (ibid 212) acknowledges this fact and therefore downplays the importance of this consideration, at least in his textual discussion.

[33] See in this context the English House of Lords judgment in *R v Jones (Margaret)* [2007] 1 AC 136, which in the context of s 3 of the Criminal Law Act 1967 clarified (at 176) in no uncertain terms that although the said section seems on its face to be a vigilante's charter (in that it allows a person to use reasonable force to prevent a crime or arrest offenders or suspected offenders), that is not in fact the case, and vigilantism is not to be tolerated: 'The right of the citizen to use force on his own initiative is ... more circumscribed when he is not defending his own person or property but simply wishes to see the law enforced in the interests of the community at large. The law will not tolerate vigilantes. If the citizen cannot get the courts to order the law enforcement authorities to act ... then he must use democratic methods to persuade the government or legislature to intervene.'

[34] As evidenced by the aforementioned judgment in *R v Jones (Margaret)* [2007] 1 AC 136 and in cases like *R v Attwater* [2010] EWCA Crim 2399 and *R v Jackson (Kenneth)* [1985] RTR 257, where the courts took a restrictive view of when certain driving offences were completed, such that the defence of prevention of crime was rendered unavailable to persons who intervened after the technical completion of the offence to apprehend the allegedly errant drivers.

unlikely that a court would grant that the interest in maintaining the social-legal order justifies the use of any private force at all in order to prevent minor and non-victimising offences such as speeding down an empty road, crossing a red light at a deserted crossing, or parking offences.[35] If so, then Sangero's unqualified acceptance of the relevance of the maintenance of the social-legal order to any proportionality calculation is suspect.

Finally, in the sense that Sangero uses the term, the 'honour' of the person attacked refers to her right to 'save face' or not to appear a coward. He says that honour is only a secondary consideration and appears to downplay its importance in his textual discussion,[36] but nonetheless treats it as a valid philosophical consideration in his tables. Such a consideration is only universally relevant if there is a (non-posited) right to 'honour'. However, Sangero cites no credible authority for the proposition that there is a right to 'honour' that is natural in the sense that it flows from legal or moral principle. The authorities he cites either unhelpfully treat the alleged right as self-evident[37] or support him only insofar as he downplays the importance of 'honour'.[38] Nevertheless, Sangero's assertion on the right to 'honour' is supported by the rhetoric used to justify 'stand your ground' rules in the (primarily American) jurisdictions that have them. For 'a true man who is without fault', it is declaimed, the notion of beating a retreat in the face of an assault is 'odious to the American ego', amounts to 'cowardice'[39] and should therefore not be required by the law. Assuming that the monopoly of force in place in these jurisdictions is as stipulated here, it would appear that they recognise a natural right to 'honour'. So, if T attacks D and D can retreat to safety, T poses a threat to D's life and to various other less central interests, including her 'honour'. The threat to D's life can be averted by retreat, but the threat to D's secondary interests (including her 'honour') cannot. Hence, force is required in order to protect these secondary claims. The next question is whether the use of force would be a proportionate response to this limited unavertable threat and, apparently, jurisdictions with 'stand your ground' laws consider it entirely proportionate to use force—even lethal force—to defend secondary interests such as one's 'honour'.

---

[35] Witness, for instance, the recent banning in England and Wales of the practice of private individuals clamping the wheels of vehicles parked without permission on private land, under s 54 of the Protection of Freedoms Act 2012.

[36] Sangero, *Self-Defence* 196.

[37] See, for instance, Kremnitzer, 'Proportionality' 188.

[38] See, for instance, RM Perkins, 'Self-Defense Re-examined' (1954) 1 *UCLA Law Review* 133, 160.

[39] M Jaffe 'Up in Arms over Florida's New "Stand your Ground" Law' (2005) 30 *Nova Law Review* 155, 160–61; A Wells, 'Home on the Gun Range: Discussing Whether Kansas's New Stand Your Ground Statute Will Protect Gun Owners Who Use Disproportionate Force in Self-Defense' (2008) 56 *Kansas Law Review* 983, 988; PL Ross, 'The Transmogrification of Self-Defense by National Rifle Association-Inspired Statutes' (2007) 35 *Southern University Law Review* 1, 10–12; O Bakircioglu, 'The Contours of the Right to Self-Defence: Is the Requirement of Imminence Merely a Translator for the Concept of Necessity?' (2008) 72 *Journal of Criminal Law* 131, 154. Contrast this with French law, under which it is clear that an attack on a person's honour will not ground a defence. See A Reed, M Bohlander et al (eds), *Defences in Criminal Law: Domestic and Comparative Perspectives* (Farnham, Ashgate, 2014) 215; C Elliott, *French Criminal Law* (London, Routledge, 2011) 110.

I for one do not think that humans self-evidently possess any natural right not to be viewed by others as possessing any particular character traits, including that of cowardice. Moreover, the liveliness of the legal and political debates over 'stand your ground' laws suggests that the claimed entitlement is far from being universally accepted as self-evident. Apart from rhetorical invocations of the American ego, no argument in favour of any natural right not to appear a coward emerges from the jurisdictions that apply 'stand your ground' rules and (thankfully) not everyone—probably not even most Americans—has that sort of ego to massage. This is not to say that it is beyond the state's power to posit a right to honour (or some variant thereof) for its citizens, and to the extent that a state does that, of course its subjects would have a right to honour. Perhaps it may create special laws to deal with bullying or with racist chants at football matches, and to the extent that it does, it grants its subjects a right not to be viewed in a certain way or to be victimised for possessing certain traits. But I doubt that there is any non-posited right not to be viewed as a coward. Even if such a right to 'honour' did exist, it is difficult to believe that one could use force, especially lethal force, to defend it.

Statman, however, offers an argument for precisely that—a general non-legislated right to honour that may be defended using lethal force. His argument builds on what he calls the 'success condition' for the private use of defensive force. He convincingly argues that the parsimoniousness constraint imports a requirement that defensive force can only be used if it has some prospect of success. Essentially, Statman's position is that D is not permitted or authorised to use defensive force if she cannot thereby avert the threat, because private force used in those circumstances would pointlessly add to the existing breaches of the monopoly of force. If so, then Statman says that we need to explain our intuitive belief that when D's life is unjustly threatened by several attackers, she is legally entitled to use lethal defensive force against as many of the attackers as possible, even if she is so outnumbered that she has no realistic prospect of saving her life by the use of that defensive force.[40] To that end, Statman tentatively proposes that the notion that force—even lethal force—can be used to defend one's honour is the most plausible (though admittedly not flawless) explanation available.

The easy response to Statman, within the parameters of this study, is that actions done in the exercise of the existential justification are outside the purview of moral

---

[40] D Statman, 'On the Success Condition for Legitimate Self-Defense' (2008) 118 *Ethics* 659. Statman also gives the example of D who can use lethal force against only two of a group of five persons bent on raping her (at 664). Assuming that even if D used such force, the rest of her attackers would not be dissuaded, Statman treats this as an instance in which the success condition would require that D not use force, since she would not be able to avoid being raped. This example is problematic. The use of lethal force may well reduce the number of instances of rape and it will definitely reduce the number of different people who rape D. To that extent, D's use of defensive force would succeed in averting some of the threats she faces. It would be a very strange iteration of the success condition that requires that D submit to multiple instances of rape because she cannot avoid being raped at least once. See also in this context D Rodin, 'Justifying Harm' (2011) 122 *Ethics* 74, 92–93. For this reason, I ignore this example and focus on Statman's stronger examples.

blame, and that explains our intuition that D is entitled to use force to defend herself against an attack on her life even if her efforts are obviously an exercise in futility. But perhaps Statman's puzzle still holds if we rephrase it in terms of posited rights. Moreover, doing so would have the added advantage of making it plausible to think of the person using defensive force in a lost cause being subsequently tried for her actions. Imagine therefore that T has appropriated D's jewellery and is about to escape by driving his (T's) car through a gated exit. D, who is at the gate, sees that T's car has already gathered so much speed that even if D shuts the gate, the car will burst through it and escape, albeit with some dents and perhaps a broken headlight. Is D legally entitled to shut the gate? Statman says that we would intuitively believe so. I accept that most people would think it unlikely that D would be punished for shutting the gate. However, for a large proportion of those people, this intuitive conclusion will be attributable, at least in part, to how unlikely it is that T (or an observer) would complain to the police about the damage to T's car on these facts. Others might reach the same intuitive conclusion because they think that even if D was tried for the damage to T's car, she would be excused from a conviction or from punishment. But in excusing D, we do not assert that she acted permissibly. Therefore, we do not support the conclusion that Statman draws. Of course, there may still be those who do believe that D is actually permitted to slam the gate shut. However, I doubt that the intuitive support for that proposition is anywhere near as pervasive as Statman imagines it is. Because I do not think that a moral state would authorise the private use of force for extracting vengeance, I see no reason why it should give D the authority to slam the gate shut on these facts. Of course, it may still excuse D for having done so. On this view of the matter, Statman's puzzle disappears, as does any need to posit a contrived solution depending on the existence of a supposed right to 'honour'.

The upshot of this discussion is that I do not agree with Sangero that the attacked person's 'honour' is a valid consideration when deciding whether there is any duty to retreat from a threat to α or, indeed, whether there is any duty to submit to a threat to β. Like Ashworth,[41] I would contend that when a threat to α may be averted by retreat, the use of force to protect α is illegitimate, even though retreat might cause some loss of face or harm D's secondary interests (ie, β). However, proportionate force may be used to protect such of D's genuine secondary interests as are threatened and as cannot be averted by retreat.

8.2.1 The Rule on Retreat

Although Sangero's analysis is flawed, it is nevertheless useful. For one, the errors in Sangero's analysis of the 'duty to retreat' illustrate the importance of distinguishing between the preconditions for in-principle access to force and subsequent

---

[41] Ashworth, 'Self-Defence' 290, 303.

constraints upon the manner in which this force may then be deployed. The conditions that comprise the Derivative Force consideration are in principle also applicable to the state in its own use of force; this is not the case for the conditions that comprise the Requirement consideration. This is why one can plausibly argue that neither the state nor an individual should be permitted to use disproportionate or excessive force to quell a threat. However, when faced with a threat to a subject's right, the state is not required to retreat,[42] although the subject concerned might well be so required. The 'duty to retreat' cannot flow from the Derivative Force consideration since it does not (even in principle) apply equally to the state and the individual; it must flow instead from the Requirement consideration. Unreflectively, Sangero applies this very idea in excluding the weight of rights that can be protected by retreat from his proportionality calculus. My own approach to the question of retreat, which flows straightforwardly from the same idea, is this: a right that can be protected by seeking state protection or by retreat does not contribute any weight in favour of a claim to stand one's ground.[43] Similarly, a threat to a core element of the social-legal order that can be averted or reduced to a threat to a non-core element thereof without resorting to the private use of force contributes no weight to a claim to stand one's ground. Thus, the Requirement consideration is not satisfied in respect of a right under threat when it may be safeguarded through state intervention or by less harmful, non-forceful means, such as retreat.

But on this model, exactly when is the Requirement consideration satisfied? Is it when the materialisation of the threat is immediate or when it is unavoidable? To explain the sense in which I employ these terms, I will use a non-legal analogy. When games between excellent chess players end decisively, they often end with one player resigning rather than being checkmated. In situations like these, the defeated player (let's call her Karpova) resigns because she sees an unavoidable checkmate several moves down the line. She may realise, for instance, that her opponent has mobilised her pieces well and has commenced an attack in which, if her opponent plays wisely, she will checkmate Karpova in five moves, and there is nothing that Karpova can do to stave off the checkmate. Karpova believes that her opponent is good enough to see this sequence of moves too, and so she decides that since the checkmate is unavoidable, she might as well resign. Alternatively, Karpova may play on in the hope that her opponent will blunder. If she does so, then it is only when her opponent reaches out to move the piece that delivers the coup de grace that checkmate is immediate. If resigning in chess is seen as an (admittedly strained) metaphor for getting in-principle access to defensive force,

---

[42] At least, not because of reasons to do with the state's monopoly of force. It might nevertheless be possible, depending on matters of state policy, for other considerations to operate in favour of retreat in special cases.

[43] See in this connection *Aznanag v CPS* (unreported) Queen's Bench Division (Administrative Court), 24 July 2015, in which the court upheld a magistrates' court's ruling that where D could have avoided a police officer's pushes by retreating, he was not entitled to grab the officer's wrist in 'self-defence'.

then should the state allow Karpova to resign as soon as she sees an unavoidable checkmate or should it insist that she wait until checkmate is immediate?

Sangero seems to argue for a scalar version of immediacy, in which the more immediate the materialisation of the threat becomes, the more defensive force is available. This is because he collapses the preconditions for access to force and its deployment into a single proportionality analysis, in which the maintenance of the (entire) social-legal order is a factor.[44] The social-legal order requires the consideration of the attacker's rights as well as the rights of the person attacked, and so Sangero's loyalties veer away from unavoidability (which facilitates earlier access to force and therefore less protection for the attacker) and towards immediacy (which delays access to force, thereby giving additional protection to the attacker). Leverick argues for a different concept that is closer to unavoidability,[45] but appears not to notice that this substantially differs from immediacy, either as Sangero uses the term[46] or as I do. Many other writers have weighed into this debate, using different terminology or the same terminology in slightly different senses.[47] As we have already seen, the rule on retreat in England and Wales seems to follow Sangero's model, relating D's access to force to the immediacy of the materialisation of the threat, but treating this immediacy as a scalar factor in a reasonableness analysis.[48] Scotland, on the other hand, insists on immediacy per se, inasmuch as it requires D to exhaust all reasonable avenues of retreat that do not enhance the risk she faces or prejudice the effectiveness of her defensive options.[49]

For our purposes, in order to determine whether it takes immediacy or unavoidability to cross the Requirement threshold, we need to identify the baseline situation that we aim to restore by authorising an exception to the state's monopoly of force. We know that this baseline situation is disturbed when D faces a threat. Thus, the absence of this threat would restore D to the baseline situation to which she is entitled. Therefore, D's baseline situation, insofar as it is relevant in this context, is the complete freedom from threats to herself or her rights. When T alters D's baseline situation by authoring a threat to D, D may use force, *if required*, to return to her baseline threat-free situation. D's use of force is required when there is no (non-forceful) way to completely nullify the threat, inasmuch as

---

[44] Sangero, *Self-Defence* 150–52, 155–56, 160–62. See also Leverick, *Killing in Self-Defence* 101, who traces the argument for immediacy to concern for the rights of the aggressor, which will be best protected by giving unpredictable chance factors such as unforeseen interruptions or a change of heart as much time as possible to end the threat without force.

[45] Leverick, *Killing in Self-Defence* 101–02.

[46] Leverick, 'Defending Self-Defence' 579.

[47] See, for instance, M Baron, 'Self-Defence: The Imminence Requirement' in L Green and B Leiter (eds), *Oxford Studies in Philosophy of Law: Volume 1* (Oxford, Oxford University Press, 2011) 228; KK Ferzan, 'Defending Imminence: From Battered Women to Iraq' (2004) 46 *Arizona Law Review* 213; and J Dressler, 'Battered Women Who Kill Their Sleeping Tormentors' in S Shute and AP Simester (eds), *Criminal Law Theory: Doctrines of the General Part* (Oxford, Oxford University Press, 2002).

[48] See n 9 above.

[49] See n 10 above.

state protection is unavailable and retreat is either impossible or will not nullify, but only postpone the materialisation of the threat. In other words, force is required when a threat is present and, without force, its materialisation would be unavoidable. Unavoidability satisfies the Requirement threshold and there is no need to wait for the materialisation of the threat to also become immediate before D is allowed in-principle access to force.

It is important to note that the unavoidability standard imports two distinct prerequisites for crossing the Requirement threshold: first, that the threat be a present one; and, second, that its materialisation be unavoidable (though not necessarily immediate). The former prerequisite has been largely neglected in academic discourse, which has instead focused on whether defensive force may be used when it gives D the best chance of averting an anticipated harm,[50] or only when T has unambiguously begun to perform the action that will harm D.[51] These two positions do not exhaust the possibilities. I have argued with my chess analogy that it is possible (i) for (what I call) a threat to present before T begins to perform the action that will actually harm D. Equally, it is possible that (ii) D's best chance of averting the anticipated harm may arise before there is a present threat of harm.[52] The standard for which I argue is a third position which would treat a threat as being present (and therefore potentially permit the use of defensive force in response to it) in (i), but not (ii),[53] because in (ii), the baseline situation to which D is entitled would not yet have been disturbed.

---

[50] Robinson, *Criminal Law Defenses* 78. See also Ferzan, 'Defending Imminence' 241–42, who recounts and critiques such an approach.

[51] Dressler, 'Battered Women' 272–75.

[52] Consider the famous Supreme Court of North Carolina case of *State v Norman* 378 SE 2d 8 (NC 1989). Here D had suffered almost 25 years of terrible physical and mental abuse from her husband T. She was too scared to press charges against T or to leave him because whenever she had tried leaving him, T had always found her and beaten her. T had also repeatedly threatened to kill her, as well as members of her family. One evening, when T had fallen into a drunken sleep after another session of violent abuse, D took a gun from her mother's house and shot T dead as he slept. Some commentators have suggested that on these facts, D seized her best chance to save herself from T's violence and impending deadly assault, because she would have been powerless to defend herself against T when T was awake and in the process of attacking her. Assuming that to be correct, this would be a case in which D's best chance of averting the anticipated harm arose before there was any present threat of harm. See in this connection WRP Kaufman, 'Self-Defense, Imminence, and the Battered Woman' (2007) 10 *New Criminal Law Review* 342, 346–48.

[53] Ferzan, 'Defending Imminence' 257–62 presents an argument along these lines, using different terminology. She argues that the imminence condition—roughly the equivalent of what I call immediacy—has conceptual purchase independently of its usefulness as evidence of the necessity of defensive force: it restricts the legitimate use of force only to responses to aggressions. In effect, she changes the imminence/immediacy condition to an aggression condition. See also in this connection Baron, 'Self-Defence' 254–55. I do not adopt Ferzan's 'aggression' proposal because it requires T to be culpable, and I think that D may also legitimately use defensive force against T when T authors a threat non-culpably. Thus, whether T is an infant who does not realise the significance of her actions or is a clumsy person who stumbles and falls towards D, it is possible to treat T as authoring a threat against D, and to permit D, subject to other conditions, to use force against T in self-defence. Note also that nothing in the assertion that D is not *permitted* to use force before she faces a present threat excludes the possibility that she may be excused from criminal liability for using force if she does do so.

The adoption of the unavoidability standard I describe then requires us to distinguish between an impending threat on the one hand and a present threat, the materialisation of which is unavoidable but not yet immediate, on the other. Because the baseline situation is only disturbed when D faces a present threat, there is occasion for D to seek access to force only in response to a present threat and not in response to an impending (but not yet present) threat. To some extent, in practical terms, the determination of when this threshold is crossed is bound to be a matter of judgment, with marginal cases being difficult to decide. However, conceptually there is a bright line separating a present threat from a future threat, and important consequences relating to the availability of defensive force turn on this distinction. I do not propose to suggest tests for making this distinction in this study—that would probably require a separate paper.[54] Nevertheless, I am confident that it is possible to make the in-principle distinction in the same way that it is possible to make the in-principle distinction between acts that are merely preparatory and attempts. A core instance of an impending threat can be distinguished fairly easily from a core instance of a present threat, the materialisation of which is unavoidable, but not yet immediate. Hence, if T, a racist, informs D, a black person, in a phone call that she (T) is coming to the marketplace, where D currently is, to kill D because D is black, T's threat to D's life is impending, but not present. Hence, at this stage, D is not pushed to respond to the 'threat' to her life in any way, including by going home to forestall it. This remains the case even if D would have no choice but to use lethal force to defend herself once T showed up on the scene.[55] On the other hand, when T starts aiming blows at D, the threat is a present one even if D knows that she can duck some or all of the blows aimed by T. At this stage, D is pushed to respond to T's threat, and if her contemplated response includes the use of force, she is required to consider retreat first.

Note that this analysis focuses entirely on the rights of D and not at all on the rights of T. This is entirely appropriate. At the Requirement threshold stage, there is no reason to insist that D be concerned with the rights of anyone else, since crossing that threshold allows D only in-principle access to force. It is not until D

---

[54] See Ferzan, 'Defending Imminence' 257–62 for one attempt along similar lines, with the slightly different concept of aggression. Ferzan uses the idea of aggression to cover almost, but not quite, the same ground as my 'present threat'. Ferzan also agrees that 'Prevention cannot be justified as [self-defence]' and therefore would also disallow the use of force to prevent an anticipated threat from being posed.

[55] But see L Alexander, 'Propter Honoris Respectum: A Unified Excuse of Preemptive Self-Protection' (2005) 74 *Notre Dame Law Review* 1475, 1479–80, who argues that D should go home because taking a life is not a proportional response to a threat to a few minutes or hours of liberty at the marketplace, even if it is proportional to a threat to D's life. I would respond by saying that even the threat to the few minutes or hours of liberty at the marketplace (presuming in favour of Alexander that it is a posited right to liberty and not merely a Hohfeldian liberty) has not yet arisen, and so D is not yet required to respond. At least some of the difficulty seems to lie in the ambiguity of the word 'threat', which is used in different senses to mean either (as I use it) a present threat or an illegitimate warning that a chain of events will be set into motion in the future, so as to precipitate unpleasant consequences (which is the sense in which I think Alexander uses it on this particular occasion).

deploys that force that she affects the rights of others. Only at that stage should she have to consider the rights of T. The difference at that stage arises because D's access to force, being derived from the state, is also subject to the same limitations that apply to the state. Those limitations are encapsulated in the Derivative Force consideration.[56]

8.2.2 The Rule on Submission

This view of the rule on retreat nicely complements the previous analysis of Sangero's theory, which had suggested that the minimal 'duty to submit' flows from a combination of the parsimoniousness and non-disproportionality constraints on the legitimate private use of force.[57] For the reasons stated previously, I would make several modifications to Sangero's model, and use the modified model to describe the minimum content of the rule on submission. This 'duty to submit' may be made more onerous by a state which legislates to further limit the amount of force it delegates to an individual, but it cannot be relaxed without becoming philosophically inconsistent with the state's claimed monopoly of force.

First, I would treat the attacked person's freedom of action as a relevant consideration only when the said 'freedom' was a Hohfeldian power or a Hohfeldian right. The recognition of an entitlement to defend a Hohfeldian liberty changes its nature from a Hohfeldian liberty to a Hohfeldian right or power. Yet norm vacuums continue to exist and, if so, then by definition they must not be legitimately defensible. I will illustrate this point using examples in section 8.2.3.

Second, for the reasons I mentioned previously, I would drop any automatic reference to a right to save face, whether it is characterised as honour or non-cowardice. If and when an overarching or limited right to honour is posited by the state, it would factor into the analysis in the same manner as any other right being threatened.

Third, I would drop Sangero's binary consideration of the aggressor's guilt and would make the analysis applicable even to an 'innocent aggressor'. The only role that this factor seemed to play in Sangero's proportionality calculus was to restrict

---

[56] This is why I think that both Sangero (*Self-Defence* 161) and Leverick (*Killing in Self-Defence* 76; 'Defending Self-Defence' 575–76) err in considering the aggressor's rights at the Requirement stage. If my analysis is correct, then there is no good reason to require D to extend the time for which she must suffer a present and operating threat. T's interests are irrelevant when considering the Requirement threshold, and so D need not bend over backwards to safeguard them by indulging the speculative possibility that T might suddenly decide to desist, or a *deus ex machina* may intervene.

[57] Note that parsimoniousness and non-disproportionality, being instances of the larger set of conditions comprising the Derivative Force consideration, also apply in other contexts in which an individual deploys force derived from the state. This is why, although it seems strange to think of them as giving rise to duties to 'submit' in those contexts, parsimoniousness and non-disproportionality also limit an individual's use of force to prevent a crime or to effect a citizen's arrest. See, for instance, in England and Wales, s 3 of the Criminal Law Act 1967.

his model to cases involving culpable aggressors so that each aggressor also threatens D's interest in the social-legal order. On the model of supervening defences that I propose, a justification may also be available to a person who repels a threat authored non-culpably. Therefore, Sangero's culpability qualification cannot be accommodated as a necessary condition within my model. Note that dropping this condition does not rule out the option of factoring in a threat to the social-legal order if it arose; it merely allows us to also address cases in which the aggression was not culpable.

Fourth, I would adopt a more nuanced understanding of the role that the maintenance of the social-legal order plays in a model of private defensive force. In support of Sangero's position, one may plausibly argue that the social-legal order performs a valuable coordination function and contributes to a sense of security amongst the public. Therefore, although the state is entrusted with the maintenance of the social-legal order, it does so for the benefit of its subjects, who retain some beneficial interest in the maintenance of the social-legal order. If so, then when T is culpable, the subjects' interest in the maintenance of the social-legal order is threatened and they ought to be entitled to defend it, using force if required. On this argument, the Requirement threshold will be met whenever state protection is unavailable, since retreat from a culpable aggressor never averts the threat to the social-legal order. Now although it is true that the subjects too have an interest in preserving the benefits of the coordinating role performed by the social-legal order, this argument makes the error of assuming that the subjects' interest in the maintenance of the social-legal order is coextensive with the state's interest. As pointed out in the previous section, modern states do not adopt that view and, indeed, it would be an implausible view to adopt. When the state is unavailable, individuals are permitted to use force to protect some elements of the social-legal order, but only once some threshold of seriousness has been crossed. This suggests that modern states recognise only a limited private interest in the maintenance of the social-legal order, such that only threats to core or foundational elements of the social-legal order are privately defensible. A threat to a core element of the social-legal order may well be averted by retreat, inasmuch as retreat might reduce the threat to the social-legal order to one involving non-core elements. If that happens, then the Requirement threshold for the defence of core elements of the social-legal order is not crossed and there is no in-principle access to force to protect the social-legal order. On the other hand, where such retreat is impossible and state protection is unavailable, the Requirement threshold for the use of force will be crossed. However, such a situation will almost inevitably coincide with some other, more directly victimising and unavertable threat, which would independently cross the Requirement threshold anyway. It is therefore unlikely that the threat to the private right to the maintenance of core elements of the social-legal order will make much of a contribution at the stage of overcoming the Requirement threshold. That said, it will contribute some weight in the subsequent Derivative Force analysis to determine how much force may be deployed once access to force is available in principle.

8.2.3 Applying the Rules on Retreat and Submission

To understand how the rules on retreat and submission translate into useful guidance, we need to consider a series of hypotheticals.[58] For the sake of simplicity, in each of the scenarios that follow, I will assume that state protection is unavailable and that all parties are fully aware of all the relevant facts.

In Case 1, D has parked in T's favourite, but not proprietary or officially designated, parking space. She is still in the driver's seat with the engine on, when T tells her that unless she moves the car, T will throw stones at it. T then picks up a stone and winds up to throw it. D can avert the stone in one of only two ways: she can either drive out of the way of the stone (and, in doing so, vacate the parking space); or she can put a bullet through T's throwing hand before T can release the stone. Even if we make the unlikely assumption that the latter course of action would not be a disproportionate response to the damage caused by a stone to the car, the appropriate response for D would still be to drive out of the parking space so as to avoid the threat to her car. Since it is possible for D to avert T's threat without resorting to force, the Requirement threshold for the use of force to protect D's car has not been crossed. Assuming for the moment that there are no other rights in play, D is not authorised to use any force against T whatsoever. Her best course of action would be to retreat and let T's comeuppance take the form of state sanction against her for her attempt or threat to damage D's car.

The obvious question that arises is: doesn't guiding D to move her car make a mockery of D's own freedom to park in that space? The answer is that it does not, partly because D's freedom to park in the space is a mere Hohfeldian liberty and partly because the guidance offered is not imperative guidance.[59] The guidance offered is not imperative, because despite the 'duty to retreat', D retains her Hohfeldian liberty to stand her ground. Doing so would not expose her to criminal liability. Hence, the choice about whether to stay or move remains hers. If she chooses to stand her ground, she will not be permitted to shoot at T's hand to defend her car, because that would not fall within the scope of any justificatory defence. However, if T did damage D's car, T could be held criminally responsible for that.

Quong would disagree, at least in the context of D's exercise of a Hohfeldian liberty to occupy a particular space. He argues that even if one has no positive normative claim to occupy a particular space, once one does occupy it, one gets at least a prima facie claim to remain in it.[60] He presents the example of Albert and Betty who are sitting in a public park, such that Betty is occupying the spot that has the best view of the lake. Albert would like to take over that space, but Quong

---

[58] I have explained the central ideas in this section in greater detail in M Dsouza, 'Retreat, Submission, and the Private Use of Force' (2015) 35 *OJLS* 727. What appears here is an adaptation of the examples referred to in that paper, focusing only on ideas relevant to this study.

[59] Sangero, *Self-Defence* 195 noticed the latter factor, but failed to appreciate its significance.

[60] J Quong, 'Killing in Self-Defense' (2009) 119 *Ethics* 507, 528–29.

argues that even if it were possible for Albert to move Betty without touching or otherwise harming or offending her, it is impermissible for him to do so. This suggests to him that Betty must have a presumptive claim-right to her location even though she is in a public park. This example is problematic for a few reasons. First, it is difficult to imagine any plausible scenario in which Albert could move Betty without touching her, harming her, offending her or tricking her, and in all those cases, it is likely that Betty's claim-right against being touched, harmed, offended or tricked does the normative work. Second, even if one could conceive of a way in which the scenario in the example could play out, this would not necessarily establish that Betty was wronged (and therefore that Betty must have had some claim-right, which was violated). It might equally show simply that Albert committed a (victimless) wrong. The state often legislates rules in order to perform its coordination functions, and a person violating these rules might cause some diffuse damage to the overall system of coordination without wronging any individual. Such an offender commits a wrong without violating any individual's claim-right. A jaywalker on a deserted street commits such a wrong. This holds true even when some individual feels particularly aggrieved by the person violating the coordinating rule. Even when a driver has to slow down because of the jaywalker and therefore loses a few seconds, it is strange to say that the driver had a claim-right not to have had to slow down. A wrong therefore need not always imply the existence of an *individual* with a claim-right. The various other intuitions that Quong explains on the basis of his theoretical claim-right to the space one occupies[61] can similarly be explained on the basis of either more established claim-rights (such as the right to one's property or one's body) or on the basis of wrongs relatable to coordination rules and not rules flowing from a directly aggrieved individual's claim-rights. Insofar as Quong took on the burden of establishing, by a process of elimination, the existence of a general claim-right to the space one occupies, he therefore fails—he is unable to eliminate these alternative explanations for the intuitions he defends. Indeed, these alternative explanations are far more plausible, since they accord with the more established theoretical concept of a Hohfeldian liberty.

Notice that the 'guidance' offered in Case 1 above to D is not that she should avoid parking in the space; it is that she should avoid the stone by *vacating* the space. The former guidance would have been imperative guidance telling her not to do something she was normatively unrestrained from doing. Of course, the state has the authority to give such guidance, but if the guidance arose because of T's illegitimate threat, the state would effectively be legitimising T's threat, which would be inappropriate.[62] On the other hand, telling D that her only justified defensive response to T's threat is to avert it by moving her car out of the parking

---

[61] ibid 526–37.
[62] But see Alexander, 'Propter Honoris Respectum' 1479–80, who differs. In my opinion, a theory that acknowledges that retreat is a condition for private access to force rather than an imperative duty will accept that until a threat is present, D cannot seek private access to force and so cannot be put to the condition of retreat for access to it.

space is perfectly legitimate, even though D has no normative obligation not to remain in the space and even though in a perfect world doing so would not require her to choose between suffering damage to her car or prosecution for shooting T. When D chooses to take *any* defensive measure, she abandons one or more alternative courses of action on which she may have embarked without legal censure. Most of the unrestricted courses of action available to us are mutually exclusive, and the mere fact that the law does not intervene to neutralise a factor that makes choosing one of them less attractive does not make the law's 'guidance' illegitimate.

Now consider Case 2. Here, T warns D that she will damage D's car if D parks in a specified space. In Scenario 1, this space is simply an empty patch of unclaimed land. In Scenario 2, the space is a designated parking space in a public car park. What norm guidance in respect of the use of force would be available to D if she wanted to park in the specified space despite T's warning in both alternative scenarios?

In both scenarios, T's threat to D's Hohfeldian right (her car) is contingent upon D exercising a particular freedom—the freedom to park in the specified space. Prior to parking in that space, since there is no present threat to her car, D cannot justifiably use force to defend her car. Now in Scenario 1, the space is merely an unclaimed patch of land. Both T and D are free to park their respective cars in that space (or to use it as they please), but neither can make a normative claim to any right to park there. T and D therefore enjoy only a Hohfeldian liberty to park in the space. Since D has no special right to remain unrestrained from parking in the specified space, D cannot legitimately use force to protect her 'claim' to park there. D would therefore be advised not to use any force to protect her 'claim' to park in the specified space and, instead, to refer the matter to the state authorities. Of course, in the absence of any legitimate guidance against parking in that space, D may, without fear of legal censure, park there anyway. Should T then proceed to threaten D's car, she would then have to examine her options in the manner described while discussing Case 1.

But consider Scenario 2. Here again, both T and D are free to park their respective cars in the identified space, but this time, their respective freedoms are also backed by an additional posited right to park there (conditional of course on the space being vacant and on the payment of a parking fee). Both T and D have a conditional Hohfeldian right to park in the space, but no right to restrain each other from parking there should the other meet the conditions. When the state posits a special provision for an individual or section of the public, it can be understood to implicitly also empower the beneficiaries of this provision to protect it within the constraints of the law—it would usually be redundant to authoritatively reiterate the lack of authoritative guidance against doing something. T's warning then constitutes a threat to D's conditional right to park in the space, and if there is no way to avert this threat (say, by convincing T to withdraw the threat) or to avail of state protection, the use of force may be required to protect D's right to park there. Of course, D would still have to ensure that the force she uses satisfies both the parsimoniousness and non-disproportionality constraints. In this case, the interests threatened would be D's claim to park in the specified space (and *not* her Hohfeldian right to her car). This remains the case even if D actually parks in the space (assuming of course that D could still protect her car by moving it).[63] One might also try to argue that T's warning, given that it is apparently culpable, constitutes a threat to D's interests in the maintenance of the social-legal order, and so this should also carry some weight in determining the maximum amount of defensive force that would not be disproportionate. However, it seems unlikely that any state would take the view that a threat to a person's in-principle access to a parking space also constitutes the sort of threat to her interest in the social-legal order that she can repel using force. In other words, a rule-of-law state would be unlikely to see T's threatened conduct as a threat to a core element of the social-legal order. Hence, while state redress for T's threat to the social-legal order would still be appropriate, private redress would not.

Ashworth argues that where there is some time lag between D becoming aware of a future threat and the threat actually presenting itself, D ought to seek police protection or inform the police of the impending threat, failing which her use of defensive force would be tainted. This, Ashworth argues, would reduce the need for the private use of force.[64] Undoubtedly, it would. However, such a stipulation does not flow from any of the constraints on the use of force, because none of these constraints becomes applicable until an individual actually needs private access to force, ie, until the threat actually presents itself. The constraints on the private use of force are not imposed as part of a system of measures calculated to minimise the need for private recourse to force. Broadly speaking, there is already such a system, and it is the legal system in general. Nothing in the state's claim to a monopoly of force ipso facto requires an individual to take pre-emptive steps to prevent threats from presenting themselves—whether those steps be avoiding 'dangerous' places, not wearing 'provocative clothes' or informing the police of anticipated threats. This is not to say that it would not be wise or useful for a person to inform the police about anticipated threats. It is perfectly competent for the state to enact the rule that Ashworth suggests. However, such a rule is not a part of the general 'duty to retreat' and, without any expressly posited rule to that effect, the failure to take such pre-emptive action should not defeat a person's subsequent claim to justification in using defensive force.

Now let us consider a different example. In Case 3, D is standing 10 feet from the edge of a high cliff. T picks up a stone to throw at D. D can avoid being hit in one

---

[63] Such a scenario would be Case 1, except that the parking space would be a designated space in a public lot. D would then be entitled to remain in place and use force not disproportionate to the threat to her right to park there (*not* the threat to her car) to defend herself against T's threat. So, for instance, if D knows that T cannot stand very loud music, she would have been entitled to remain in place and drive T away by playing some music very loudly on her car's music system. But if that did not work, I doubt that she would have been entitled to use physical force against T. D's most favourable legal option would then be to protect her car by vacating the space.

[64] Ashworth, 'Self-Defence' 295–96. *cf* Alexander, 'Propter Honoris Respectum' 1479–80, who recommends retreat in such cases.

of two ways: she can either sidestep the stone by moving one foot closer to the cliff; or she can pre-emptively throw a stone at T's hand, thereby injuring T and preventing her from throwing the stone. Purely to avoid cluttering up the argument with too many variables, let us assume that T's threats to D's right to avoid being hurt and her liberty to remain in place do not constitute threats to D's interest in the maintenance of the social-legal order.[65] In Scenario 1, T has only one stone. In Scenario 2, T has 11 stones and D does not have the option of retracing her steps once she has moved.

In Scenario 1, as will be clear from the foregoing discussion, my opinion is that the only non-criminal way in which D can avoid being hit by the stone is to move one foot closer to the cliff. Some commentators refer to the English Court of Appeals decision in *Redmond-Bate v DPP*[66] and suggest that in English law, in cases falling short of fatal force, there is no duty to make a safe retreat from the scene if one's presence is lawful.[67] In that case, the appellant, a Christian fundamentalist, was preaching from the steps of a cathedral. A crowd of about 100 people, some of whom were hostile, gathered and, fearing a breach of the peace, the police officer asked the appellant to stop preaching. She refused and was arrested for, and convicted of, wilfully obstructing the police officer in the execution of his duty. Her conviction was set aside on the grounds that the police officer had no right to call upon the appellant to desist from lawful conduct, unless it gave rise to a reasonable apprehension that it would provoke violence by interfering with the rights and liberties of others. I doubt that this decision can support the proposition for which it has been marshalled. The *Redmond-Bate* case did not involve the evaluation of a claim to justification made by an actor who could have averted a threat by retreat, but instead chose to maintain her lawful presence and take more serious defensive measures. The court was actually asked to consider whether the appellant's Hohfeldian liberty (or arguably even Hohfeldian right, given that she had, in advance, agreed her course of conduct with the police) to preach from the steps of a cathedral could legitimately have been curtailed because of the likelihood that her continued exercise of it would provoke an illegitimate response from an angry mob that had gathered to berate her. It was, in effect, the same question as in Scenario 1 in Case 2 discussed above, and the court reached the same conclusion. The fact that in *Redmond-Bate* the appellant was already present at the cathedral, whereas in Scenario 1 in Case 2, D is not yet present in the parking space does not effectively distinguish the two cases. The key question in both cases is whether

---

[65] The assumption that T's threat to D's claim to remain in place does not threaten a core element of the social-legal order is admittedly more plausible than a similar assumption in respect of D's right to avoid being hurt. If contrary assumptions were adopted in respect of either of these rights, then D's related interest in the maintenance of core elements of the social-legal order would weigh into the Derivative Force analysis to determine the outer limit of defensive force that would not be disproportionate.

[66] *Redmond-Bate v DPP* [2000] HRLR 249.

[67] Simester, Spencer et al, *Simester and Sullivan's Criminal Law* 810.

a person's Hohfeldian liberty can legitimately be constrained in response to an illegitimate threat, and the answer in both cases is 'No'.[68] The *Redmond-Bate* case is not authority for the proposition in support of which it has been marshalled, and that proposition is unsound, not just doctrinally, but also philosophically.

Now consider Scenario 2. What steps would D be justified in adopting to avoid being hit? Assuming that doing so does not increase the danger faced by D or prejudice the effectiveness of her defensive option, must D move towards the cliff for as long as she can without going over the edge and only then throw her own stone at T's hand, or can she throw her stone at once? To require D to sidestep the stones for as long as possible might arguably provide added insurance against any misperception by D of the situational facts, including T's intentions. It might also give T a chance to reconsider her actions and voluntarily cease her attack, or allow for some unforeseen intervention—say, a siren from a passing ambulance unnerving T—to cause the attack to cease without the need for force. This question goes to the heart of whether the Scottish rule requiring retreat until cornered is based on a philosophical principle.

The answer, I would suggest, has to do, first, with D's perception of the threat and, second, with D's duties (or the absence thereof) towards T. Since D's norm-reasoning has to be assessed entirely within the contours of her subjective perception, the answer to how D should behave depends on how D honestly perceived the threat to herself. Did she (Situation 1) believe that T would keep throwing stones until D could no longer avoid them without falling over the cliff? Or did she think that T would stop short of doing that (Situation 2)? If she thought the latter, then any claim that D might make to legitimately use force would fall at the Requirement threshold. Hence, the only appropriate defensive response for D would be to sidestep the stone. She must do this for as long as she continues to believe that T will not simply force her over the edge of the cliff. If, after a few such sidesteps, D comes to believe that T is not going to stop until D cannot sidestep the stones any longer, then Situation 2 merges into Situation 1.

What then is the conduct guidance available to D in Situation 1? There is nothing to stop the state from positing an express retreat-until-cornered condition for legitimate private access to the use of force, and it may well choose to do so for prudential reasons, in which case the question posed is straightforwardly answered. However, let us consider the position when there is no such stipulation. The only source of any guidance to retreat within the model I defend comes from the Requirement constraint, which is satisfied by unavoidable rather than immediate threats. If D believes that T will keep throwing stones until T hits D,

---

[68] See in this connection Ashworth, 'Self-Defence' 295–96. See also *R v Field* [1972] Crim LR 435, in which the appellant was warned in advance that some persons were coming to attack him, but instead of fleeing, he stood his ground. During the ensuing attack, the appellant used lethal force to defend himself against one of his attackers. The Court of Appeal in England and Wales set aside his conviction, holding that the fact that he had stood his ground instead of fleeing did not disentitle him from using force to defend himself.

then D is faced with a present and unavoidable threat, and not a contingent threat. Sidestepping the first stone will not avert the threat—it will merely postpone it without affecting its unavoidability. Since it is impossible to avert the threat by means other than injuring T's hand, the Requirement threshold for the D's use of force is crossed. D is not required to retreat or delay her response, and may legitimately defend herself using force that satisfies the parsimoniousness and non-disproportionality constraints.

Sangero would disagree. He advocates waiting until the last possible moment at which defensive action would be effective, in order to give the aggressor the chance to unilaterally withdraw her threat. This, he argues, would best safeguard the rights of the aggressor as well as the person attacked.[69] That is, of course, true, but, I would argue, not germane. As I mentioned in section 8.2.1, since crossing the Requirement threshold allows an agent only in-principle access to force, consideration for the rights of the aggressor is not material at that stage. Those concerns are accommodated in the Derivative Force analysis applicable to determining the appropriateness of the planned response. Hence, a person who perceives a threat to herself and who cannot avoid the threat or invoke state protection is permitted to use proportionate defensive force without having to indulge the speculative possibility that her attacker may have a sudden change of heart.

In determining the disproportionateness or otherwise of D's most parsimonious defensive option, it is important to correctly quantify the variables in play. Here, D is faced with the choice of either submitting to injury by stoning or dying by falling off a cliff. D can reduce the magnitude of the threat she faces by choosing to avoid the more serious threat—the threat to her life. In effect, she can 'retreat' from the threat to her life, albeit by choosing a course of action that involves facing the lesser threat of injury by stoning. Hence, the only inevitable and unavoidable threat that D faces from T is the threat of injury by stoning. Her response must be proportionate to that threat. It might still be argued that the amount of defensive force that would not be disproportionate should depend on whether D thinks that T's purpose is to hit D as many times as possible or just once. Surely, if D believed the former, then she could respond with more force than if she believed the latter? I think that this assertion would be wrong, because the argument on which it is based clandestinely reintroduces the assumption that D is *entitled* to stand her ground when (on the facts stated in the hypothetical at least) all D has is an unrestricted freedom to stand her ground. Since there is no such legal entitlement, D is not entitled to stand her ground (although she would incur no blame if she did, provided that standing her ground was all she did). If D retreats until it is no longer safe to retreat, she will be hit by one stone.[70] Therefore, if D chooses to stand her ground despite having an avenue of safe retreat, the escalation in the

---

[69] Sangero, *Self-Defence* 161.
[70] Since this is a hypothetical example, let us assume that D does not have acrophobia and would be able to retreat to the edge of the cliff without a heightened perception of the risk to herself.

amount of threat she faces is attributable to D's own choice.[71] The unavoidable threat that D faces is only the threat of injury by being struck by one stone, and her response must not in any case be disproportionate to that unavoidable threat. In summary, in Case 3, Scenario 2, Situation 1, D can use defensive force at once, without having to sidestep any stones and without waiting until she is teetering on the edge of the cliff. However, the defensive force that she uses must be parsimonious and must not be disproportionate to the amount of unavoidable threat she faces—the threat of being hit by one stone. If there is no non-disproportionate yet effective response available to D—say, the only way in which she can stop T is to shoot her dead—then she cannot legitimately take any defensive action. Her best (legitimate) course of action would then be to sidestep the stone for as long as it is safe to do so and then to suffer the injury by stoning. She would have to rely on the criminal law to punish T and might also claim compensation from T under civil law. D could also legitimately stand her ground and risk greater injury. If as a result T injured D more severely, T would face greater consequences under both criminal and civil law.[72]

But consider yet another variation: what if T were throwing acid-filled packets instead of stones such that any packet that hit D would kill her—how would the normative guidance given to D change? When the threat is to D's life, an existential justification will be available to her, and if D acts under the existential justification (which, it must be remembered, is a very limited justification), she will not have to refer to any additional Requirement or Derivative Force consideration. Hence, if D acts under an existential justification, she can defend herself against T's acid-filled packets by shooting T dead without violating any criminal law norm.

We can now consider a case that is usually treated as meriting special normative treatment—where the aggressor threatens the attacked person such that the latter can only avoid the threat by retreating from her home or similar place of refuge. The Model Penal Code has a special rule to recognise the absence of a 'duty to retreat' in the face of an attack in a dwelling place.[73] For Sangero, the 'immunity of the dwelling' is an important part of autonomy, and so if an agent faces attack in her dwelling, there is automatically a greater weight (as part of the autonomy consideration) in favour of the use of defensive force without retreat.[74] Leverick, on the other hand, rejects the notion that the dwelling place merits any special treatment, returning to the argument that the life of the aggressor is worth more

---

[71] Though again, if T hits D several times, T remains punishable under the criminal law by the state for the harm actually caused to D by the several strikes. Nevertheless, the extent of D's potential criminal liability is not strictly relevant for determining the amount of defensive force that would be permissible.

[72] In reality, the proportionality calculus is (and must inevitably be) much more rough and ready than this in order to take into account the psychological stresses faced by D in an emergency threat situation. The hypothetical example described in the main text should therefore be understood as an exercise in philosophical norm clarification rather than as a practical demonstration of how the courts should determine the proportionality of D's defensive response.

[73] Model Penal Code, §3.04(2)(b)(II)(1).

[74] Sangero, *Self-Defence* 266–68.

than any sentimental attachment that the attacked person may have to her dwelling place.[75] I think that at least in some respects, Leverick argues across and not against Sangero's position. Certainly, when comparing individual factors, the life of the aggressor is far more valuable than the special interest of a person in the sanctity of her dwelling place. Nevertheless, I think Sangero is correct to acknowledge that there is something about the dwelling place that makes retreat from it a greater sacrifice than retreat from a public place. This 'something', I think, is the fact that a person is generally understood to have a posited right to remain in her dwelling, as opposed to the mere Hohfeldian liberty to remain in a public place. A threat to an agent's person that can be averted only by retreat from her dwelling place therefore also constitutes an independent threat to her right to remain in her dwelling place. If there is no safe way to avert this threat and no way to invoke state protection, the Requirement threshold is breached and, in principle, force may be used to defend this right. Again, the corollary of this conclusion is not that the agent can use the amount of force requisite to repel the threat to her right to remain in the dwelling place—she must still only use force that satisfies the parsimoniousness and non-disproportionality constraints in order to be justified in her actions. Nevertheless, in most jurisdictions, the posited right to remain in one's dwelling is understood as a particularly strong right,[76] and therefore the proportionate response may involve a relatively greater amount of force than, say, the protection of one's posited right to park in an unoccupied public parking space.[77] Therefore, although the same set of rules apply to cases in which a person may only escape an attack by retreating from her dwelling place, the special nature of the posited right to remain in one's dwelling place does explain why retreat from a dwelling place is considered a special case.

A final clarification is called for at this stage. The foregoing discussion on the 'duty to retreat' and the 'duty to submit' has been focused on the question of what guidance D can be given ex ante in order to act in a manner that is permissible and justified. However, rationale-based excuses refer to an altogether different system of normative guidance. It therefore remains possible that, depending on the prevalent societal attitudes, a person who does not prefer effective retreat to the use of defensive force, or who uses required but disproportionate or non-parsimonious

---

[75] Leverick, *Killing in Self-Defence* 84–85; Leverick, 'Defending Self-Defence' 577.

[76] Many explanations of why this is seem to suggest that humans naturally relate to the dwelling place in a special manner—perhaps as an expression of their autonomy, as Fletcher, *Rethinking Criminal Law* 868 and Sangero, *Self-Defence* 266–68 suggest, or perhaps because of sentimental factors, as Leverick, *Killing in Self-Defence* 83 argues. It may well be that there is something intrinsic in humans that makes them especially protective of their dwelling place, and perhaps an argument could be made that this is, in some manner, a feature constituent of a human. If that argument can be convincingly made, it might necessitate some minor adjustments to the arguments made herein, but for the present purposes, I will not attempt to make either the argument or the consequential adjustments. I will assume here that our special protectiveness of our homes is not a constituent behavioural tendency and that it is posited into our law either by legislation or by norm-clarification through adjudication. (I refrain, however, from actually expressing a positive opinion to that effect.)

[77] See in this connection Ashworth, 'Self-Defence' 294.

defensive force instead of submitting to a threat may still be completely or partially excused from criminal liability.

8.3 Implications for Persons Suffering Defensive Action

As I have made clear in sections 3.2.3 and 3.3.4, in my view a person suffering justified defensive action is not under any duty to submit to it. Obviously, the same also applies when the defensive action is not justified, but is subsequently found to merit excusing. However, as I pointed out in section 8.2, at least in the context of threats to posited rights, the range of responses available to such a person continues to be restricted by proportionality constraints.

Furthermore, in section 3.3.3, I also suggested that a person who justifiedly affects the rights of another does not ipso facto become liable to compensate the persons affected by her actions for any loss they suffer. At this stage, it would be apposite to expand a little on this proposition. Compensation is usually a civil remedy and is usually premised on a finding of fault on the part of the defendant. Undoubtedly, there are cases in which no-fault liability is imposed,[78] but those are the exceptions rather than the norm. Therefore, before suggesting that an agent should compensate the victims of her defensive actions, we should ascertain whether any finding of fault can be made in respect of the agent.

Straightforwardly, a person who is justified acts without fault in respect of her norm-reasoning. Hence, her norm-reasoning does not provide any basis for either criminal liability or civil liability to compensate. However, this does not settle the matter. She may nevertheless be at fault in respect of her functional reasoning. If she was careless or negligent in perceiving or analysing situational facts, then although her justification will avert criminal liability, she could still suffer civil liability to compensate on the basis of the fault relatable to her functional reasoning. On the other hand, if, in addition to her norm-reasoning, her functional reasoning was also impeccable, then no finding of fault can attach to her. In such a case, the only civil liability that can be imposed on her is the exceptional no-fault liability, provided that it is applicable on the special facts of the case.

---

[78] In addition, there are forms of liability that even conceptually are not fault-predicated. Thus, the final bearer of the economic burden of a loss may be decided by contractual risk-apportionment between parties, or statutory stipulations to the same effect (usually made for public policy purposes), or insurance (though the insurer will usually be subrogated to any right to recover from the person taking the defensive action, if she is liable). Furthermore, some theorists argue that certain forms of restitutionary liability flow simply from the existence of property rights which can be vindicated by the owner of property against persons holding it without any need to establish fault. I venture no opinion as to these genres of liability, except to say that just like no-fault liability in tort, if they do arise, they do so on their own terms and not as a corollary of any defensive action.

When a person affects the rights of another but successfully invokes a rationale-based excuse to avoid criminal liability, then irrespective of the quality of her functional reasoning, she remains at fault in respect of her norm-reasoning. Although her supervening defence exempts her from criminal consequences, she may nevertheless suffer civil consequences arising out of her deficient norm-reasoning. Of course, the fact that there is a basis for imposing civil liability does not imply that it is inevitable, or even that it should be. In deciding on whether to award compensation, the civil court considers several factors, including factors that overlap with the considerations relevant to deciding on the availability of a rationale-based excuse. Hence, the civil law may well refuse to award compensation for the same reasons that the criminal law considers germane in deciding to excuse the agent from criminal liability. Nevertheless, in principle, fault-based liability is not excluded in such cases.

When a person who affects the rights of another successfully invokes a necessity defence (but not a paradigm justification), the situation is slightly more complicated. Assuming that no paradigm justification was available, the agent will have displayed deficient norm-reasoning and so, in principle, fault-based civil liability may be imposed. However, necessity is a special case of supervening exculpation. The consequences of successfully claiming a defence of necessity will depend on the contours of the defence posited in each jurisdiction, but if the defence conforms to the general suggestions made in Chapter 7, then a court that finds that the agent acted out of necessity will be deeming her to have acted norm-blamelessly. If so, the defence of necessity should carry with it the same consequences in relation to compensation as a paradigm justification defence. I think that this is a desirable stipulation for the state to posit for two reasons. First, if consequentialist considerations so overwhelmingly favour the action that a necessity defence is deemed appropriate, the chances are that one would not want to create an economic disincentive to performing the action. Second, because exempting persons who are deemed to be justified from fault-based liability imposes a significant undeserved loss on the person who suffers the defensive action, the judiciary is likely to adopt a restrictive view of when consequentialist considerations merit the grant of a necessity defence. This will minimise the deeming provision's weakening effect on the concept of a right.

8.4 Implications for Third Parties

The implications of the model of rationale-based defences that I defend for third parties have already been alluded to at various points in the foregoing arguments. However, for the sake of completeness, I will summarise my views on the main points of interest in this section.

First of all, we have found no normative basis for any norm that, in the absence of special facts, imposes on an onlooker ('O') the duty to help another person ('D') who is facing a threat to her constituent or posited rights. It is irrelevant whether D would have been justified in, or excused for, using force to defend her rights.

Second, in section 3.3.4, I have argued it is quite possible for more than one party in an emergency situation to be justified while acting at cross-purposes to each other. The same approach applies to third parties to a conflict as well, and they too can react to the situation as they perceive it. Therefore, in a fight between D and T, if onlooker O perceives T to have been the party at fault, then she can then invoke an authority norm to intervene by accessing D's existential immunity (or an analogous posited immunity) to defend D's threatened right as appropriate. Alternatively, if O perceives D to have been the party at fault, she may intervene to assist T in a similar manner. In neither case would O attract norm-blame for her intervention, although depending on the quality of her functional reasoning in perceiving and interpreting the situational facts, she may attract functional blame and any liability attaching to that blame. Similarly, if O's intervention, though effective in diffusing the threat situation, does not affect the rights of any other person, then (assuming that only rules that flow from the recognition of a private right are applicable) she has nothing for which to answer—she would have acted within the scope of her Hohfeldian liberty even though she intervened and would not attract norm-blame. However, if O intervened against the interests of a party that she believed not to have been at fault (either because the other party was at fault or because the threat was authored blamelessly), she would, in principle, incur norm-blame and criminal liability. This is because in such a situation, O would not be acting within the scope of any authority norm when intervening, and therefore any harm she caused to the rights of either D or T would amount to a violation of one of the duty norms applicable to her. However, she may still be able to show that her norm-reasoning merited a defence of necessity, or at least a rationale-based excuse.

Third, whenever O chooses to intervene by using force against the rights of any or both of the primarily concerned parties, she too has to demonstrate that she meets the preconditions for the legitimate private use of force. As such, she too must demonstrate that the Requirement for the use of force (ie, that state protection was unavailable, that the perceived victim could not have safely avoided the threat without the use of force and that she herself could not have diffused the situation without using force) and that the force she employed was parsimonious and not disproportionate to the threat.

8.5 Implications for the State

As will have become apparent by now, the model that I have proposed is more than a model of rationale-based defences. It also makes propositions as to the general connection between the criminal law, liberalism and morality. To that extent, it imposes certain limits upon the legislative and executive powers that can be exercised by a perfectly moral state. In this section, I provide a brief overview of the most significant of these limitations, while also suggesting some measures that the state can employ to mitigate some of the harsher consequences of the robust role played by the concept of the tragic in this theory.

8.5.1 Legislative Powers

As I have explained in section 3.3, when the state chooses to posit rights, it also posits the structure of norms that support them. The structure of posited norms described in section 3.3 was merely an example of a set of such norms. Those norms were fashioned to be compatible with, and closely analogous to, the norms that exist for the protection of constituent rights, so that they may also benefit from the same intuitive appeal possessed (I hope) by the norms described in section 3.2. Nevertheless, a perfectly moral state can have a system of posited norms that looks very different from those described in section 3.3. Most states, for instance, posit a right to property, but make it subject to the state's right to compulsorily acquire it in times of emergency. Similarly, most states posit a right to liberty (which is different from a Hohfeldian liberty), but make it subject to the state's power to curtail it by way of punishment or, in exceptional cases, preventative detention. Gur-Arye elegantly describes the practice of defining a right such that it may be withdrawn or curtailed upon the occurrence of a specified contingency, as the creation of powers.[79] These powers are often vested in the state or its functionaries.

However, a moral state's legislative powers are restricted in respect of the structure of norms that support the constituent rights, which I described in section 3.2. Any state that does not apply those norms to the letter is not a perfectly moral state. One would be hard-pressed to find any perfectly moral state, and some might see this as suggesting that the model proposed in this study does not conform to our moral intuitions. However, although there are far too many states that purport to have the moral authority to take away a subject's constituent right to life, there undoubtedly exists significant anti-death penalty moral sentiment, as evidenced by the protests one witnesses each time a person is executed. Similarly, inhuman punishments such as the amputation of the limbs of thieves generate considerable moral denunciation across the world. Although there are pockets of the world in which slavery continues to exist in one form or the other, the systematic instrumental use of persons meets unanimous condemnation in liberal states. The fact then that there is probably no perfectly moral state does not mean that the model of a moral state described in this study does not conform to our moral intuitions. It seems more likely to me that we have simply learnt to rein in (and to

---

[79] M Gur-Arye, 'Justifying the Distinction between Justifications and Power (Justifications vs. Power)' (2010) 5 *Criminal Law and Philosophy* 293. See also M Gur-Arye, 'Can the War against Terror Justify the Use of Force in Interrogations?' in S Levinson (ed), *Torture: A Collection* (Oxford, Oxford University Press, 2004) 189–91.

rationalise the reining in of) our moral intuitions in order to accommodate the political, historical and social pressures of the world outside the perfect one in which philosophy can dwell.

8.5.2 Executive Powers

The state does not exist in the state of nature; it is a political creation. The question of what the state is empowered to do is therefore also a question of normative political philosophy. However, even without delving too deeply into issues of political philosophy, it is probably safe to assume that, normatively, we would want the state to be a moral state. If we wanted to create a moral state, we would want and permit the state to act in accordance with the precepts of our preferred view of morality, as translated into a morally distinctive criminal law. A state created with that underlying intention would therefore implicitly be made subject to the core restrictive conduct norms in its criminal law, but would also implicitly be empowered to act in a manner expressly permitted by the criminal law's permissive conduct rules. Conversely, it would not be implicitly empowered to act *outside* the domain of the permissive rules of the criminal law—that power would have to be given to it by the polity that creates it. Hence, criminal law theory is not the source of the state's powers to perform coordination functions—those powers probably derive from the concerned polity's normative political philosophy. Furthermore, by definition, any polity committed to morality cannot empower the state to act *against* the precepts of morality.

This means that both individuals and moral states with liberal criminal law systems have the power to act as permitted by the criminal law's conduct rule system (by way of its justifications). The same equivalence of power between the individual and the state does not apply to conduct that is not recognised as morally permissible by the criminal law. However, in respect of matters not governed by the criminal law, the state can be empowered (or can empower itself in the name of the polity) to act. Unlike humans, though, a moral state is simply not constituted with (and cannot be given) the power to act contrary to moral guidance. This proposition has implications on the availability of rationale-based excuses to the state, because conduct that is merely excused is always morally wrongful. An excuse is available to humans because humans, being naturally constituted with the purposive agency to choose their own actions, may choose to act in accordance with or in defiance of the guidance of morality. Even when they act in defiance of morality, if their reasoning was no worse than the benchmark for reasoning that is normatively expected of agents in that society, they might be excused from criminal liability. The state has no constituent purposive agency—it merely has the agency given to it, ie, the agency to act morally, or as empowered by the polity. It does not have the constituent agency to act immorally and, furthermore, no moral state can be empowered by its polity to act immorally. Therefore, when the state acts contrary to moral guidance, it acts, in a sense, ultra vires its powers.

The grant of a rationale-based excuse in respect of an action does not function as a ratification thereof, since the action remains morally wrongful. As such, even if the state were to be granted a rationale-based excuse, that would not cure the ultra vires nature of its action, and so it would remain an inappropriate action. In fact, I doubt that the morally wrongful action of a state could be ratified and thereby retrospectively made permissible in a moral state at all, for the same reason that it is not possible to prospectively empower a moral state to act immorally—to do so would contradict the state's claim to being a moral state. For that reason, it is conceptually incoherent to suggest that the grant of a rationale-based excuse to a moral state could even theoretically make the concerned state action permissible with retrospective effect.

Moreover, excuses exculpate by demonstrating that the agent's reasoning was no worse than the benchmark for reasoning that is normatively expected of agents in that society. The state is not an ordinary agent and therefore comparing its reasoning with that of the ordinary agent is like comparing apples and oranges. The state is not expected (even by its polity) merely to reflect the mores of its subjects—it also has a role to play in shaping these mores and must lead by example. As such, I believe that while a rule-of-law moral state has the implicit power to act in a manner that would be justified, it has no analogous authority to choose to act in a manner that might (merely) have been excused if the state had been human.[80] If a state so acts, it acts immorally and would no longer be a moral or rule-of-law state.

But what about the special defence of necessity? Can a state invoke necessity in its defence when it contravenes the conduct rule system that underlies the criminal law for overwhelming consequentialist reasons? The foregoing analysis of the conceptual authority of a moral state would suggest that the answer is no—the necessity defence is a retrospective deeming fiction created by the state in respect of what is essentially excused conduct. If a moral state cannot be retrospectively empowered to act immorally by the grant of a rationale-based excuse, it also cannot be retrospectively empowered to act immorally by the grant of a necessity defence.

However, this does not conclude the matter. Recall that in sections 3.3 and 8.5.1, it was noted that when positing rights, the state can define them such that they are defeasible. Thus, for instance, property may be subject to compulsory state acquisition and, under the doctrine known as eminent domain or compulsory purchase, subject to conditions as to the public nature of the motivating need and compensation, it invariably is. When the state acquires property under the doctrine of eminent domain, it does not commit a prima facie offence—instead, it purports

---

[80] See M Gur-Arye, 'Legitimating Official Brutality: Can the War against Terror Justify Torture?' (2003) dx.doi.org/10.2139/ssrn.391580, 24; and SH Kadish, 'Torture, the State and the Individual' (1989) 23 *Israel Law Review* 345, 354. Y Lee, 'The Defense of Necessity and Powers of the Government' (2009) 3 *Criminal Law and Philosophy* 133, 137–38 takes the contrary position on the basis that some excuses may also guide conduct, and that conduct that accords with the guidance offered by the criminal justice system is permissible not just for individuals, but also for the state. I have already set out my views on why this argument fails in section 4.3.

to exercise a power.[81] As such, these acquisitions do not call for supervening justification. Judicial review of an acquisition focuses on whether the power of acquisition has been validly exercised rather than whether the state deserves criminal blame for acquiring the property. Although the doctrine of eminent domain is generally understood to apply to property, there is no reason why other posited rights cannot also be definitionally limited in the same way.[82] The posited right to liberty is an example of a non-property posited right that is definitionally limited. It is definitionally limited so that it is subject to state curtailment for fault (incarceratory punishment) or in the overriding public interest (preventive detention). Generally, when positing a right, the state reserves the power to curtail or compulsorily acquire it, either for fault or without fault but for compensation and in the overriding public interest.

In relation at least to posited rights, then, the state may in effect do the same acts as an individual may do when she successfully claims a defence of necessity, except that when the state does it, it is technically exercising a power in the public interest rather than claiming a defence in respect of the violation of a right. Presumably, when the state purports to exercise a power to curtail a posited right, it would first have to fulfil certain procedural formalities, whereas no such formalities would apply when it purports to justifiedly use defensive force against the same set of rights. One other difference is that usually the state would have to compensate a person who faultlessly suffers a curtailment of her posited right because of the state's exercise of its power. Intuitively, neither of these results is particularly troubling.

However, even this line of argument does not permit a moral state to compulsorily curtail or acquire constituent rights. When the state recognises constituent rights, it merely recognises the limits of its own powers. It does not define the contours of the constituent rights and so it cannot definitionally limit them. As such, no matter what the consequences of not doing so, a truly moral state cannot claim any power to kill, torture,[83] physically or mentally maim or enslave any human. In terms of the model for which I have argued, my answer to the ticking bomb hypothetical[84] is an unqualified rejection of the permissibility of any state

---

[81] For the classic statement of the power of eminent domain, see J Lewis, *A Treatise on the Law of Eminent Domain in the United States* (Chicago, Callahan & Company, 1888/1909) 1–2.

[82] Alternatively, an incorporeal right like a chose in action can also in principle be treated as property for the purposes of the doctrine of eminent domain and be made subject to state acquisition. See generally JA Blumenthal, 'Legal Claims as Private Property: Implications for Eminent Domain' (2009) 36 *Hastings Constitutional Law Quarterly* 373.

[83] In the sense that I have used the term in section 5.5.

[84] A typical statement of the ticking bomb hypothetical is as follows: 'to avert a mass killing: could it not be right to torture an uncooperative suspect credibly believed to know the (densely populated urban) location of a ticking bomb? The danger is imminent, the potential disaster great, potential victims innocent, helpless and numerous, and the suspect uncooperative'. See C Card, 'Ticking Bombs and Interrogations' (2008) 2 *Criminal Law and Philosophy* 1, 3. The answer to this hypothetical (and variations thereon) has been hotly contested for more than two centuries and a variety of different answers have been proposed. Bentham, for instance, argued that we should choose the lesser of the evils, even if

torture that affects the suspect's constituent elements, because such actions would involve treating the suspect as non-human—as a mere repository of information.

This analysis leaves the state powerless to use defensive force for the sort of consequentialist reasons that might push a person to respond despite not being justified. However, we must remember that the state functions through humans, who may well in their individual capacity follow their (societal) conscience. In doing so, they would choose to act without the protection of the state machinery and outside the colour of the state's claim to power, thereby laying themselves open to personal criminal liability. However, if the cause is sufficiently important, it is not in principle inconceivable that they might be excused from criminal liability. The state, however, would continue to be vicariously responsible for the extra-legal actions of its agents and may well suffer vicarious criminal or non-criminal liability.[85]

8.5.3 Social Functions

Strictly, the arguments made in this study do not generate any obligations for the state in respect of the social functions that it performs. However, I am aware that in externalising tragic losses and arguing for limiting the availability of both criminal and civil redress in respect of them, the model I defend may cause some intuitive uneasiness. This uneasiness can be mitigated, at least to some extent, by various social policy initiatives, which, though not mandated by the model that I defend, are certainly compatible with it.

For instance, as mentioned previously in section 8.1, it is fairly common in many jurisdictions for states to respond to tragedies and disasters by making ad hoc ex gratia payments to the victims or their kin. If the state formalised this practice by setting up an insurance-like model of state compensation for all tragedies, including human-authored ones, it could provide some compensation for the undeserving victims of justified or necessary action. Unlike the criminal law, which focuses (or ought to focus) on the guilt of the accused, the proposed system of compensation would focus on verifying the undeserved nature of the loss suffered

---

that were torture. See WL Twining and PE Twining, 'Bentham on Torture' (1973) 24 *Northern Ireland Legal Quarterly* 305, 345–46. Others, like Kadish, 'Torture' 346, argue that torture might, in principle, be justifiable, but only in extreme circumstances. Card, 'Ticking Bombs' builds upon this proposition and says that these circumstances would be so unrealistic that torture is practically unjustifiable. Still others maintain the absolute position that torture is not justifiable in any circumstances. See, for instance, J Waldron, 'What are Moral Absolutes Like?' (2011) *NYU School of Law, Public Law Research Paper No 11–62* dx.doi.org/10.2139/ssrn.1906850. My own conclusions, in respect of the kinds of torture that I address, are in line with those of Waldron.

[85] For instance, in *Ashley v Chief Constable of Sussex Police* [2008] UKHL 25, the police were held liable in tort for negligently killing a suspect in circumstances where the direct perpetrator could arguably have claimed a self-defence justification, albeit that he was negligently mistaken as to the true facts. There is no reason why the same should not apply where the direct perpetrator is merely excused and not justified.

by the victim and providing compensation. A state that could afford to set up such a system and that used it to complement the model of rationale-based defences described in this book would avoid making false blaming judgments while nevertheless securing its subjects against undeserved harm to their rights. My broader analytical point is that while the model of rationale-based defences that I defend cannot achieve both the above objectives, both these objectives can be achieved in a manner compatible with the model I defend. Further, I suggest that in refraining from trying to achieve both goals, one saves the model of rationale-based defences from being pulled in opposite directions and being stretched out of shape.

Conclusion

I began this study by noting that most modern theories of justification and excuse are premised on what I called the 'wrongness hypothesis'—the idea that a justification negates the objective wrongness of the prima facie offence, whereas an excuse negates the defendant's blameworthiness for causing the prima facie offence, whilst (usually) leaving its wrongness intact. The wrongness hypothesis is incapable of proof—it is merely a suggestion as to the logical structure that would best serve to understand, explain and critique a certain set of criminal law defences. It is a plausible candidate to serve that purpose, but it is certainly not the only plausible candidate. Although the wrongness hypothesis has been the basis of many comprehensive models of criminal defences, each of these models has been shown to generate some intuitively dissonant outcomes and, as such, none of them has been completely convincing. Therefore, I experimentally rejected the wrongness hypothesis in favour of an alternative hypothesis to see if it would generate a better model. I called this alternative hypothesis as to the structure of criminal law defences the 'quality of reasoning' hypothesis—the idea that justifications and rationale-based excuses were differentiated based on the quality of the reasoning demonstrated by the defendant in choosing to commit the prima facie offence. While cataloguing the most important prima facie outcomes generated by the quality of reasoning model, I found that each of the outcomes was intuitively at least plausible, even if there remained scope for theorists to find other outcomes more intuitively appealing. Perhaps the point is better explained by stating that I found at least some academic support for each of the outcomes generated by the quality of reasoning model. I thus concluded that even if any particular outcome was not presently the dominant view, it could not be said about it that it was completely implausible. Since none of the outcomes generated by the quality of reasoning model were implausible, the model itself was not implausible and therefore merited deeper consideration.

But, of course, this made no positive case in favour of the quality of reasoning model. At best, it showed that this model, like various competing models, could not be dismissed out of hand. It would appeal to those who agreed with the outcomes it generates, but it would not convince those who grudgingly came to accept that the said outcomes were not completely implausible. This latter class of people might still find other models of justification and excuse more appealing. For this reason, I spelled out the links between key propositions made in the quality of reasoning model and a set of widely shared intuitions about the criminal law. These intuitions were as follows:

1. At the trial stage, the criminal law is concerned with adjudicating on the defendant's criminal blame. It does so by reference to previously articulated conduct guiding rules, core instances of which are designed to minimise wrongful interferences with rights.
2. The criminal law is morally distinctive—at least the core tenets of the criminal law draw from logically prior moral norms.
3. The morality that links to the criminal law in this way is a human-centric morality—it is premised on the notion that the continuation of the human species is good.
4. Beings that are recognisably part of the human species have certain constituent elements which include life, a human form and purposive agency, and engage in constituently human behaviours like protecting their own constituent elements by any means possible and recognising the equal humanity of others.
5. A recognisable modern system of criminal law would be committed to liberal tenets of non-interference. As such, it would, at its core, not contain guidance relating to or permit interference with matters that lie in the private domain of a person (or persons united by mutual consent).
6. The modern state enjoys a monopoly over the legitimate use of force in the non-private domain.

If these foundational intuitions resonated with the reader, then the argument based on the quality of reasoning model could proceed. It proceeded as follows.

First, I argued that since human morality is premised on the notion that the continuation of the human species is good, the ontology of a 'human being' is logically prior to (and hence outside the remit of) such a morality. Therefore, any guidance that requires humans to be other than human would be internally incoherent. Hence, the human constituent elements are 'off-limits' for human morality, and any other code of conduct guidance (including the criminal law) that claims to be morally derived. Such codes can never issue legitimate guidance requiring that a person interfere with, or to suffer an interference with, any human constituent element (including constituent behaviours), because this guidance would require a human to be other than human. Accordingly, morality cannot guide a person to kill or maim another person, or to suffer being killed or maimed. At the same time, it cannot guide a person not to engage in constituently human behaviour directed towards protecting human constituent elements. Nor can it guide a person to ignore the equal humanity of other humans and to instead treat them as mere means to be deployed towards an end (even where that end is the person's own survival). In Hohfeldian terms, these constituent elements are immune to morality's guidance (and consequent evaluation). However, when human constituent behaviours conflict, morality can offer guidance, since neither course of action could be said to be the actions of a human merely being human.

Next I noted that states that claim to be moral (by reference to the aforementioned human morality) and claim to have a morally derived criminal law tend to vest these limits of the human morality with the trappings of rights. When they do so, a person's immunity to guidance requiring her to submit to a curtailment of her life, her bodily integrity, her purposive agency or her constituently human behaviours becomes rights against such guidance and, consequently, rights to these constituent elements. I call these rights 'constituent rights' and describe the guiding rules that a liberal state, committed to avoiding busybody interference, would issue in order to protect these rights.

Thereafter, I identified other rights that the state might posit in exercise of its political powers. These rights would relate to things that humans do not already constituently possess, but which are considered valuable for a good life. I set out one possible system of guiding rules that a liberal state might posit to protect these rights. In describing this system of rules, I use the rules applicable to constituent rights as a template in order to capitalise on the intuitive plausibility of those rules.

I treated the composite of the guiding rules designed to protect constituent rights, and those designed to protect posited rights, as the rules at the core of the modern liberal criminal law's conduct guidance. Some of this guidance is conduct-restricting and some of it permits conduct that is prima facie forbidden. I argue that the criminal law's conduct restricting guidance is captured by offence definitions in the criminal law, whereas justifications should be understood as capturing the criminal law's conduct permitting guidance. A person should be taken to be criminally blameless when she chooses to comply with the guidance (both conduct-restricting and conduct-permitting) that was applicable to the circumstances with which she thought she was faced. Hence, a person who successfully claims a justification is not criminally blameworthy.

Next I argued that even conduct that merits criminally blame may be excused from such blame if it accords to societal normative expectations (as opposed to the criminal law's morally derived normative expectations). Hence, if society would normatively expect one of its members to respond to a situation in the same manner as the defendant did, then it would be hypocritical for it to use its criminal law to single out the defendant as being especially deserving of blame. The defendant would have shown herself to be no worse than the society to which she belongs, and so society would have a very good (albeit not conclusive) reason not to single her out for condemnation. The defence that the criminal law may choose to grant such a defendant would be a rationale-based excuse. However, even if it does excuse the defendant from criminal blame, this does not automatically translate into an exemption from non-criminal blame (say, in tort law) or liability that is not predicated on blame (say, in terms of contractual or statutory risk allocations).

Finally, I argued that lesser evils necessity ought to be conceived of as a special case of rationale-based excuse, in which the defendant acts not just as society normatively expects her to act, but, in fact, as society positively wants her to act (even though this does not accord with the criminal law's conduct guidance). In order to promote such conduct, the criminal law may, within certain limits, deem such conduct to have been justified and may treat the defendant as having been criminally blameless.

In order to illustrate the practical effects of a system of criminal law with these features at its core, I considered a series of vexed questions, including whether a person is ever under a duty to retreat from or submit to an aggression (whether warranted or not), and what the state and its functionaries can do in a 'ticking time-bomb situation'. I also considered questions relating to the options available to a third party to a threat situation. In each case, I suggested answers based on the logic of the system of criminal law described in this study.

If both the foundational intuitions enumerated previously and the arguments advanced on the basis of those intuitions appeal to people who have different outcome intuitions, then this study will have offered them good reasons to reconsider their outcome intuitions and, as a consequence, their overall assessment of this model.

I was mindful of the fact that in generating a particular intuitively plausible outcome, the quality of reasoning model simultaneously ruled other plausible alternative outcomes out of the criminal law. For instance, in adopting the position that D deserves no criminal blame when she unreasonably believes that a situation calls for self-defensive force and therefore inflicts undeserved harm on V, the quality of reasoning model rules out of the criminal law the very plausible intuition that D should be liable in such a situation *because* of the unreasonableness of her beliefs. However, my belief that this intuition should not shape the criminal law does not entail its complete rejection. Instead, intuitions like this one remain valid intuitions and can often be accommodated in blaming enterprises other than the criminal law, or in enterprises that generate liability other than criminal liability. Hence, the unreasonableness of one's epistemic beliefs should give rise to a kind of blame unrelated to the criminal law and its conduct-guiding rules, but which could supply a basis for liability in tort, or the laws of unjust enrichment, or restitution. Although these forms of liability are also concerned to different extents with blaming the defendant, their core concerns are not the *moral* blameworthiness of the defendant, and so the liabilities they impose do not carry morally loaded labels. The model of rationale-based defences that I describe focuses entirely on ensuring that the morally loaded label 'criminal' is fairly imposed upon only deserving defendants. Unlike many competing models, it does not *also* attempt to do justice to the victim by providing the victim with the satisfaction that any undeserved harm has been redressed. It may do so incidentally, but where the interest in fairly labelling the defendant clashes with the interest in providing redress to a victim who has suffered an undeserved harm at the hands of the defendant, the model I defend stands squarely and unabashedly behind the former interest. In that sense, this model sets up a system of criminal law that is much more modest in its ambitions than most competing theoretical models and, indeed, than most competing criminal law systems actually in place. Personally, I doubt that it is possible for one system of criminal law to always meet both objectives (viz fairly imposing morally loaded labels and providing redress to all victims) perfectly. Traditionally, the redressal of undeserved harms has been the domain of tort law or the law of restitution, and the redistribution of undeserved gains has been the domain of the law of unjust enrichment. The decision rules that operate in those domains of law are focussed primarily on providing fair redress to the victim or on redistributing gains equitably. I think that there is value in keeping the decision rules that operate in those different domains of law conceptually separate, so that each set can achieve its unique objective perfectly rather than all of them achieving several divergent objectives imperfectly. Keeping the sorts of blaming judgments that are important for civil law outside the core realm of the criminal law also secures that criminal convictions will be better able to perform the role that they are perceived to have in popular imagination—conveying morally loaded blaming judgments. For that reason, this model is desirable.

None of this is conclusive proof that the model of rationale-based defences that I present here is correct—indeed, I doubt that it is possible to provide any such proof. However, I hope that it does supply strong reasons to believe that the quality of reasoning-based model described here is a very good description of how the criminal law should be, because it is plausible, well founded and gives rise to desirable outcomes.

BIBLIOGRAPHY

Alexander, L, 'Lesser Evils: A Closer Look at the Paradigmatic Justification' (2005) 24 *Law and Philosophy* 611.
——, 'Propter Honoris Respectum: A Unified Excuse of Preemptive Self-Protection' (2005) 74 *Notre Dame Law Review* 1475.
Alexander, L and Ferzan, KK, 'Results Don't Matter' in PH Robinson, SP Garvey and KK Ferzan (eds), *Criminal Law Conversations* (Oxford, Oxford University Press, 2009) 147–53.
——, 'Against Negligence Liability' in PH Robinson, SP Garvey and KK Ferzan (eds), *Criminal Law Conversations* (Oxford, Oxford University Press, 2009) 273–81.
Aristotle, *Nicomachean Ethics*, trans D Ross and L Brown (Oxford, Oxford University Press, 350 BC/2009).
Ashworth, AJ, 'Self-Defence and the Right to Life' (1975) 34 *Cambridge Law Journal* 282.
——, 'The Doctrine of Provocation' (1976) 35 *Cambridge Law Journal* 292.
——, 'Ignorance of the Criminal Law, and Duties to Avoid it' (2011) 74 *MLR* 1.
Ashworth, AJ and Horder, J, *Principles of Criminal Law* (Oxford, Oxford University Press, 2013).
Austin, JL, 'A Plea for Excuses' (1956–57) LVII *Proceedings of the Aristotelian Society* 1.
Bakircioglu, O, 'The Contours of the Right to Self-Defence: Is the Requirement of Imminence Merely a Translator for the Concept of Necessity?' (2008) 72 *Journal of Criminal Law* 131.
Baron, M, 'Justifications and Excuses' (2005) 2 *Ohio State Journal of Criminal Law* 387.
——, 'The Provocation Defense and the Nature of Justification' (2009) 43 *University of Michigan Journal of Law Reform* 117.
——, 'Self-Defence: The Imminence Requirement' in L Green and B Leiter (eds), *Oxford Studies in Philosophy of Law: Volume 1* (Oxford, Oxford University Press, 2011) 228–66.
Beale, JH, 'Retreat From a Murderous Assault' (1903) 16 *Harvard Law Review* 567.
Berman, MN, 'Justification and Excuse, Law and Morality' (2003) 53 *Duke Law Journal* 1.
——, 'Lesser Evils and Justification: A Less Close Look' (2005) 24 *Law and Philosophy* 681.
Berman, MN and Farrell, IP, 'Provocation Manslaughter as Partial Justification and Partial Excuse' (2011) 52 *William and Mary Law Review* 1027.
Blumenthal, JA, 'Legal Claims as Private Property: Implications for Eminent Domain' (2009) 36 *Hastings Constitutional Law Quarterly* 373.
Bohlander, M, 'Transferred Malice and Transferred Defenses' (2010) 13 *New Criminal Law Review* 555.
Bratman, ME, 'Planning Agency, Autonomous Agency' in *Structures of Agency: Essays* (New York, Oxford University Press, 2007) 195–221.
——, 'Reflection, Planning, and Temporally Extended Agency' in *Structures of Agency: Essays* (New York, Oxford University Press, 2007) 21–46.
Brettschneider, C, 'The Rights of the Guilty: Punishment and Political Legitimacy' (2007) 35 *Political Theory* 175.
Brudner, A, 'A Theory of Necessity' (1987) 7 *OJLS* 339.

Brugger, W, 'May Government Ever Use Torture? Two Responses from German Law' (2000) 48 *American Journal of Comparative Law* 661.

Byrd, BS, 'Wrongdoing and Attribution: Implications Beyond the Justification-Excuse Distinction' (1987) 33 *Wayne Law Review* 1289.

——, 'Till Death Do Us Part: A Comparative Law Approach to Justifying Lethal Self-Defense by Battered Women' (1991) 1 *Duke Journal of Comparative & International Law* 169.

Card, C, 'Ticking Bombs and Interrogations' (2008) 2 *Criminal Law and Philosophy* 1.

Chan, W and Simester, AP, 'Duress, Necessity: How Many Defences' (2005) 16 *King's College Law Journal* 121.

Christopher, RL, 'Mistake of Fact in the Objective Theory of Justification: Do Two Rights Make Two Wrongs Make Two Rights...?' (1994) 85 *Journal of Criminal Law and Criminology* 295.

——, 'Unknowing Justification and the Logical Necessity of the Dadson Principle in Self-Defence' (1995) 15 *OJLS* 229.

Cohen, GA, 'Casting the First Stone: Who Can, and Who Can't, Condemn the Terrorists?' (2003) 58 *Royal Institute of Philosophy Supplement* 113.

Colvin, E, 'Exculpatory Defences in Criminal Law' (1990) 19 *OJLS* 381.

Crisp, R and Cowton, C, 'Hypocrisy and Moral Seriousness' (1994) 31 *American Philosophical Quarterly* 343.

Curry, O, 'Who's Afraid of the Naturalistic Fallacy?' (2006) 4 *Evolutionary Psychology* 234.

Dan-Cohen, M, 'Decision Rules and Conduct Rules: On Acoustic Separation in Criminal Law' (1984) 97 *Harvard Law Review* 625.

——, 'Reply' in PH Robinson, SP Garvey and KK Ferzan (eds), *Criminal Law Conversations* (Oxford, Oxford University Press, 2009) 24–28.

Dershowitz, A, *Why Terrorism Works: Understanding the Threat, Responding to the Challenge* (New Haven, Yale University Press, 2002).

Dillof, AM, 'Transferred Intent: An Inquiry into the Nature of Criminal Culpability' (1997) 1 *Buffalo Criminal Law Review* 501.

Dressler, J, 'Reassessing the Theoretical Underpinnings of Accomplice Liability: New Solutions to an Old Problem' (1985) 37 *Hastings Law Journal* 91.

——, 'Battered Women Who Kill Their Sleeping Tormentors' in S Shute and AP Simester (eds), *Criminal Law Theory: Doctrines of the General Part* (Oxford, Oxford University Press, 2002) 259–282.

Dsouza, M, 'The Power to Consent and the Criminal Law' (2013) http://ssrn.com/abstract=2225267.

——, 'Undermining Prima Facie Consent in the Criminal Law' (2014) 33 *Law and Philosophy* 489.

——, 'Criminal Culpability after the Act' (2015) 26 *King's Law Journal* 440.

——, 'Retreat, Submission, and the Private Use of Force' (2015) 35 *OJLS* 727.

Du Bois-Pedain, A, 'Book Reviews—Self-Defence in Criminal Law by Boaz Sangero and Killing in Self-Defence by Fiona Leverick' (2009) 68 *Cambridge Law Journal* 227.

Duarte d'Almeida, L, *Allowing for Exceptions: A Theory of Defences and Defeasibility in Law* (Oxford, Oxford University Press, 2015).

Duff, RA, 'Choice, Character, and Criminal Liability' (1993) 12 *Law and Philosophy* 345.

——, 'Rule-Violations and Wrongdoings' in S Shute and AP Simester (eds), *Criminal Law Theory: Doctrines of the General Part* (Oxford, Oxford University Press, 2002) 47–74.

——, *Answering for Crime* (Oxford, Hart Publishing, 2007).

——, 'Towards a Modest Legal Moralism' (2014) 1 *Criminal Law and Philosophy* 217.

Duff, RA and Marshall, SE, 'Public and Private Wrongs' in J Chalmers, F Leverick and L Farmer (eds), *Essays in Criminal Law in Honour of Sir Gerald Gordon* (Edinburgh, Edinburgh University Press, 2010) 70–85.

Eldar, S and Laist, E, 'The Misguided Concept of Partial Justification' (2014) 20 *Legal Theory* 157.

Elliott, C, *French Criminal Law* (London, Routledge, 2011).

Eser, A, 'Justification and Excuse' (1976) 24 *American Journal of Comparative Law* 621.

Eubanks, CL, 'Subject and Substance: Hegel on Modernity' (2005) 6 *Loyola Journal of Public Interest Law* 129.

Feinberg, J, *The Moral Limits of Criminal Law Volume 1: Harm to Others* (Oxford, Oxford University Press, 1987).

Ferzan, KK, 'Defending Imminence: From Battered Women to Iraq' (2004) 46 *Arizona Law Review* 213.

——, 'Justifying Self-Defense' (2005) 24 *Law and Philosophy* 711.

——, 'Self-Defense and the State' (2008) 5 *Ohio State Journal of Criminal Law* 449.

Finkelstein, CO, 'On the Obligation of the State to Extend a Right of Self-Defense to its Citizens' (1999) 147 *University of Pennsylvania Law Review* 1361.

——, 'A Puzzle about Hobbes on Self-Defense' (2001) 82 *Pacific Philosophical Quarterly* 332.

——, 'Responsibility for Unintended Consequences' (2005) 2 *Ohio State Journal of Criminal Law* 579.

Fletcher, GP, 'The Right Deed for the Wrong Reason: A Reply to Mr. Robinson' (1975) 23 *UCLA Law Review* 293.

——, *Rethinking Criminal Law* (Boston, Little, Brown & Company, 1978).

——, 'Rights and Excuses' (1984) 3(2) *Criminal Justice Ethics* 17.

——, 'The Right and the Reasonable' (1985) 98 *Harvard Law Review* 949.

——, 'The Nature of Justification' in S Shute, J Gardner and J Horder (eds), *Action and Value in Criminal Law* (Oxford, Clarendon Press, 1993) 175–86.

Fox, D, 'Non-excludible Trustee Duties' (2011) 17 *Trusts & Trustees* 17.

Gardner, J, 'Justifications and Reasons' in AP Simester and ATH Smith (eds), *Harm and Culpability* (Oxford, Clarendon Press, 1996) 103–29.

——, 'The Gist of Excuses' (1998) 1 *Buffalo Criminal Law Review* 575.

——, *Offences and Defences* (Oxford, Oxford University Press, 2007).

Gardner, J and Tanguay-Renaud, F, 'Desert and Avoidability in Self-Defense' (2011) 122 *Ethics* 111.

Gardner, MR, '"Decision Rules" and Kids: Clarifying the Vagueness Problems with Status Offense Statutes and School Disciplinary Rules' (2010) 89 *Nebraska Law Review* 1.

Garza Jr, A, 'Hegel's Critique of Liberalism and Natural Law: Reconstructing Ethical Life' (1990) 9 *Law and Philosophy* 371.

Gewirth, A, *Reason and Morality* (Chicago, University of Chicago Press, 1978).

Grabczynska, A and Ferzan, KK, 'Justifying Killing in Self-Defence' (2009) 99 *Journal of Criminal Law and Criminology* 235.

Greenawalt, K, 'The Perplexing Borders of Justification and Excuse' (1984) 84 *Columbia Law Review* 1897.

——, 'Distinguishing Justifications from Excuses' (1986) 49(3) *Law and Contemporary Problems* 89.

Gross, O, 'Are Torture Warrants Warranted? Pragmatic Absolutism and Official Disobedience' (2004) 88 *Minnesota Law Review* 1481.

Gur-Arye, M, 'Should a Criminal Code Distinguish between Justification and Excuse?' (1992) 5 *Canadian Journal of Law and Jurisprudence* 215.

——, 'Legitimating Official Brutality: Can the War against Terror Justify Torture?' (2003) http://dx.doi.org/10.2139/ssrn.391580.

——, 'Can the War against Terror Justify the Use of Force in Interrogations?' in S Levinson (ed), *Torture: A Collection* (Oxford, Oxford University Press, 2004) 183–98.

——, 'Justifying the Distinction between Justifications and Power (Justifications vs. Power)' (2010) 5 *Criminal Law and Philosophy* 293.

——, 'Human Dignity of "Offenders": A Limitation on Substantive Criminal Law' (2012) 6 *Criminal Law and Philosophy* 187.

Hart, HLA, 'The Ascription of Responsibility and Rights' (1948) 49 *Proceedings of the Aristotelian Society* 171.

——, *The Concept of Law* (Oxford, Clarendon Press, 1961/1994).

——, *Punishment and Responsibility* (Oxford, Oxford University Press, 1968).

Hayton, D, 'The Irreducible Core Content of Trusteeship' in AJ Oakley (ed), *Trends in Contemporary Trust Law* (Oxford, Oxford University Press, 1996) 47–62.

Hegel, GWF, *Phenomenology of Spirit*, trans HP Kainz (Pennsylvania, Pennsylvania State University Press, 1807/1994).

Hobbes, T, *Leviathan* (London, Yale University Press, 1651/2010).

Hohfeld, WN, *Fundamental Legal Conceptions as Applied in Judicial Reasoning and Other Legal Essays*, ed WW Cook (New Haven, Yale University Press, 1919).

Honneth, A, 'From Desire to Recognition: Hegel's Account of Human Sociality' in D Moyar and M Quante (eds), *Hegel's Phenomenology of Spirit* (Cambridge, Cambridge University Press, 2008) 76–90.

Horder, J, 'Redrawing the Boundaries of Self-Defence' (1995) 58 *MLR* 431.

——, 'Transferred Malice and the Remoteness of Unexpected Outcomes from Intentions' [1996] *Crim LR* 383.

——, *Excusing Crime* (Oxford, Oxford University Press, 2004).

Hruschka, J, 'Imputation' (1986) 3 *Brigham Young University Law Review* 669.

——, 'Justifications and Excuses: A Systematic Approach' (2005) 2 *Ohio State Journal of Criminal Law* 407.

Hsieh, N, Strudler, A and Wasserman, D, 'The Numbers Problem' (2006) 34 *Philosophy & Public Affairs* 352.

Hurd, HM, 'What in the World is Wrong?' (1994) 5 *Journal of Contemporary Legal Issues* 157.

Husak, DN, 'Justifications and the Criminal Liability of Accessories' (1989) 80 *Journal of Criminal Law and Criminology* 491.

——, 'Conflicts of Justification' (1999) 18 *Law and Philosophy* 41.

——, 'On the Supposed Priority of Justification to Excuse' (2005) 24 *Law and Philosophy* 557.

——, 'Mistake of Law and Culpability' (2010) 4 *Criminal Law and Philosophy* 135.

Jaffe, M, 'Up in Arms over Florida's New "Stand Your Ground" Law' (2005) 30 *Nova Law Review* 155.

Jones, GE, 'On the Permissibility of Torture' (1980) 6 *Journal of Medical Ethics* 11.

Kadish, SH, 'Respect for Life and Regard for Rights in the Criminal Law' (1976) 64 *California Law Review* 871.

——, 'Torture, the State and the Individual' (1989) 23 *Israel Law Review* 345.

Kasachkoff, T, 'Killing in Self-Defense: An Unquestionable or Problematic Defense?' (1998) 17 *Law and Philosophy* 509.

——, 'Comment and Reply to Suzanne Uniacke's "A Response to Two Critics"' (2000) 19 *Law and Philosophy* 635.

Kaufman, WRP, 'Self-Defense, Imminence, and the Battered Woman' (2007) 10 *New Criminal Law Review* 342.

Kramer, MH, *Objectivity and the Rule of Law* (Cambridge, Cambridge University Press, 2007).

——, 'Is Law's Conventionality Consistent with Law's Objectivity?' (2008) 14 *Res Publica* 242–43.

——, *The Ethics of Capital Punishment: A Philosophical Investigation of Evil and its Consequences* (Oxford, Oxford University Press, 2011).

Kremnitzer, M, 'Proportionality and the Psychotic Aggressor: Another View' (1983) 18 *Israel Law Review* 178.

Lawler, R, 'Taurek, Numbers and Probabilities' (2006) 9 *Ethical Theory and Moral Practice* 149.

Lazar, S, 'Necessity in Self-Defense and War' (2012) 40 *Philosophy & Public Affairs* 3.

Lee, Y, 'The Defense of Necessity and Powers of the Government' (2009) 3 *Criminal Law and Philosophy* 133.

Leverick, F, *Killing in Self-Defence* (Oxford, Oxford University Press, 2006).

——, 'Defending Self-Defence' (2007) 27 *OJLS* 563.

Lewis, J, *A Treatise on the Law of Eminent Domain in the United States* (Chicago, Callahan & Company, 1888/1909).

Lisska, AJ, 'Finnis and Veatch on Natural Law in Aristotle and Aquinas' (1991) 36 *American Journal of Jurisprudence* 55.

Locke, J, *Two Treatises of Government and a Letter Concerning Toleration* (New Haven, Yale University Press, 1690/2003).

Lübbe, W, 'Taurek's No Worse Claim' (2008) 36 *Philosophy & Public Affairs* 69.

Marshall, SE and Duff, RA, 'Criminalization and Sharing Wrongs' (1998) 11 *Canadian Journal of Law and Jurisprudence* 7.

——, 'Reply' in PH Robinson, SP Garvey and KK Ferzan (eds), *Criminal Law Conversations* (Oxford, Oxford University Press, 2009) 248–52.

McMahan, J, 'Self-Defense and the Problem of the Innocent Attacker' (1994) 104 *Ethics* 252.

Mill, JS, *On Liberty* (New Haven, Yale University Press, 1859/2003).

Moore, MS, 'Choice, Character, and Excuse' (1990) 7(2) *Social Philosophy and Policy* 29.

——, *Placing Blame: A Theory of the Criminal Law* (Oxford, Oxford University Press, 2010).

Moore, MS and Hurd, HM, 'Punishing the Awkward, the Stupid, the Weak, and the Selfish: The Culpability of Negligence' (2011) 5 *Criminal Law and Philosophy* 147.

Morris, N, 'The Future of Imprisonment: Toward a Punitive Philosophy' (1974) 72 *Michigan Law Review* 1161.

Nourse, VF, 'Reconceptualizing Criminal Law Defenses' (2003) 151 *University of Pennsylvania Law Review* 1691.

Nozick, R, *Anarchy, State, and Utopia* (New York, Basic Books, 1974).

Ormerod, D and Laird, K, *Smith and Hogan's Criminal Law* (Oxford, Oxford University Press, 2015).

Perkins, RM, 'Self-Defense Re-examined' (1954) 1 *UCLA Law Review* 133.

Philips, M, 'The Justification of Punishment and the Justification of Political Authority' (1986) 5 *Law and Philosophy* 393.

Plaxton, M, 'John Gardner's Transatlantic Shadow' (2013) 39 *Queen's Law Journal* 329.

Posner, RA, 'Torture, Terrorism, and Interrogation' in S Levinson (ed), *Torture: A Collection* (Oxford, Oxford University Press, 2004) 291–98.

Prosser, WL, 'Transferred Intent' (1967) 47 *Texas Law Review* 650.

Quong, J, 'Killing in Self-Defense' (2009) 119 *Ethics* 507.

Raviv, A, 'Torture and Justification: Defending the Indefensible' (2004) 13 *George Mason Law Review* 135.

Raz, J, *Practical Reason and Norms* (Oxford, Oxford University Press, 1975/1999).

Redding, P, 'Georg Wilhelm Friedrich Hegel' in *The Stanford Encyclopedia of Philosophy* (Summer 2012 Edition) http://plato.stanford.edu/archives/sum2012/entries/hegel.

Reed, A, Bohlander, M et al, (eds), *Defences in Criminal Law: Domestic and Comparative Perspectives* (Farnham, Ashgate, 2014).

Robinson, PH, 'A Theory of Justification: Societal Harm as a Prerequisite for Criminal Liability' (1975) 23 *UCLA Law Review* 266.

——, 'Criminal Law Defences: A Systematic Analysis' (1982) 82 *Columbia Law Review* 200.

——, *Criminal Law Defenses Volume 2* (Minnesota, West Publishing Co, 1984).

——, 'Rules of Conduct and Principles of Adjudication' (1990) 57 *University of Chicago Law Review* 729.

——, 'Competing Theories of Justification: Deeds versus Reasons' in AP Simester and ATH Smith (eds), *Harm and Culpability* (Oxford, Clarendon Press, 1996) 45–70.

——, 'The Bomb Thief and the Theory of Justification Defenses' (1997) *Criminal Law Forum* 387.

——, *Structure and Function in Criminal Law* (Oxford, Clarendon Press, 1997).

Rodin, D, 'Justifying Harm' (2011) 122 *Ethics* 74.

Ross, PL, 'The Transmogrification of Self-Defense by National Rifle Association-Inspired Statutes' (2007) 35 *Southern University Law Review* 1.

Sangero, B, *Self-Defence in Criminal Law* (Oxford, Hart Publishing, 2006).

Segev, R, 'Fairness, Responsibility and Self-Defence' (2005) 45 *Santa Clara Law Review* 383.

Sendor, BB, 'Mistakes of Fact: A Study in the Structure of Criminal Conduct' (1990) 25 *Wake Forest Law Review* 707.

Simester, AP, 'Mistakes in Defence' (1992) 12 *OJLS* 295.

——, 'Responsibility for Inadvertent Acts' (2005) 2 *Ohio State Journal of Criminal Law* 601.

——, 'Intoxication is Never a Defence' [2009] *Crim LR* 3.

——, 'Wrongs and Reasons' (2009) 72 *MLR* 648.

——, 'On Justifications and Excuses' in L Zedner and JV Roberts (eds), *Principles and Values in Criminal Law and Criminal Justice* (Oxford, Oxford University Press, 2012) 95–112.

——, 'A Disintegrated Theory of Culpability' in DJ Baker and J Horder (eds), *The Sanctity of Life and Criminal Law* (Cambridge, Cambridge University Press, 2013) 178–203.

Simester, AP, Spencer, JR, Stark, F, Sullivan, GR and Virgo, GJ, *Simester and Sullivan's Criminal Law: Theory and Doctrine* (Oxford, Hart Publishing, 2016).

Simester, AP and von Hirsch, A, *Crimes, Harms, and Wrongs* (Oxford, Hart Publishing, 2011).

Simmonds, NE, 'Introduction' in WN Hohfeld, *Fundamental Legal Conceptions as Applied in Judicial Reasoning* (Aldershot, Ashgate, 2001) ix–xxix.

Simons, KW, 'Self-Defense: Reasonable Beliefs or Reasonable Self-Control?' (2008) 11 *New Criminal Law Review* 51.

Smith, SB, 'Hegel's Critique of Liberalism' (1986) 80 *American Political Science Review* 121.

Stark, F, 'Necessity and Nicklinson' [2013] *Crim LR* 949.

Statman, D, 'On the Success Condition for Legitimate Self-Defense' (2008) 118 *Ethics* 659.

Steinhoff, U, 'Self-Defense as Claim Right, Liberty, and Act-Specific Agent-Relative Prerogative', (2016) 35 *Law and Philosophy* 193.

Stewart, H, 'The Role of Reasonableness in Self-Defence' (2003) 16 *Canadian Journal of Law and Jurisprudence* 317.

Tadros, V, *Criminal Responsibility* (Oxford, Oxford University Press, 2005).

Tanguay-Renaud, F, 'Individual Emergencies and the Rule of Criminal Law' in F Tanguay-Renaud and J Stribopoulos (eds), *Rethinking Criminal Law: New Canadian Perspectives in the Philosophy of Domestic, Transnational, and International Criminal Law* (Oxford, Hart Publishing, 2012) 21–54.

Taurek, JM, 'Should the Numbers Count?' (1977) 6 *Philosophy & Public Affairs* 293.

Thomson, JJ, 'Self-Defense' (1991) 20 *Philosophy & Public Affairs* 283.

Thorburn, M, 'Justifications, Powers, and Authority' (2008) 117 *Yale Law Journal* 1070.

——, 'Criminal Law as Public Law' in RA Duff and S Green (eds), *Philosophical Foundations of Criminal Law* (Oxford, Oxford University Press, 2011) 21–43.

——, 'The Constitution of Criminal Law: Justifications, Policing and the State's Fiduciary Duties' (2011) 5 *Criminal Law and Philosophy* 259.

Twining, WL and Twining, PE, 'Bentham on Torture' (1973) 24 *Northern Ireland Legal Quarterly* 305.

Uniacke, S, *Permissible Killing* (Cambridge, Cambridge University Press, 1994).

——, 'In Defense of Permissible Killing: A Response to Two Critics' (2000) 19 *Law and Philosophy* 627.

——, 'Rights and Relativistic Justifications: Replies to Kasachkoff and Husak' (2000) 19 *Law and Philosophy* 645.

Von Hirsch, A and Ashworth, A, *Proportionate Sentencing* (Oxford, Oxford University Press, 2005).

Waldron, J, 'What are Moral Absolutes Like?' (2011) *NYU School of Law, Public Law Research Paper No 11-62* dx.doi.org/10.2139/ssrn.1906850.

Wallace, RJ, 'Hypocrisy, Moral Address, and the Equal Standing of Persons' (2010) 38 *Philosophy & Public Affairs* 307.

Wells, A, 'Home on the Gun Range: Discussing Whether Kansas's New Stand Your Ground Statute Will Protect Gun Owners Who Use Disproportionate Force in Self-Defense' (2008) 56 *Kansas Law Review* 983.

Westen, P, 'An Attitudinal Theory of Excuse' (2006) 3 *Law and Philosophy* 289.

Williams, B, 'A Critique of Utilitarianism' in B Williams and JJC Smart, *Utilitarianism: For and against* (Cambridge, Cambridge University Press, 1973) 77–150.

INDEX